T0339671

# The Rise and Fall of Franklin Delano Roosevelt

# THE RISE AND FALL OF FRANKLIN DELANO ROOSEVELT

ROBERT UNDERHILL

Algora Publishing
New York

Library of Congress Cataloging-in-Publication Data

Underhill, Robert, 1920-
  The rise and fall of Franklin Delano Roosevelt / Robert Underhill.
      p. cm.
  Includes bibliographical references.
    ISBN 978-0-87586-948-3 (soft cover : alk. paper)—ISBN 978-0-87586-949-0 (hard
cover : alk. paper)—ISBN 978-0-87586-950-6 (ebook)  1. Roosevelt, Franklin D. (Franklin
Delano), 1882-1945. 2. Presidents—United States—Biography. 3. United States—Politics
and government—1933-1945. I. Title.
    E807.U54 2012
    973.917092—dc23
    [B]

                                    2012031579

Printed in the United States

Some are born great; others achieve greatness, and some have greatness thrust upon them.

— Shakespeare, Twelfth Night, Act II, Scene III.

And some persons destroy it themselves.

— Author

## ACKNOWLEDGMENTS

"Writing a book," according to Winston Churchill, "is an adventure. To begin with, it is a toy and an amusement. Then it becomes a mistress; next it's your master; then it becomes a tyrant. The last phase is that just as you are about to be reconciled to your servitude, you kill the monster and fling him to the public."

A chronicler less succinct than Churchill might add that a book never comes from its writer alone but is an outgrowth of experiences and detail being gathered since infancy, though only a few of these outstanding relatives, friends, students, teachers, writers, and colleagues who have shaped my thinking can be suitably credited in these few pages.

My teaching career spanned several generations of students who challenged ideas and freely pitched in worthwhile ones of their own. Additionally, notable colleagues were Keith Huntress, Clarence Mattterson, and Kelly Kehlenbeck — all Iowa Staters

Librarians ought to be listed as associates among authors, and I have been helped immeasurably by librarians at several institutions: the Franklin Delano Library at Hyde Park, the Harry S Truman Library at Independence, and the Herbert Hoover Library at West Branch. In addition to these Presidential Libraries, I've drawn on works at the Deering Library at Northwestern, the Harper Library at the University of Chicago, the Parks Library at Iowa State University, and the Ames Public Library.

Like most scribes, I've tried out on friends and relatives sample phrases, anecdotes, and instances gleaned while building pages in my manuscript. Friends and readers like Fred and Terry Schlunz, Margaret Maitland, and the eight members of an informal book club have been innocent and especially patient in listening to my spiels and test runs.

This is not my first book, so computers are not entirely new to me. Nevertheless, at least mine baffles consistently. Without my friend and computer guru, Professor Herb Harmison, my computer would be useless.

Dr. Ken Mills is a working psychologist with considerable knowledge about electronic instruments. He also is my son-in-law and has generously given leadership and guidance in getting this manuscript into actual publication.

On a personal level, I owe more to my two daughters, Susan and Sandy, than I can ever express, let alone repay. Sandy's courage despite adversities and illnesses was an inspiration, and no one could have followed my writings more carefully than she. Unfortunately, Sandy passed away before this manuscript could be finished, but without her devotion the work would not have been undertaken.

My daughter Sue has been monitor, critic, and editor-in-chief. Sue has fine judgment honed by teaching expertise. She read early versions of the manuscript, made suggestions on organization, and then with eagle eyes went through every revision. When Sue read a chapter and found passages out of place or caught me rambling, she would brush aside my nostalgic cobwebs and urge me to get back to historical facts — facts which I hope each reader will find interesting and pertinent.

A reader finding mistakes or shortcomings in this book will understand that such lapses come entirely from the author.

—Robert Underhill

# TABLE OF CONTENTS

# FOREWORD

It is said that an experienced oceanographer can examine an incoming tide and learn of events which happened far out at sea. Likewise, those who study an historical event will be drawn into examining happenings leading up to it. The rabble in arms that sparked the Revolutionary War can be understood only by knowing something about disgruntled settlers in colonial America when ruled by overseers from abroad. Those who want to understand our country's Civil War will have to study sectional rivalries, differing social patterns, and economic conditions in the North and South during that period.

At the equator, the earth's diameter is approximately 25,000 miles, and maps tell us that from the Balkan Peninsula to Hawaii is nearly half that distance — a space demanding over fifteen hours of flight time for most travelers. Connections between an assassination in Sarajevo, Yugoslavia in 1914 and an attack on Pearl Harbor, Hawaii in 1941 — twenty-seven years later, therefore, might appear at first blush to be unrelated. The years between the two dates, slightly more than one-third of a human's life span according to modern reckoning, would seem long, yet with instantaneous communication and in the world's history, the interlude becomes infinitesimal.

World War I reduced most of Western Europe to rubble, and in the aftermath of that debacle extreme poverty, due in large part to the harshness of peace treaties, swept over the defeated nations. The hardships of those times made it inevitable that some governments would attempt recovery through authoritarian and military means. Choosing such routes were Spain, Germany, Italy, and the USSR (Union of Socialist Soviet Republics). In the United States, conditions first flourished and then after the stock market crashed in 1929 sank into a Great Depression. Stresses were very grave, but rather than resorting to arms American citizens yielded to reforms instituted through measures of the New Deal.

Meanwhile, totalitarian leaders in Germany and Italy, encouraged by huge rearmaments programs, began encroaching upon neighboring governments. Austria, Czechoslovakia, Hungary, Romania, and smaller nations were taken over by Nazis, thereby adding to a *Reich* which *der Fuhrer* (the leader) and his cohorts claimed would last a thousand years. Driven by that zeal, the German Wehrmacht (armed forces) in 1939 invaded Poland, and another World War was begun. The die once cast could not be undone.

Governments during the period marking World War II were not without defects, yet despite lapses and mistakes made by the U.S. Administration in Washington between 1939 and 1945, the accumulated errors did not equal either of two major ones committed by wartime enemies: 1) Hitler's judgment in invading the Soviet Union, and 2) Japan's decision to attack Pearl Harbor.

# CHAPTER 1. EUROPE AFTER THE FIRST WORLD WAR

> "With supreme irony, the war to "make the world safe for democracy" ended by leaving democracy more unsafe than at any time since the collapse of revolutions in 1848."
>
> — James Harvey Robinson

Countries in central Europe were competing with one another, and relations already were sour in June of 1914 when Archduke Francis Ferdinand of Austria was assassinated by young Bosnian revolutionaries — recognized as agents of a terrorist Serbian society dedicated to overthrow Austrian control. As the murderous event became known, citizens throughout the world were outraged and sympathetic toward Austrian claims for satisfaction.[1]

Aware of the assassination plot, the Serbian government had done nothing to stop it or even warn the Austrian government. Most of the Austrian crown council favored immediate declaration of war against Serbia, but the declaration was delayed a month until the end of July, when Austria formally declared war on Serbia.

Meanwhile, Russian governments in turmoil undertook a general mobilization program. Germany interpreted this program as a threat to its own eastern frontier and sent a 12-hour ultimatum to Russia, demanding cessation of military preparations on the German frontier. The twelve hours passed, and Germany, having received no reply to its ultimatum, declared war on Russia on August 1, 1914. German diplomats next sent an inquiry to Paris asking what attitude France would take in the German–Russian dispute. The reply was non-committal, declaring only that France would be guided by her own interests. Next Germany offered England a promise not to attack France if England would guarantee French neutrality.

England rejected the German offer, and after wide-ranging arguments in the British cabinet voted to give France assurances to protect the coast against a German attack. The British vote came because of "moral obligations" arising from previous naval agreements.

Very quickly, Germany launched an invasion of Luxemburg and demanded that Belgium give permission for German troops to cross Belgian territory. When that demand was rejected, Germany declared war on Belgium and France. After that statement was released, other nations issued formal declarations of war: England on Germany, Austria on Russia, Serbia on Germany, France on Austria — the list seemed to draw in every nation. Thus it was called a World War.

The United States was able to stay out of actual combat for nearly three years, but complex questions about former treaties, trade, transportation, and safety in the shipping lanes confronted combatants and neutrals. The odds against U.S. involvement were insurmountable.

On May 7, 1915, off the coast of Ireland, the Lusitania was sunk by German submarines. The sinking claimed 1198 lives, including 120 American citizens, and the disaster set off a furor that spread across America from east to west. The furor added more tension to disputes between American and Allied governments over questions of contraband and blockade.

In Washington, D.C., American foreign policy was in disarray; not all members of President Woodrow Wilson's cabinet agreed with him. He struck a strong note, nevertheless, and in a public speech defined his administration's policy vis-à-vis the European war. The U.S. intended to continue shipping supplies to Allied countries and would demand reparations from Berlin for the sinking of the Lusitania along with a promise that in the future such actions would not be repeated.

William Jennings Bryan, Secretary of State, insisted such a decision could only lead to war, but an adamant Wilson could not be swayed. Bryan resigned his position in protest and was replaced by Robert Lansing. The day after Bryan's resignation, President Wilson sent a stronger note to Germany and a third one a month later. The German government gave assurances that in the future no ocean liners would be sunk without warning and without offering choices for the safety of non-combatants. Those assurances were reasonably well observed for more than a year.

The U.S. stepped up its shipping to Allies though, and when the year of 1917 began, Germany resumed its submarine attacks. The U.S. Department of State released a Zimmerman note which showed that Germany had attempted to enlist Mexico into supporting Germany's position in the war. Attitudes in the U.S. toward Germany hardened, and when more American ships were sunk, President Wilson in April of 1917 asked Congress to declare a state of war between the U.S. and Germany.

Cruelties and sufferings during World War I were horrendous and would go on until November 11, 1918. After that surrender date, the Allies immediately took over the occupied and former western German territories. The following January a Peace Conference formally met in Paris.

During World War I — the War to End All Wars — more than 10 million Europeans had been killed, 7 million more permanently disabled, and 15 million others wounded. Widespread destruction in lands formerly held by Western Allies — Belgium, the Netherlands, and France most notably — was beyond description. The actual cost was incalculable, but writers later estimated that this war's prosecution had cost nations of Europe six and a half times as much as the total national debt of the entire world for the preceding one hundred years. Much of Western Europe was left in shambles, and citizens throughout the stricken lands had to struggle to stay alive.

In January of 1918, President Wilson in an address to the U.S. Congress outlined a peace program consisting of Fourteen Points. It was not until nearly a year later — in mid December, 1919, however, that Wilson sailed to Europe, where in Paris, he was received with wild enthusiasm.

At the Peace of Paris or the Treaty of Versailles as it became better known, the Big Four consisting of representatives from the U.S., Britain, France, and Italy held meeting after meeting to discuss aspects of peace. Very quickly Wilson's idealistic Fourteen Points receded into the background, as the victorious governments sank into quarrels over how to manage post war Europe. In contrast to Wilson's dreams, the Treaty of Versailles was harsh, brutal, and punitive.

George Clemenceau, representative from France, most of all wanted to extract revenge from Germany. Citizens throughout his nation smoldered in anger, believing that Germany alone had brought on war. In consequence, Germany had to be punished and that nation's ability to start another war had to be destroyed.

The defeated enemy, Germany, was not invited to the peace conferences, nor was Russia. The latter country had made a separate peace with Germany in 1917, and was feared by the victorious Allies because of the rise of revolutionary Bolsheviks.

The Central Powers were to be punished severely. Terms of the harsh Versailles Treaty ordered that France would control the Saar Valley, rich in coal and iron, for a minimum of 15 years, and would regain the Alsace-Lorraine territory — a contested region in northeastern France. A buffer zone known as the Rhineland lying between France and Germany would be demilitarized, and German colonies would be divided between France and Britain. Altogether, Germany lost 13.5% of its land and 12.5% of its population. The German navy was confiscated; Germany was allowed no planes, artillery, or submarines, and its army would be limited to 100,000 members. A new German government would be forced to pay reparations amounting to more than 132 billion marks, and finally, a War Guilt clause in the Treaty ordered Germany to bear full responsibility for the war.

The Allies bore the brunt of the World War I debt and suffered the most material damages, but living conditions throughout the defeated nations were unbelievably grim. Hunger was widespread; demobilized Deutschland soldiers came home to find their families destitute and little or no work for themselves. In the first years after the war inflation hit all of Europe as pent up demand was released and production fell off due to a shortage of new materials. The combination of high demand and scarcity sent prices soaring even in the best managed countries. In Britain a pound sterling bought in 1919 about one third what it had bought in 1914. French prices approximately doubled during the war and got worse during the 1920s. Inflation was even worse in other belligerent countries.

France and Britain owed war debts to the U.S., and in order to pay those obligations, the French demanded reparations in gold from Germany. Germany was unable to pay, and in retribution the French seized industrial towns in the Ruhr Valley. Germany's response was to print more money, resulting in even higher inflation.

The march of French troops into the Ruhr Valley quickened the descent of the German mark. On Armistice Day, 1918, one mark was equal to seven American dollars and forty-five cents. Five years later in 1923, the value of marks to a dollar had plunged to 50,000 to one. One historian described the unbelievable inflation:

> The last payment of railway expenses by the Weimar Government to the Committee of Guarantees for a trip to Berlin had required seven office boys with huge wage-paper baskets full of [twenty-mark] notes to carry

the full sum from the office down to the railway station. Now it would take forty-nine office boys.[2]

The end of the war left Europe with hordes of unemployed former soldiers, and facing such hardships many veterans joined right or left groups to stage revolts in a number of areas. Most of these splinter movements were unsuccessful. Communist revolts in Hungary and Germany failed, but farther south in Italy — a late entry into the war on the side of the Allies — fascist Blackshirts led by Benito Mussolini came to power.

The winter of 1920-1921 was severe throughout Europe and particularly bad in Germany. A large segment of the population in that country went to bed hungry, and food riots were rampant. Numerous groups emerged, and among them was one called the German Workers Party. At first, the meetings were small — less than a dozen members attending — but one of the leaders was always there, an orator spilling out denunciations, threats, and promises.

The fourth son of a civil servant, Adolf Hitler was born April 20, 1889, in a village not far from Vienna. When the boy was about four years old, his father, a customs official, moved from Vienna to the German side of the Danube River. The young boy began playing with children more oriented toward Germany than Austria, and the lad's lower Bavarian dialect would remain with him throughout his life.

In the spring of 1906, Adolf's mother permitted her seventeen-year-old son to visit Vienna, a Mecca for art, music, and architecture. The visit resulted in Adolf's longer-lasting move to Vienna the following year with the purpose of studying art. He submitted samples of his work to the Art Academy, but they were returned with the verdict: "Test drawings unsatisfactory." Hitler was not the only disappointed aspiring artist at the time; a contemporary, Marc Chagall, was rejected by the Academy of Art in St. Petersburg the same year.[3]

Disappointed and downcast, young Adolf Hitler decided his future lay in architecture rather than in painting and drawing.

In the first month of 1914, the twenty-five-year old Hitler received an official Austrian notice to "present himself for military service" at Linz. He asked for a delay and returned to Vienna where he eked out a meager living painting posters and post cards. He was in Vienna when the assassination of Archduke Ferdinand occurred. Angry mobs swarmed through Vienna's streets, and war fever soon swept the entire country. Hitler volunteered for army service, was accepted, and assigned to the Bavarian Fifteenth Regiment.

His first actual combat came in a battle near Ypres in Belgium. Under heavy fire, and now a regimental dispatch carrier, Hitler found a medic who helped him carry a wounded comrade to a dressing station. For the action, Hitler was recommended and received an Iron Cross, 2nd Class, an award uncommon for a mere corporal and one for which he was inordinately proud.

He participated in more front line action, and in the summer of 1916 his regiment moved south. His good luck was still with him until October, when at the Battle of the Somme he was wounded and had to be evacuated to a field hospital. Upon recovery he was reassigned to a replacement battalion in Munich where he found the mood of other soldiers despicable. No one honored the front line soldier, and most had lost confidence in the army. The military, according to malcontents around him, was undermined by Jews and Communists! Nearly every clerk was a Jew and nearly every Jew a clerk. Moreover, Jews were behind the lines, plotting for the overthrow of the Fatherland. The weed seeds of anti-Semitism planted first in Hitler's mind during his postcard months in Vienna grew fast in this period of his military service.

Returned to his regiment, Hitler went back into battle, was gassed, and had lost his eyesight temporarily the first week in November when he learned that Germany was going to surrender. At the war's end he, like thousands of other German soldiers, was not ready to accept defeat. In their minds, Jews had sold out to the enemy while true Germans were doing the actual fighting and dying in the front lines.

Disgruntled groups sprang up everywhere in impoverished Germany. In Berlin, Spartacists, a far leftist group named after the slave who centuries earlier had led a rebellion against the Romans, took to the streets to make revolution with the help of demobilized sailors. Similarly elsewhere, Communists were waiting to take over. To a huge May Day crowd in Moscow's Red Square, Lenin boasted, "The working class is celebrating its anniversary freely and openly not only in Soviet Russia, but in Soviet Hungary and Soviet Bavaria."

In Munich, the *Freikorps* (Free Corps), an armed rightist group attempted a coup but was put down by Austrian police. *Freikorps* numbers grew, and Hitler shared with its members feelings of shame and distrust of a home front now disintegrating into Bolshevism. The Spartacists, openly admitting to Communist allegiance, called for revolution, but the *Freikorps* using announcements in newspapers and on billboards gathered strength in their call for former soldiers and sailors to rise and join in the move to repulse the Communists. Most likely, all of Germany would have gone Communist if it had not been for this *Freikorps*, which was able to crush the threatening Red cells in the Fatherland.

In America, where the Great Depression was at its worst, most citizens were not paying much attention to events overseas; there were too many problems here at home. Adolf Hitler, when mentioned, was ridiculed and seen as a minor copy of the stronger man in Italy, Benito Mussolini.

In early 1933, *Time* magazine, Henry Luce's weekly, gave a tongue-in-cheek report of Hitler's visit to the prestigious *Reichpresident* Paul von Hindenburg. Cheeky enough to seek appointment as Chancellor, the mustachioed Austrian supplicant was asked by Hindenburg, "With what power do you seek to be made Chancellor?" An undaunted Hitler shot back, "Precisely the same power Mussolini used in his march on Rome." Time's report continued to lampoon Hitler, his "beer-backed Bavarians," and their programs:

> The Nazi program consists of stentorian appeals to every form of German prejudice. Essentially, Nationalists and patrioteers, the Nazis insert "Socialist" into their party's name simply as a lure to discontented workers. . . . Today it is no exaggeration to state that the Nazi Party is pledged to so many things that it is pledged to nothing. . . . In so far as it has a doctrine, National Socialism promises the bulk of the German people whatever they want.[4]

In 1919 the German Workers Party was only a tiny splinter group when Hitler joined it in Munich. He was put in charge of propaganda and devoted his energy in building the party which soon was renamed *Nationalsozialistisch Deutsche Arbeitpartei*, abbreviated into "Nazi." Hitler's unrelenting propaganda through the party's newspaper, *Volkischer Beobachter*, and in public harangues, built the original sect into an ever larger and more effective political force. In speeches at meetings every day and evening, Hitler polished his talent for magnetism and leadership. At the same time, he gathered around him a coterie of Nazi leaders who would become infamous — including Alfred Rosenberg, Rudolph Hess, Hermann Goering, and Julius Streicher.

In building the Nazi party, Hitler preached that its greatest danger came from Marxism, with that doctrine's insistence upon internationalism and class conflict. Behind all Marxism, of which Communism was the present expression, one would find the Jew, who for Hitler was the very incarnation of evil.

Hindenburg and others in the reigning German government tendered Hitler several offices, all of which he turned down. He wanted absolute power, and in January, 1933, Hindenburg succumbed and offered the chancellorship. In that office, Hitler immediately set about creating an absolute dictatorship. He got the president's assent for a new election on grounds that a majority in the *Reichstag* — the governing body — could not be obtained. Then a fire in the *Reichstag* on the night of February 27, 1933, was engineered by the Nazis but attributed by them to have been the work of a Communist plot. The disaster gave Hitler and his minions an excuse to mount an intensified campaign of violence and to issue decrees overriding guarantees of freedom.

Unchallenged in his position as head of the Nazi party and Chancellor of Germany, Hitler paid less attention to internal matters. Obsessed with pan-Germanism and the myth of Aryan superiority, foreign policy became his overriding interest. Today it was Germany, but tomorrow it would be the entire world (*Deutschland heute: Morgen die ganze Welt!*). He and Nazis faithful would lead the Third *Reich* on a quest for more living space (*Lebensraum*).

## CHAPTER 2. AMERICA'S GREAT DEPRESSION

> The land had been overturned in a great speculative frenzy to make money in an unsustainable wheat market. . . . The rains disappeared — with no sod to hold the earth in place — the soil calcified and started to blow. Dust clouds boiled up, ten thousand feet or more in the sky, and rolled like moving mountains...
>
> — Timothy Egan in *The Worst Hard Times*

---

For America and for most of the world, just prior to the First World War, manufacturing enough furniture, appliances, and equipment to serve people's needs seemed to be the major economic challenge. John D. Rockefeller, Cornelius Vanderbilt, and Andrew Carnegie — titans of earlier generations — were confident that whatever they constructed in railroads or produced in oil and steel, Americans would consume. As the nation industrialized, however, conditions changed, and enlarging public demand usurped the challenges of production.

With ever lessening dependence upon hand skills, efforts shifted from production methods toward increasing consumption. It was necessary to convince people that they needed more — larger homes, new inventions, different furniture, this year's vehicle, appliances, and gadgets of every description. Along with rosy incomes and larger industrial production arose another enterprise — a huge venture with staggering societal impact. That venture was advertising — the planting and promotion of *wants* in people.

Advertisements before 1920 usually were limited to small notices discreetly placed on back pages of newspapers and magazines. As the volume of advertising swelled, promotion agencies — specialists in the art of hype — began dominating billboards, newspapers, and the new medium of radio. In the second half of that decade, President Herbert Hoover speaking at a conference of advertising executives declared, "In the past, wish, want, and desire were the motive forces of economic progress. Now you have taken over the job of creating desire."[1]

For ten years following the end of World War I, most of America prospered. For nearly everyone except farmers, incomes rose and living became easier. World War I had helped turn American agriculture into a world grocery. Prices for corn and hogs rose to levels undreamt of by the Founding Fathers. A bushel of corn brought as high as $20 and one full-grown hog $330. Spurred by this "golden age" for land and the commodities it produced, farmers began taking on debt to expand their operations. They didn't have to worry as long as demand and prices for beef, pork, and corn remained high. The bubble for agriculture burst soon after Armistice Day, however, when in Europe country after country, strapped for cash, started putting heavy tariffs on imported foodstuffs. With such markets closing, prices for land and agricultural commodities in the United States began to shrink. After the Wall Street crash in 1929, demand and prices plummeted, and those who tilled the soil found themselves in deep financial distress.

As the Depression worsened, the vise on agriculture tightened; the spirit of rebellion raised itself even in the usually conservative and placid Midwest. Serious trouble began in August, 1931, when the Iowa Governor called out the National Guard to quell what became known as the "Cedar County Cow War," so named over armed resistance to a new state law requiring veterinary inspection of dairy cattle. In central Iowa, a mob of unruly farmers attacked a veterinarian's car, and a cadre from the Guard set up machine guns at farm-to-market roads in other sections of the state to prevent similar groups from forming.

The wave of farm foreclosures that swept over the country in the first years of the 1930s decade put cracks in the foundations of law. There were "penny auctions," where neighboring farmers with weapons or clubs on display would turn up at a foreclosure sale — a conspicuous warning that outside bids would not be welcome — then the farmers would bid only pennies for the distressed property.

In 1933 before the growing season began, Midwestern farmers had formed what they called the "Farmers' Holiday Association," a movement for a mass agricultural strike in the coming year. Some journalists, a few professors, politicians, and businessmen viewed the movement as a possible forerunner to the kind of autocratic revolution that had put the Bolsheviks in power in 1917, Mussolini's fascists in Italy in 1922, and Hitler's Nazis in Germany.

Two innovations helped rescue American agriculture during the decade of the 1930s: mechanization and hybrid corn. In the first half of that period, a farmer considered mildly prosperous might have four horses — only one farm in four could boast a tractor, usually Harvester's Farmall or Deere's Waterloo Boy. By the end of that decade, most farmers had come to realize that mechanized tractors were worth the investment because they not only saved time and labor but freed up several acres that used to be needed to raise oats for horse feed.

Hybrid corn, a development coming from Henry Wallace's Pioneer Corporation in Iowa, produced even more dramatic changes. Traditionally, a yield of 50 bushels per acre was considered average. With the new hybrids, the average doubled, and in some cases even tripled. Farmers in Ohio, Indiana, Illinois, Iowa, Kansas, and Nebraska were rejuvenated with new aspirations.

Moreover, in the aftermath of World War I, new techniques of mass production increased the efficiency per man-hour by over 40 per cent. This gigantic spurt in the output of goods demanded a corresponding surge in consumption and buying power — the latter boosted by advertising. While many with funds to invest did so, countless others did too — people owning little but fanciful dreams now speculated in stocks. Customers of limited means were encouraged to buy products or stocks on credit. Citizens large and small succumbed to the fervor of Wall Street, a bastion of power since the mid-nineteenth century. Advertisers, business associates, and friends convinced wage-earners to invest their life savings, but when Black Friday occurred in 1929, they held only paper or ticker-tape figures — neither of which would buy groceries or pay the mortgage.

In October, 1929, the stock market, honeycombed with credit extended in the form of brokered loans, crashed of its own weight, calling to account the millions of deals contracted with agencies who sold anything and everything to people without means to pay.

The era of prosperity ended. Most observers and advisors had been indifferent to the lack of actual buying power, and President Herbert Hoover after leaving the White House would write, "A margin of some thousands . . . got too much of the productive pie for the services they performed . . . Another margin of some 20 per cent got too little."[2]

Across the land there were enough confrontations and violence between desperate groups and law enforcement agencies to cause serious historians to wonder if the nation was being stampeded toward a state which would be governed either by the radical right or the radical left. Several European nations were choosing the former course.

In February, 1933, the State of Minnesota banned mortgage foreclosures on farms and homes. The sentiment spread to other states, and the Minnesota Act was reviewed by the U.S. Supreme Court where it was sustained by a 5 to 4 decision.[3]

In 1932, roughly one quarter of the U.S. population lived on farms, and almost none of the farmers had shared in the prosperity of the era. Farmers had been considered the most conservative of citizens, yet it was in Iowa — the state with more than one-quarter of America's top grade soil — that sunburned men reached for pitchforks and shotguns.

The market crash merely worsened their already deplorable lives. They were getting less than twenty-five cents for a bushel of wheat, seven cents for a bushel of corn (some even burned it for fuel), a dime for a bushel of oats, a nickel for a pound of cotton or wool. Sugar brought three cents per pound, hogs and beef two and a half cents a pound, and apples, if flawless, were at forty cents for a crate of two hundred.

Translated into purchasing power, such prices meant that a wagon load of oats would barely buy a pair of four-dollar Thom McAnn shoes. A bushel of wheat might buy slightly more, but with mortgage interest at $3.60 an acre, another $1.90 in taxes, the wheat farmer was losing $1.50 on every acre he tilled.[4]

Before October 1929, across the U.S. cities of various sizes were blossoming with new industries. Within a couple of months after the crash, employment might run as high as 50%. Local banks failed, taking all the deposits with them. The devastation struck all levels. State and local assistance programs quickly ran out of food; malnourished children struggled to live in homes their parents couldn't afford to heat; some died.

No small wonder the Hawkeye State teetered on the brink of anarchy. Dairymen in northwest Iowa boycotted milk creameries in Sioux City. In addition to keeping milk from their own dairy herds off the market, angry men set up road blocks to prevent anyone from delivering milk to Sioux City processors. Protestors were taking up arms against a system that paid them two cents a quart for milk that distributors in Sioux City sold for eight cents.

Farm strikers and sheriff deputies were injured in confrontations around Sioux City, Des Moines, Council Bluffs, Clinton, and other Iowa towns. Near Cherokee, Iowa, fourteen strikers were wounded when nine masked men opened fire and threw tear gas bombs into their camp. A deputy sheriff at Council Bluffs was killed when a riot gun was accidentally fired, and a South Dakota man was mortally wounded when he tried to move a truck load of milk past the blockade into Sioux City.

In April, 1933, dozens of farmers forced their way into the O'Brien County Courthouse in northwestern Iowa where on the third floor a sheriff was scheduled to sell the land of another farmer unable to keep up his mortgage payments. On the second floor, twenty sheriff deputies armed with ax handles were prepared to deal with trouble makers. Irate farmers rushed the deputies, but in the bloody fight the deputies won out and the angry mob was repulsed.

The mob of farmers, still inflamed and abetted by swigs of homemade liquor moved toward LeMars, a town of 8,000, twenty-five miles northeast of Sioux City. In a courtroom there, District Judge C. C. Bradley was conducting a hearing on another farm foreclosure. The mob had swelled to 100 persons, and as they pushed their way into the court chambers they refused to take off their hats or snub out their cigarettes. Judge Bradley banged his gavel and called for respect for the law, but his action only fueled more anger in the dozen or more men who swarmed the bench, grabbed him, and demanded a promise that he would sign no more farm foreclosures.

Sixty-three years later the *Des Moines Register* gave an account of what happened next.

> The judge trembled, and color drained from his face. But he would not give in to the mob's demands. The men around him began slapping and hitting him.
>
> Bradley was blindfolded, led from the courthouse, put in a truck, and driven out of town. Encircled by his tormentors, Bradley was crowned with a greasy hubcap. A rope was tossed over a telephone line crossbar and a noose draped around his neck. Men began to hoist him into the air. But still he would not give in to the mob's demands.
>
> Bradley fainted and slumped to the ground. The mob, frightened by its own murderous potential, broke up and ran. Bradley was shaken but not badly hurt. [5]

Discontent was not limited to the hinterlands, for in the eyes of Americans all over the country the stock market crash and the Great Depression that followed it discredited not only big business but financial institutions as well.

## Chapter 3. Franklin Roosevelt: The Early Years

*I have always been a great believer in heredity.*

— Franklin Roosevelt's Mother

---

The history of the United States in the ten years between 1930 and 1940 might well be called the era of Franklin D. Roosevelt. True, he was not elected President until November, 1932, but wheels pushing him toward that office had begun turning earlier.

The 1880s had been an age of moguls — an age that displayed poverty and wealth, unrest and stability — an age when thousands of unemployed workers searched for jobs, bread, and shelter while a few fortunate others built half-million-dollar yachts and sumptuous mansions. Horatio Alger's rags-to-riches writings encouraged entrepreneurs, and mainly because there were vast natural resources and unsettled territories, there was enough evidence to support his thesis.

The Scottish immigrant Andrew Carnegie, Colossus of Pittsburgh, amassed millions through producing steel, and Cornelius Vanderbilt made a fortune in steamboats; his descendants added to their founder's enormous wealth. The Vanderbilts lived in a fifty-four-room Renaissance mansion a few miles to the north of where Franklin Roosevelt was born, but despite the wealth started by Cornelius and enlarged by his son W. H. Vanderbilt, Franklin's father would always consider the Vanderbilts as *nouveaux riches*, yet to be accepted in the best levels of society.

Neither the Delano nor the Roosevelt family in New York State had firsthand knowledge of poverty. On the Delano side, a Flemish seafarer, Philippe de la Noy Delano, had settled in Massachusetts very early in the seventeenth century. The first Roosevelt — Claes Martenszen van Roosevelt — came from Holland to New Amsterdam in 1613. The descendants of these two progenitors married within English families in New England so consistently that future generations would become ever more English in orientation and outlook.

Warren Delano Roosevelt, grandfather of Franklin D., was a China merchant in the early nineteenth century and no doubt trafficked in opium as did most traders in those times. After amassing a fortune, Warren Roosevelt retired to a handsome estate in the Hudson River Valley. His daughter, Sara, was born there as well as another daughter and a son. The family traveled extensively — to China, to Europe several times, and to the Suez Canal. Daughter Sara was twenty-five and well on the route to spinsterhood when she met James Roosevelt, a fifty-one-year-old widower and fifth cousin to Theodore Roosevelt. James fell in love with Sara, and the two were married in October, 1880.

Two years later the couple was living in their home at Hyde Park, N.Y. when their son Franklin Delano Roosevelt entered this world. On January 30, 1882, the proud father wrote in his diary, "At a quarter to nine my Sallie had a splendid large baby boy. He weighs 10 lbs. without clothes." Franklin Roosevelt was the only child the couple would have, and he grew up among the landed gentry living along the Hudson River.

Sara once described Franklin's arrival:

> [He] . . . was plump, and nice . . . born right here in this house; one never went to hospitals in those days . . . I realize how much more scientific hospital care is today, but I am old-fashioned enough to think it's nicer for a baby to be born in his own home. I've passed the door of that sunny, upstairs room many hundreds of times in my long life, and oh! So often I've remembered that there my son first saw the light of day . . .[2]

All accounts picture Franklin Roosevelt as a bright, handsome, and happy infant — constantly in the company of an adoring, watchful mother and surrounded by servants. Born to the purple, he entered a boyhood that had few rivals if measured by comforts, travel, security, formal training — all the privileges enjoyed at the time by the few families with wealth and high social position. Franklin was taken to Europe for the first time when he was three, and thereafter he spent a few months of each year abroad. In the course of his boyhood, he had a series of nurses, governesses, and tutors — seven different ones by the time he was fourteen — and at that age his mother enrolled him at Groton, a private school in Massachusetts.

The decade in which Franklin Roosevelt was born also introduced other boys destined to play important roles in history. In West Branch, Iowa, a boyish Herbert Hoover went skinny-dipping among willows down by the railroad bridge, used bent pins and butcher string to catch green sunfish, and picked potato bugs for a penny a hundred. Winston Churchill in 1882, the year of Franklin Roosevelt's birth, was an eight-year-old youth having trouble with schoolwork. In that decade in Georgia — not the U.S. State but the onetime kingdom of Georgia on the southern periphery of Russia — Josef Dzhugashvili, son of a peasant cobbler, was a pock-marked youth three years old. Josef lived in a leaky adobe hut in a land seared by national strife; the world would come to know him as Joseph Stalin. In central Italy, Benito Mussolini, son of a socialist blacksmith, slept on a sack of corn leaves. He later was sent away to school, where he ate at third-class tables before being expelled at the age of eleven.

Three years before the decade ended, in a small northern Austrian town near the German border a child was born who turned into a moody, introspective young man with ambitions for becoming an artist. At fifteen he was orphaned, but he later served in the German army and won the Iron Cross, an uncommonly high decoration for a mere corporal. Few people could understand his complex personality, but from 1933 until his death in a bunker outside Berlin in 1945, the words and actions of Adolf Hitler shook the world.

Although his boyhood was far different from theirs, years later Franklin Roosevelt would have to contend with all these men. He knew nothing about poverty, school troubles, hunger, or family strife. His early education was by tutors in his home, and his watchful mother, Sara, kept it there as long as she could.

From Groton, Franklin went to Harvard, following the path of other boys in his economic and social class. At Harvard, he was an average student, getting grades seldom above a B and failing in several examinations. Nevertheless, he graduated from Harvard and then went to Columbia University, where he studied law from 1904 to 1907.

Eleanor Roosevelt was Franklin's fifth cousin and daughter of Theodore Roosevelt's younger brother, Elliott. Her mother was pretty Anna Hall, whom Elliott married in 1883, a year after Franklin's birth. Elliott — the black sheep in the Roosevelt family — became Franklin's godfather but was an alcoholic who never found solid footing in the world.

Elliott died a drunkard's death in 1894, and by then the ten-year-old Eleanor was in the custody of great aunts or other relatives. She knew her father only slightly because he shuttled between flings and drinking bouts in Berlin, Paris, and New York; nevertheless, she sent him endearing notes sprinkled with childish adoration.

Eleanor's mother died on December 7, 1892, after a lingering illness. By this time Eleanor was separated from her and living with various relatives, and she apparently felt more sympathy for her absentee father than for her mother. Her father did not come to see her immediately after her mother's funeral, but in memoirs Eleanor would write that her mother's death must have been a terrible tragedy for her father because he now had:

> [n]o hope of ever wiping out the sorrowful years he had brought upon my mother, and he had left her mother as guardian of her children. My grandfather did not trust my father to take care of us. He had no wife, no children, no hope.[3]

Without either parent, Eleanor's childhood was lonely and troubled. By the time she was eleven, she was in the custody of Grandmother Hall who would her to Allenswood School for Girls in England. At Allenswood, Eleanor fell under the demanding tutelage and supervision of Mlle. Marie Souvestre, a guardian young Eleanor came to admire and adore second only to her father. The headmistress' motherly concern for Eleanor extended to her clothes, her health, and her grooming. Eleanor spent three years at Allenswood, which she would describe as "the happiest years of my life."

In 1902 when Eleanor was approaching eighteen, Grandmother Hall insisted that she return to America where she could make her entry into society as a debutante. New York City then was a bisected metropolis; there was the section where Eleanor's family and friends lived — a section marked by resplendent homes, fine clothes, carriages, and other attributes of wealth. On the other side was the huddle of East Side slums where two thirds of the city's inhabitants lived in a total of slightly more than 90,000 tenements.

Soon after returning to New York, Eleanor joined the Junior League and was assigned to do volunteer work at a settlement house in the Lower East Side of Manhattan. This first assignment touched off a lifetime advocacy for the underprivileged and a concern for those who for one reason or another were not getting their needs met.

Eleanor and Franklin had known each other slightly as children and as teenagers. In 1902, after they met by chance on a train, they began courting secretly. A year later Eleanor came to Groton to visit Franklin and to attend a football game between Harvard and Yale. The next day, a Sunday, he proposed marriage.

Sara, Franklin's mother, was devastated when she heard what her son had done without consulting her. She prevailed upon them both to delay their marriage for at least a year, and during that time she took Franklin on an extended cruise expecting and hoping that he would change his mind. He did not.

Franklin's and Eleanor's marriage was scheduled for March 17, 1904, in New York City, and two weeks before that time the engaged couple went to Washington D.C. to attend Uncle Theodore's inauguration. Theodore had defeated rival Alton B. Parker by a landslide tally of more than 2.5 million votes and had agreed to give the bride away at Franklin's marriage. The wedding ceremony purposely had been set for a day Theodore had assured them he could attend.

The rites took place in the home of Cousin Susie and Mrs. Ludlow on Seventy-Sixth Street in New York City, and outside that day traces of winter were still on the streets. Yet the weather was balmy; everywhere open windows were filled with spectators. Guests arrived in sumptuous carriages; little boys surrounding them shouted as they pushed one another around in the street awaiting arrival of President Teddy.

Inside the home, Sara, mother of the groom, immaculate in white silk trimmed with black lace, was ushered to a seat in the front. Bridesmaids in taffeta moved with measured steps down the circular stairway before marching sedately up the aisle. Behind them came the bride on the arm of her famous uncle. Eleanor's satin gown was adorned with rose-point Brussels lace, and the veil covering her long hair was secured with a diamond pin that had belonged to her mother.

Although on this wedding day attention centered on the bride, relatives knew that Sara Roosevelt was going to be matriarch of the family. She meant to dominate her son's married life the way she had controlled his childhood and youth.

Franklin had to finish the year at Columbia Law School before the newly-weds could leave for a three-and-a-half-month honeymoon trip to Europe. He did finish the year at Columbia — after a fashion — receiving failing grades in two subjects.

In London, the couple walked themselves weary, and Franklin bought rare books, prints, and wrote his mother that he was spending "thousands of dollars" on clothes. Eleanor, more parsimonious, bought a few clothes and linens. In Paris, they dined at out-of-the-way places, and

Franklin, whose French was not nearly so good as Eleanor's, would try to get along with the *patrons.*

In Italy, the disparity was greater, for while her Italian was only fair, his was almost non-existent. They enjoyed tea at the Lido, but at the beach Eleanor's strait-laced attitudes surfaced in letters she wrote Sara: "It is a lovely island with a splendid beach, but I never saw anything like the bathing clothes the ladies wear . . . but Franklin says I must get accustomed to it as France is worse."

Eleanor didn't like mountain climbing, and she let her new husband accompany another young lady up the Dolomite Alps in northern Italy. Eleanor confessed she had been uneasy over that pairing until she and Franklin had left for St. Moritz. The drive there was wonderful, and she was thrilled when Franklin leaped out of the coach to pick some wild flowers for her.

In Paris again, Eleanor found clothes she had ordered were awaiting her fittings. As the honeymoon drew near its end, she cabled Sara that she and Franklin were anxious to get home and see "mother" again.

Arriving back in New York City, Franklin had a brief stint with a law firm before deciding an attorney's life was not for him. As a young married couple the two were well off financially even if not as wealthy as others in their crowd. Franklin had a $5,000 a month income from a $100,000 trust fund, and Eleanor had an annual income of $7,000. Moreover, Sara could be counted on for generous checks on holidays and special purposes. Eleanor, shy and anxious to avoid confrontation, made no protest when her husband agreed to Sara's offer of living in one of two adjoining houses on East 65th Street.

# Chapter 4. FDR: Emerging Politician

> "Well, if we've caught a Roosevelt, we'd better take him
> down and drop him off the dock."
>
> — Big Tim Sullivan, Political Boss in the Bowery

---

After gaining admission to the Bar of New York State, Roosevelt left Columbia University without completing a degree there and joined a well-established law firm. His three-year practice of law was "more or less casual," and in 1910 he opted for active politics. Departing from the Republican fold of his cousin Theodore, Franklin ran a colorful and successful campaign for the New York Senate.

Not all Tammany leaders were pleased to welcome the handsome, young aristocrat into their ranks. Among incoming members of the Assembly at Albany, "Big Tim" Sullivan, political boss of the party in the Bowery, when first spotting Franklin speaking in cultured language, cigarette holder held firmly in his mouth, and gold pince-nez glasses across his nose, is supposed to have said, "Well, if we've caught a Roosevelt, we'd better take him down and drop him off the dock."[1]

Franklin Roosevelt served in the New York Senate from 1911 until 1913, and in the latter year President Woodrow Wilson appointed him Assistant Secretary of the Navy, a post he held for the next seven years. Roosevelt's unwavering support of the Democratic national leadership won him the vice-presidential nomination on the James M. Cox ticket in 1920.

A year later, a sudden and severe attack of polio at his summer home in Campobello, New Brunswick, left Franklin apparently a hopeless invalid, but during the next seven years he fought his way back to health, used his leisure for study and correspondence, and emerged from forced retirement no longer just a likeable, wealthy playboy, but a man with deep political ambitions.

Roosevelt's political comeback got a major boost at the Democratic National Convention in 1924, where he nominated New York Governor Alfred E. Smith for president. Roosevelt called Smith the "happy warrior of the political battlefield." Delegates at the convention erupted; the applause was deafening, and Roosevelt's concluding sentences were drowned out by shouts of approval. Smith did not win the nomination and the Democratic nominee, John W. Davis, was defeated by Republican Calvin Coolidge in that November, but as a party stalwart Franklin Roosevelt's position had been secured.

Four years afterward, Governor Smith again asked Roosevelt to make the nominating speech. Franklin's speech on this second occasion was good but not as compelling as the "Happy Warrior" one. An outcome, however, came at the New York state convention in 1928 when the Democrats nominated Roosevelt to succeed Smith as governor of the Empire State. During this race for the governorship, Franklin traveled by automobile, which permitted him to stop at crossroads, shake hands, and make a few remarks. His campaigning was so vigorous that it rebutted any who suggested that his health was not strong enough to hold public office.

As early as midnight on election eve in 1928, it was clear that Democrats were not going to win the presidency, but in New York the race for governor was exceedingly close. Not until the next day did Franklin Roosevelt learn that his hard campaigning had brought him a hairbreadth victory. Almost immediately, his closest advisers, led by James Farley and Louis Howe, began developing strategies aimed toward winning the presidential nomination for him in 1932.

Due to the debacle of '29, financiers, banks, and big business by 1930 had lost respect, yet despite stories of millionaires and brokers committing suicides, most men and women of wealth had enough to tide them over. Alarms spread rapidly though after December, 1930, when the Bank of the United States in New York City was closed by order of the State Assembly.

In the congressional elections of 1930, Republicans, in their first setback since 1916, lost their majority in the Senate; in the House their majority shrank from 103 to 2. Two years later the GOP held its convention in Chicago and re-nominated President Hoover and Vice President Charles Curtis. The lethargic Republican gathering produced no surprises, but delegates were confident; they remembered being trounced in 1928 and now were convinced their rivals were badly divided.

Debris left by Republicans in the Chicago Stadium had hardly been swept away before Democrats began coming in. In contrast to the convention just concluded, the Democratic meeting was exuberant, rowdy, and bitter, yet it would become a landmark in the nation's history.

There was a free-for-all battle for the presidential nomination. Al Smith, the party's candidate in 1928, wanted it again. Speaker of the House, "Cactus Jack" Garner of Texas, had sizeable support, and other potential nominees included William MacAdoo (President Woodrow Wilson's son-in-law), Newton D. Baker (Wilson's Secretary of State), Owen D. Young, who had helped engineer a financial recovery for the German Republic, and two governors of U.S. states — Harry F. Byrd of Virginia and "Alfalfa" Bill Murray of Oklahoma. All of them were being challenged by Franklin D. Roosevelt of New York.

One by one the contenders were eliminated, and Roosevelt was named on the fourth ballot with approval from all his opponents except Smith, who, after a period of sulking, finally yielded valuable support.

Franklin Delano Roosevelt was fifty years old and still considered by many as a wealthy playboy in politics. Walter Lippmann, dean of American journalists for more than thirty years, viewed Roosevelt as a likeable sort of fellow, but dismissed him as "an amiable . . . pleasant man who, without any important qualifications for the office, would very much like to be President."

In truth, Roosevelt in 1932 brought considerable experience to the ticket. He had attended three prestigious schools — Groton, Harvard, and the Columbia Law School — had tried law practice and business for a couple of years, married Eleanor Roosevelt, niece of his cousin Theodore whom he greatly admired, had served as Assistant Secretary of the Navy, and had been a vice-presidential nominee on the losing Cox ticket in 1920. His speeches at national conventions in 1924 and 1928 had impressed countless Democratic Party leaders. From the governor's chair in the Empire State, he had done so well that in 1930 he had been re-elected by a whopping 700,000 votes. Only stubborn opponents could deny that he was a *bona fide* contender for the presidency.

When the stock market crashed in 1929, Franklin Roosevelt had been in the Governor's chair in Albany, N.Y. less than a year. In those years, presidential inaugurations didn't take place until March, and it was on the fourth day of that month in 1933 that FDR was sworn in as the nation's thirty-second president. The weather in Washington that day was cold, and across the land, families struggled under conditions even more chilling. The Great Depression was at its lowest. *Fortune* magazine estimated that 28% of the population — 34 million men, women, and children — were without any income — and this estimate didn't even include 11 million farm families.

Factories, which a few years earlier had striven to fill orders, laid off their workers, locked gates, and closed — some forever. In cities, soup kitchens and bread lines kept some of the employed alive but just barely. Wretched shanty towns grew like weeds on the margins of once prosperous urban districts.

# CHAPTER 5. SEIZING THE CROWN

> The President is the nation's Number One Voice. When
> he speaks, he speaks for America.
>
> — James Reston, *New York Times* Columnist

On March 4, 1933, the date of his first inaugural as President, Franklin Roosevelt with outgoing President Hoover sitting by his side did not
merely assent when Supreme Court Justice Charles Evans Hughes asked
the words in the Constitution; instead the incoming Chief Executive repeated each phrase before adding his own, "I do." Then turning to the
crowd, he declared:

> This is a day of national consecration, and I am certain that many Ameri-
> cans expect that on my induction into the presidency I will address them
> with a candor and a decision which our present situation impels.

> This great nation will endure as it has endured, will revive and prosper...
> Let me assert my firm belief that the only thing we have to fear is fear it-
> self — nameless, unreasoning, unjustified terror, which paralyzes needed
> efforts to convert retreat into advance. [1]

Indeed, the nation was in shambles. At fifty-one years of age, Roosevelt, despite the debilitating effects of polio, was a vigorous, healthy bull
of a man, muscular and strong especially in his upper torso. Ready to
work long, late hours into the night, he could function well for days at a
time with little sleep. At first there was no overall plan or grand strategy;
every crisis would be dealt with as it arose. The time called for action of
almost any sort, and he was determined to supply it.

Public treasuries were bankrupt, and in larger cities where relief measures were making their pitiful starts, a stigma accompanied every family's application. The prevalent feeling was that somehow poor people were responsible for the worsening tragedy.

In a special session of Congress, a flurry of legislation was passed — almost all of which came from the new Chief Executive. In that hectic period which historians would label the Hundred Days, Congress passed in quick succession:

March 9 — Legislation to reopen the banks on a sound basis.

March 10 — Legislation to effect economics in government.

March 13 — Modification of the Volstead Law to permit light wines and beer.

March 16 — Legislation for relief of agriculture (AAA).

March 29 — Legislation for supervision of sale of securities (SEC).

April 3 — Legislation to save farm mortgages from foreclosure (FCA).

April 5 — Civilian Conservation Corps created (CCC).

April 10 — Legislation for Tennessee Valley Authority (TVA).

April 13 — Legislation to save small-home mortgages from foreclosure (HOLC).

May 4 — Legislation for relief of railroads.

May 17 — Legislation to establish the National Recovery Administration (NRA).

May 20 — Legislation for relief of the oil industry.

Bills became law so rapidly that considerable confusion arose; more than sixty agencies were created to help revive the shattered economy in one way or another. The numerous alphabetical agencies often overlapped, and the confusion was abetted by competition among directors of the various agencies. The prime example was a mix-up between the WPA and the PWA.

The WPA (Works Projects Administration) was patterned after the Emergency Relief Act set up in New York State while Roosevelt was its Governor. Like its forerunner, the federal WPA's primary purpose was to provide minimum paying jobs for unemployed workers, and the bill creating it gave the President authority to "recommend and carry on small useful projects designed to assure a maximum of employment in all localities." Under the provisions of WPA millions of men dug ditches, shoveled snow, raked leaves, tended cemeteries, guarded public properties, or engaged in other tasks necessary to keep a community going. Roosevelt put Harry Hopkins in charge of WPA, and it was his responsibility to see that millions of destitute individuals were given work by some agency.

By March, 1936, the WPA rolls reached a total of more than 3,400,000 persons, and by June 1943, when it was officially terminated, the agency had spent more than $11 billion. Thus WPA was by far the largest Federal employer and spender.

Hopkins was not without rivals in FDR's administration, and his chief one was formidable Harold Ickes, irascible Secretary of the Interior. FDR himself contributed to the rivalry by never making clear which one of the two he favored, and as a result the mammoth Work Relief Bill through which Congress authorized the spending of billions set up both WPA and PWA — the latter being an abbreviation for Public Works Administration.

The Public Works Administration had been created in order to increase employment and business by "pump-priming," i.e., the raising of popular consuming power through use of public monies. Although increased later, the original authorization for PWA was $3,300 million, and the agency was placed under the authority of Secretary Harold Ickes. PWA's purpose lay in construction of dams, bridges, roads, and other public infrastructures. After a project was authorized, however, wages for men employed on it had to be administered through Hopkins — chief administrator for all Work Relief Measures. In addition to a personal rivalry between Hopkins and Ickes now was added a mixture of the two agencies. A distinguished speech writer and associate of FDR at the time admitted:

> I was one of the large number of Roosevelt supporters who, during the New Deal years, could not understand what was the difference between WPA and PWA, and why there should have been two of them with the same three initials. Actually, the difference between the two organizations was fundamental: it was the difference between two opposed philosophies; essentially the difference between Hopkins and Ickes. The former had the point of view of a welfare worker — that the main object was to get the greatest possible number of people to work in the shortest possible space of time and that the productivity of the work that they performed was a matter of only secondary importance.
>
> Ickes had the point of view of a businessman (albeit an exceptionally liberal one); he believed that the best way to relieve unemployment on a long-range basis was to "prime the pump" by subsidizing private enterprise for the construction of massive, self-liquidating projects.[2]

Ickes charged that Hopkins deliberately chose those same three initials in order to garner credit from the projects which were under the administration and supervision of Ickes's agency — the Public Works Administration, but Ickes's accusation was never corroborated.

# Chapter 6. Advisors and Aides

> I write the pretty mottoes which you find inside the crackers.
>
> — William S. Gilbert

---

Those who study executive power will note that the higher the office, the greater the need for advisors. That was true with FDR. Although he would listen to many opinions, he most often acted from his own impulses and judgments.

Niccolo Machiavelli, oft misunderstood political philosopher of the early sixteenth century, observed:

> The first impression one gets of a ruler and of his brains is from seeing the men he has around him. When they are competent and faithful one can always consider him wise, as he has been able to recognize their ability and keep them faithful. But when they are the reverse, one can always form an unfavorable opinion of him because the first mistake he makes is in making his choice.[1]

No one can study the career of Franklin Roosevelt without considering the impact Eleanor had on him.

Franklin ran his first political race in 1910 and won election from Duchess County as a senator in the New York State Assembly. Eleanor played almost no part in this first campaign, being pregnant and having delivered Elliott, their child, only two months before the election. In Albany she was talked about as the wife of one of the state's most up and coming young politicians. Only after her husband got into the Presidency did Eleanor's persistent political convictions have significant impact.

She first met Harry Hopkins, who would become one of FDR's closest aides, in 1928 when her husband was running for Governor of the State of New York. Three years after his narrow victory in that race, Governor Roosevelt revealed his social philosophy in an address to the State Legislature:

> One of these duties of the State is that of caring for those of its citizens who find themselves the victims of each adverse circumstance as makes them unable to obtain even the necessities for mere existence without the aid of others. That responsibility is recognized by every civilized Nation.[12]

FDR took the philosophy with him into the White House, and his statement of it helps explain many alphabetical agencies during the New Deal and others in the three and a half years of World War II.

In 1890, Harry Hopkins, the son of a harness maker in Sioux City, Iowa, was born, the fourth of five children. Harry's father was a *bon vivant* who found diversions in his skill as a bowler. His mother, when not caring for husband and children, put her efforts into work for the Methodist Church and achieved considerable prominence in the good deeds carried out by that faith. There can be little doubt that son Harry inherited some of his missionary zeal from his mother.

Hopkins' father also was an occasional salesman, and when the family moved to Chicago young Harry came down with a severe case of typhoid which was the beginning of a life-long bout with recurrent digestive illnesses. He returned to Iowa in 1912 to enroll at Grinnell College, and when he was on the verge of graduation from that school four years later, one of his professors recommended him for a position as counselor at a camp for needy children at Bound Brook, New Jersey. It was there that Hopkins first came into contact with the problems of East Coast slums.

As the chief executive in New York, Governor Roosevelt in 1929 set up an agency called the Emergency Temporary Relief Administration and upon recommendations from subordinates chose Harry Hopkins to head it. The appointment brought Hopkins into Eleanor's attention because of her perpetual concern for the underprivileged, and thus began a long and significant collaboration.

In 1933 when nearing the end of his First Hundred Days, FDR brought Hopkins into the Federal Government by naming him chief administrator of the newly-created Federal Emergency Relief Agency, patterned af-

1

ter the one previously set up in New York. That summer Hopkins in his new role spoke out in Detroit debunking the idea that assistance from government agencies was a form of charity. In his judgment, the Federal Government had the obligation, without any pretense of dependence upon private or business groups, to provide relief to citizens needing it. His speech received scant attention from the press, but ideas in it became gospel of the Federal Emergency Relief Agency and the bedrock for numerous offshoots during FDR's presidential administrations. In advocating social and humane measures, Eleanor and Hopkins were sometimes joined by curmudgeonly Secretary of the Interior Harold Ickes.

As war clouds gathered and even more after actual fighting had begun, Roosevelt relied more and more upon Hopkins as an aide whom he could trust for frankness and confidentiality. By-passing the Department of State, FDR sent Hopkins to London to meet Churchill in December of 1940, and from there on to Moscow for a personal appraisal of Stalin. When it came to dealing with other world leaders throughout the war years, Hopkins would remain as FDR's single most confidential aide

Another person FDR relied upon — albeit somewhat less than Hopkins — was Henry Morgenthau, Jr., a neighbor from Duchess County. Morgenthau like Roosevelt came from a well-to-do family, had ideals of his own, and shared FDR's hatred for oppression.

After a brief service in the Navy during World War I, young Henry Morgenthau married, returned to New York State and tried his hand first at raising potatoes, cabbages, squash, rye, and beef cattle. Then he settled more on a dairy herd and tending his apple orchards as well as publishing a weekly newspaper called the *American Agriculturist*. His ventures into agriculture were successful enough to add to the considerable wealth he had inherited.

In 1920 when Roosevelt received the Democratic vice-presidential nomination, Morgenthau served as chairman of the notification ceremonies held at Hyde Park, and that occasion marked the beginning of a long political linkage between him and FDR.

Morgenthau and his wife Elinor (spelled differently from the Eleanor in Franklin's life), were friends who gave comfort to FDR and Eleanor during the former's long rehabilitation from poliomyelitis. Occasionally, the Morgenthaus accompanied the Roosevelts on their houseboat *Narooco* in cruises around the Florida Keys. Both families supported the Presidential candidacies of Alfred Smith in 1924, and four years later when

Smith was nominated again, Roosevelt was selected as the Democratic nominee for the Governorship of New York State.

Smith, a victim of Coolidge prosperity and anti-Catholicism, suffered a humiliating defeat, but Roosevelt won the Governorship, and as the Empire State's newly-elected chief administrator he appointed Morgenthau to be chairman of its Agricultural Advisory Commission.

Morgenthau met Harry Hopkins most likely sometime around 1926 or 1927 when both were working for New York State Government. The two men shared concerns for social problems, some of which included reducing unemployment ranks and improving the lot of the poor. While still working under the aegis of Governor Roosevelt, Morgenthau solicited lists of young men from fellow social workers in New York City and personally organized a precursor of the New Deal's National Youth Administration, the federal agency that later would provide employment for thousands of college aged youths.

Even in the New York years, Morgenthau and Hopkins were fiercely loyal to Franklin Roosevelt and aware of his aspirations. In personality, Hopkins, profligate and fond of playing man-about-town, was almost opposite to Morgenthau, who was restrained and far more conservative in thought and behavior.

In May, 1932, when FDR was enacting plans for capturing the White House, he sent Morgenthau on a trip through the Middle West to question farmers, newspaper editors, and farm experts about agricultural depressions; more particularly, Morgenthau was to find out what such opinion makers thought of the presidential candidacy of Franklin Roosevelt.

Henry A. Wallace of Iowa, agricultural economist and editor of the influential *Wallace's Farmer*, told Morgenthau at their first meeting that if low prices persisted he expected either revolution or state socialism to come about. [23]

According to Wallace, only by controlling the national market and limiting domestic production could farm prices be raised. Morgenthau wasn't convinced; he agreed that prices ought to be raised, but he always had believed that could be accomplished best by distributing more industrial output, not in reducing crop and livestock production. Nevertheless, he reported his findings to FDR, and as voters soon learned though numerous federal agencies, it was Wallace's agricultural con-

2

cepts, not Morgenthau's, that FDR took with him when he moved into the White House.

The "Corn/Hog" ratio that Wallace developed paid farmers to plow under their crops and dispose of surplus hogs — often with shotguns. The program worked; in Iowa, for example, the herd of 10 million hogs was cut in half by 1935, and prices edged upwards from their all-time low of 1932. Moreover, Wallace's "Ever Normal Granary" pushed corn prices up from worthless to $1 per bushel by 1936.

Appointed Secretary of the Treasury in 1934, Henry Morgenthau would serve in that post for eleven years. During the span he supervised the sale of more than $200,000,000 worth of government bonds to finance America's defense and war activities. He was one of Roosevelt's most loyal Cabinet members and considered himself one of the President's closest confidants.

Throughout his tenure, Morgenthau offered FDR ideas and suggestions which grew into needed programs. It was he who first proposed to President Roosevelt the creation of the New Deal's Civilian Conservation Corps, the government agency that put young men to work on reforestation and related projects.

Franklin Roosevelt was sometimes forthright with Morgenthau; after all, he had more in common with this Dutchess County neighbor than with most persons around him. But in truth he revealed very little of himself to others. Even with Morgenthau, there were bounds not to be crossed. FDR announced as much once when the two men were having a discussion after a lunch together. The conversation took place in the late spring of 1935, not long after the U.S. House of Representatives had passed a veterans' bonus bill which FDR as well as his predecessor President Hoover opposed. FDR had stated publicly that he was against any legislation conflicting with his budget estimates or discriminating in favor of special groups.

Understandably, veterans were antagonized, and Morgenthau was instructed to concentrate his own energy in attempting to drum up support for his chief. By the third week in May, when FDR and Morgenthau were alone after lunch, the President indicated he was wavering. According to notes in Morgenthau's diary,

> FDR said, "Patman [the Congressman who had sponsored the bonus bill in the House] asked me point-blank this morning if I was against all bonus legislation or whether I had an open mind, and I told him I had an open mind because how could I know what they might pass."

I had a sort of sinking feeling and found myself sort of gradually crumpling up, and I said, "If you want me to go on, please do not talk that way to me because I am building a bonfire of support for you in your veto message."

He said rather quickly with a smile, "Let's agree that I will not talk to you about any compromise if you will not talk to me about any bonfire. In other words, never let your left hand know what your right hand is doing."

I said, "Which hand am I, Mr. President?"

And he said, "My right hand," he said. "But I keep my left hand under the table."

This is the most frank expression of the real FDR that I ever listened to and that is the real way he works.[34]

There were others in FDR's early Brain Trust. David Lilienthal, Rex Tugwell, and Tommy (the Cork) Corcoran to name a few. During those years in office FDR tended to listen to other persons before stating his own judgment. As months passed, his innate self-confidence soared and he would guide a conference the way he chose, often pleasing an attendee but actually engaging in distraction. And as more years went by, he would dispense with information gathering conferences, issue an edict by executive action, and then tell aides and lieutenants why the action he had taken.

Franklin Roosevelt had numerous advisors and craftsmen who helped draft messages and speeches. His most able and dedicated aide in this vital aspect of the Presidency was Samuel Rosenman. FDR and Rosenman first met in 1928 when the latter was running for the Governorship of the State of New York.

Rosenman began amassing material on such matters as labor legislation, unemployment insurance, better housing, education, and public health. He would categorize his findings and place them in large red manila envelopes, each properly labeled by subject matter. He showed his system to Roosevelt, who was impressed enough that four years later when he launched his own run for the Presidency he asked Rosenman to join the team. Rosenman accepted and rose to become the chief speech writer throughout the more than twelve years FDR was in office.

Ideas change as they are phrased, and no one within FDR's entourage and his eminence in office was more valuable than his veteran speech writer, Sam Rosenman. Rosenman would be joined by other wordsmiths, including playwright Robert Sherwood and presidential confidante Har-

3

ry Hopkins. Others might claim to have contributed ideas and phrasing, of course, and no doubt did so upon occasion, but none could match the reliance FDR placed upon Rosenman. Adolf Berle, Assistant Secretary of State in 1940 wrote that all of FDR's writers were talented and devoted to their chief. Berle then added a caveat:

> Hopkins and Sherwood, along with Federal Judges Felix Frankfurter and William O. Douglas were a highly intelligent crew — and, except for Sam Rosenman, as unscrupulous a crew as was ever put together. Rosenman is square. Harry Hopkins is nice and likeable, but would commit murder for the President. The rest of the bunch would commit murder on general principles, either for the President or for themselves. How you can put any of the saving grace of solidity of character into this bunch is a question I've been unable to solve.[5]

## Chapter 7. FDR: First Media President

Roosevelt's words, like regiments, went, yea go, marching
on. There was a voice... We shall not soon hear its like again.

— T. V. Smith, Philosopher, University of Chicago, 1948

By the time Franklin Roosevelt entered the White House, the role of media had become crucial to the success of a presidency in bringing about significant changes in domestic or foreign policies or even administering existing ones. Masterful as he was in reading manuscripts before microphone and upon the dais, FDR did not rely upon those performances alone for communicating with the American public. In press conferences, he was equally adept if not even more so. Few presidents would match his success in establishing favorable, lasting relationships with working members of the press. At the outset of his administration, the press usually referred just to newspapers and magazines, but soon radio, photography, and newsreels were added to media he could use for persuading the citizenry. He seemed to enjoy his twice-weekly meetings with the Washington press corps. In all, he held 998 press conferences, most of which he conducted like a friendly, informal schoolmaster presiding over a seminar of attentive students. He was able to influence the news gathering by the very exclusiveness of attendees, for the gatherings were limited in attendance to correspondents who had credentials from either the House or Senate Press Galleries or from the White House Correspondents Association. Moreover, only accredited correspondents could ask questions or make comments.

Cultivation of the press did not begin with FDR's presidencies. Almost at the outset of our government, Thomas Jefferson won a strong ally in Phillip Freneau, a journalist whose 1792 *National Gazette* became such an adversary of the Federalists that President George Washington cursed "that rascal Freneau." And from the administrations of Jefferson through Jackson the press was courted by awarding printing contracts to newspapers that were serving as presidential mouthpieces.

Andrew Jackson had Amos Kendall and Francis Blair as powerful friends in the press. Later, Theodore Roosevelt had William Loeb, Jr., and Woodrow Wilson had Joseph Tumulty as personal advisors who influenced presidential style so that it would be reported more favorably.

A legislature, be it state or federal, speaks with many voices, an able executive with one. Few can dispute that FDR was one of the most eloquent spokesmen in the nation's history; not only persuasive at the rostrum, he was unsurpassed when it came to using press conferences as forums to advance his own interpretations of news events or the goals of his administration. His talents in this regard were abetted by radio, which had grown tremendously since the beginning of the century. During that time political power in the U.S. had tilted away from legislatures to executives. Radio reduced the effectiveness of multiple voices in an assembly and enhanced the persuasiveness of the single-voiced strong executive. FDR was foremost among those in this category.

FDR established a high standing with most reporters; most of whom were impressed with his political acumen and craftsmanship. Leo Rosten, chronicler and analyst of the Washington press corps during the 1930s, concluded that Roosevelt's bonhomie with reporters sprang from the fact that he was not so much trying to give them stories for an avid public but rather to get them to frame those stories in ways favorable to him.[1]

Franklin Roosevelt has to be considered the first of the media presidents; it was he who created the modern news conference. He was unsurpassed when it came to using press conferences as forums to advance his own interpretations of news events or the goals of his administration. Presidential meeting with members of the press had roots in forerunners, but it was FDR who used such gatherings often enough and in such fashion as to make them indispensable to the nation's leader.

FDR was one of the first politicians to recognize that radio technology helped put more power into the executive branch of government. The larger the government grew, the greater the power held by the administrator at its head, whether it be at the state or federal level. The emergence of the U.S. as one of the world's great industrial powers elevated its president even further. The office swelled into gigantic proportions, and as it did with its ever growing power and authority, FDR grew more secretive, seldom sharing his private thoughts and more guarded in his statements.

The perceptive Charles E. Bohlen, an American diplomat who spent a lot of time with Roosevelt later in the war, summarized FDR's personality:

> [He] was a world figure of monumental proportions . . . Yet I cannot say he was a likable man. He preferred informal relationships which were informal merely in structure. He could not stand protocol in the accepted sense of the word but was quick to resent the slightest departure from the respect normally accorded the President of the United States, and the aura of the office was always around him.[14]

Franklin's cousin Theodore had called the presidency a "bully pulpit" and had used it to great advantage in preaching the strenuous life or for flaying the "malefactors of great wealth." FDR also viewed the presidency as a pulpit for moral leadership. "I want to be a preaching President," Franklin once said, "like my cousin." And preach he did.

He became an orator of rank soon after being elected Governor of New York. In those early speeches he tried to make his messages warm, intimate, and aimed at specific individuals in the audience. After polio had crippled him, Roosevelt's actions on the platform were severely limited. He usually used one arm to rest on the lectern, steadying himself as he spoke, and the other hand then was free to turn the pages of his manuscript. In his day there were no such contrivances as teleprompters, so he spoke either extemporaneously or from a manuscript. He preferred the latter for several reasons, one of which was the confidence which came from his superb ability to read with feeling. Whatever he lacked in bodily gestures while speaking he made up for with his resonant voice and expressive vocal patterns.

For the most part, during FDR's first eight years in office, Congress passed the bills he requested one after another in quick succession. One of the country's most brilliant politicians, he knew the value of gestures, slogans, and catch phrases. Hitler established the stiff right arm as the Nazi salute, and Mussolini's strut became a sure sign of his appearance. Churchill's fingered V after 1940 signified victory by the Allies. Clare Boothe Luce, critic and playwright in her own domain and wife of influential publisher Henry Luce, when asked what she thought would be the most apt sign for FDR, moistened her index finger and pointed it upwards to test force and direction of the wind. Her gesture was not far wrong, for FDR felt it absolutely necessary to ascertain public sentiment before taking major steps in international diplomacy. The polling indus-try had become a vital accessory to political success.

Understandably, throughout most of his first two terms in office most of FDR's rhetoric was directed toward the country's terrible economic condition. Within two weeks of taking office, he gave his first fireside chat. The fireside chats, as they soon were dubbed by the press, were informal, short messages, none lasting more than thirty minutes. To lis-teners gathered by radios in living rooms across the nation the talks may have sounded like informal remarks thought up on the spur of the mo-ment; contrary to that impression they were planned and crafted very carefully.

# CHAPTER 8. SUPREME COURT IMBROGLIO

> The court plan is not liberal. A liberal cause was never
> won by stacking a deck of cards, by stuffing a ballot box, or
> by packing a court.
>
> — Senator Burton K. Wheeler

Passage of the Banking Act helped shore up financial institutions, and the Triple A was in place to revitalize the nation's distressed farmers. One more measure was needed — a shotgun law which would stimulate industrial and business activity, thereby reducing unemployment. With those goals in mind, a bill prepared by Democratic stalwarts drew little debate and was passed hurriedly by the 73rd Congress on the day it adjourned, June 16, 1933.

Named the National Industrial Recovery Act, later shortened simply to the NRA, the program would become one of the New Deal's most touted and yet most controversial enactments. The act aimed to revive industrial and business activity and to cut down on unemployment — the most visible sores of the Depression.

Actions under codes and agreements were exempt from operations of antitrust laws, and courts could issue injunctions against violators. A high-minded idea, the NRA was based on the principle of industrial self-regulation, operating under government supervision through a system of fair competition codes. Fair trade codes had been set up and used by industrial and related associations in the period following the First World

War. With the New Deal in full flow, the NRA was begun with new, fair competition codes to be approved by the President and enforceable by law.

The President was given authority to prescribe the codes and to make agreements or approve voluntary agreements.

One section of the NRA Act, Section 7a, guaranteed labor's right "to organize and bargain collectively through representatives of their own choosing." Title II of the established the Public Works Administration (WPA). FDR put crusty Secretary of the Interior Harold I. Ickes in charge of the WPA, which during its lifetime and under his aegis spent a total of $4,250 million on more than 34,000 public projects.[1]

The President first picked General Hugh S. Johnson to head the NRA. Johnson had graduated from West Point in 1903 and had helped draft the Selective Service Act used during World War I. At the end of that conflict, he had left army service and had campaigned vigorously for FDR in the '32 election.

At the outset of the NRA, Johnson was highly recognized for his prior achievements and was chosen by *Time* magazine as its 1933 "Man of the Year." "Old Iron Pants," as he was called, threw his evangelistic style into promoting the NRA, and its symbol, the "blue eagle," flew in store windows and business establishments across the nation.

Almost immediately, the colorful, outspoken, and opinionated Johnson began to rankle business leaders. They complained he was dictatorial, and it was not long before he was criticized for having fascist tendencies. By 1934 his reputation had lost much of its luster.

FDR's naming of Ickes to lead the WPA put Hugh Johnson in a subservient role. Humiliated and angered, Johnson's language grew more intemperate as he came under attacks by officials within the Administration and increasing volleys from the public. Some historians ascribe his fall to inherent contradictions in the NRA; others attribute it to his acknowledged drinking. Whatever the cause, he was faltering badly by 1934, and FDR replaced him. Although Johnson's enthusiasm had lost most of its vigor when the '36 election rolled around, he still supported FDR.

Eight months after the seminal NRA Act had been passed by Congress, a National Recovery Board, primarily to enforce labor's right to collective bargaining, was established. Three months later, this body submitted a gloomy report, alleging that to the detriment of small businesses, the parent NRA agency was encouraging monopoly and cartelization.

Charged with enforcement of collective bargaining practices, the NLRB could ban company unions as well as employers for interferences with union organizing.

The Board was given authority to investigate an employee's charge of unfair labor practices (such as intimidation, espionage, discrimination, etc.), and could summon the employer for a trial hearing. If the charges were upheld by the NLRB, it could issue a "cease and desist" order enforceable by federal courts.

Business and financial leaders saw such measures as intrusions upon their basic rights. Adverse reactions to the NRA mounted, and even some old guard New Dealers broke ranks. Then a legal case, the formal name of which was *Schechter Poultry Corporation vs. United States*, set off nationwide repercussions as it percolated its way to the Supreme Court.

The challenge had originated when the Schechter brothers, operators of a Brooklyn poultry business, were convicted of violating the NRA's Live Poultry Code by selling diseased chickens and by disregarding the code's wage-and-hour provisions. When appeals reached the Supreme Court, attorneys for the Administration insisted that the grave economic emergency had made codes and empowerment of the President necessary.

The Court brushed aside such arguments, and in May 1935, passed a unanimous decision ruling that in approving the National Industrial Recovery Act, Congress had exceeded its authority. "Extraordinary conditions do not create or enlarge constitutional powers," ruled the nation's highest tribunal.[2]

During his first press conference following that judicial decision, an embittered President Roosevelt asserted that the Court's action had rendered the powers of the federal government to "the horse and buggy age." There already was enough controversy, but FDR's statement denigrating the Court's judgment made the bubbling stew rise higher.

His opponents fought back in Congress, in newspapers and magazines, and over air waves. On one Sunday evening during prime time listening hours, a leading businessman used the Columbia Broadcasting System to retaliate to FDR's "horse and buggy"-age metaphor.

The speaker admitted that throughout history there indeed had been great changes. Society had moved from cartwheel, to stagecoach, to saddlebags, pony express, telegraph, steamboats, railways, automobiles, and even to airplanes. Families now owned automobiles, and parking lots at Detroit were filled to overflowing. However, individual men and women had made the achievements and had done so without government shackles such as the NRA.

"If you want something done, you must do it yourself." If one man can do it, others can and will. It was the man in the driver's seat who brought progress to society. "Free enterprise," the speaker insisted, "is the spinal cord of progress."[3]

Former President Herbert Hoover, Senators Hiram Johnson, William Borah, Gerald Nye, and other Republican spokesmen jumped into the debate along with scribes from the media. One of the latter, acerbic H. L. Mencken, wrote that in 1932 America had been told utopia was on its way, and he added:

> Wizards of the highest amperage . . . were on hand to do the job, and they were armed with new and infallible arcana. . . But what did these wizards turn out to be? Once on the job they were the sorriest mob of mountebanks ever gathered together at one time — even in Washington . . . vapid young pedagogues, out-of-work YMCA secretaries, third-rate journalists, briefless lawyers, and soaring chicken farmers. . . As for the President, he has survived for a long time through the very flexibility of his principles. . . If he became convinced tomorrow that coming out for cannibalism would get him votes . . . he would begin fattening a missionary in the White House backyard come Wednesday.[4]

Conservative critics attracted converts, and in the summer of 1935 Republican prospects began looking up. Roosevelt's popularity sagged in the next winter, and in August of the following year the GOP won a congressional election in Rhode Island. The Republican upsurge continued in November when the party captured the city of Philadelphia and the New York State Assembly.

Herbert Hoover led the old guard in speeches denouncing regimentations of the New Deal, but he offered only past formulas: retrenchment, a balanced budget, the gold standard, the tariff, and return of relief measures to control by the states.

In addition to Hoover, other possible Republican candidates for the presidency included Senators William E. Borah from Idaho and Arthur H. Vandenberg of Michigan, and Frank Knox, publisher of the Chicago Daily News. Then a dark horse, Governor Alfred M. Landon of Kansas, joined the nomination-seeking pack.

Republicans held their convention in Cleveland the second week in June, 1936, and on the first ballot chose the dark horse, Alfred Landon, to lead their ticket. Landon was the only Republican governor elected in 1932 who survived the Democratic land-slide two years later and was an old Bull Mooser, more liberal than the party that nominated him. He did not see the New Deal as a plot to undercut American institutions and in fact had supported some New Deal programs.

Landon could boast of a balanced budget in his home state, and it was thought would win agricultural votes throughout the Midwest. A sincere, plain-speaking man with little magnetism, Landon lacked the style of FDR; journalists called him a "Kansas Coolidge." He had declined to fly to Cleveland to accept the nomination for fear such a gesture would appear to be aping his opponent's dramatic flight to Chicago four years earlier.

For their convention, Democrats met in Philadelphia during the last week in June. The gathering was more coronation than convention, for there was no question FDR would be chosen again. Senator Alben Barkley of Kentucky delivered the keynote address, and in it gave a sonorous defense of the New Deal, addressing also the furor caused by the Supreme Court's decision.

"Over against the hosannas of Hoover for the tortured interpretation of the Constitution of this nation," intoned Barkley to uproarious applause from delegates, "I place the tortured souls and bodies of its working men, women, and children." The trouble lay not with the Constitution , he said, but with the men who interpreted it. The Democratic Party wanted the Court to treat the Constitution "as a life-giving charter, rather than an object of curiosity on the shelf of a museum."[5]

Barkley's language reinforced FDR's convictions, and the election that fall was lackluster. Landon's tours and unpretentious campaigning failed to convince many voters. Democrats garnered nearly twenty-five million votes compared with sixteen million given Republicans. Results from the electoral college were even more overwhelming: for Democrats 98.49 percent, or 523 votes — 46 states — all states except Maine and Vermont; and for Republicans, 1.51 percent, or 8 votes — two states.[6]

Buoyed by the size of his victory and with his dander up from the rebuke suffered by the Supreme Court rulings, Roosevelt vowed to continue the fight. Particularly galling was his realization that he was the first American President to serve a four-year term without being able to name a single Supreme Court Justice. To him it was obvious the body was dominated by conservatives who used their own economic and social biases to interpret the Constitution.

He talked the matter over with advisors, some of whom recommended taking the problem to congressional leaders. After all, Congress had the power to reenact laws voided by the Supreme Court and to raise the number of justices required to invalidate a Congressional Act from a simple majority to perhaps six or even seven votes. Other confidants suggested launching arguments for a constitutional amendment, but FDR learned that two thirds of Congress and three quarters of state legislatures were necessary for a constitutional amendment. Opponents could easily choke off that avenue.

Besides, FDR insisted, the trouble lay not in the Constitution itself but in the old men interpreting it. The President asked his attorney general to search files for any precedents, and the search revealed a plan proposed in 1913 under President Woodrow Wilson — an idea for empowering the President of the United States to appoint a new federal judge for every one with ten years of service who had reached the age of seventy and failed to retire. There was nothing sacred about the actual number of justices on the Supreme Court. John Adams had cut the original six members down to five, and Jefferson had upped the membership to seven.

Twenty-three years prior to the Civil War, the Court was set at nine, and under Lincoln's administration it had increased to ten. After the Civil War, the Court was decreased to eight members, and in 1869 increased again to nine, its membership in 1936.

FDR pounced on the scheme offered by his attorney general, saying it was "the answer to a maiden's prayer." Spokesmen on the other side, equally fervent, immediately labeled it "court packing." By the end of January 1937, FDR was ready to fire his weapons.

On the thirtieth of that month, while movie stars and other celebrities were assembling downstairs in the White House for his annual Birthday Ball, FDR held a private luncheon upstairs with only four trusted associates. After dishes had been cleared, he read aloud a letter from his attorney general — one of the attendees — recounting workloads and delayed cases on dockets of judicial courts everywhere, including the Supreme Court.

Then came his stunning revelation: he was going to submit a proposal dealing with judges in any federal court — including the Supreme Court — who had reached the age of seventy. The plan, in essence, provided that whenever a judge of that age in any federal court refused to avail himself of his existing statutory opportunity to retire on a pension, an additional judge should be appointed to that court by the President with approval of the Senate. There was no discussion by attendees at the luncheon — just FDR's announcement.

A White House Judiciary Dinner was scheduled for February 2, 1937. In accordance with custom, all members of the Supreme Court were invited. Other guests that evening brought the number of attendees to slightly over ninety. Toasts were drunk honoring the Court and discussion over cocktails more serious than usual. After the meal, the ladies retired to the Blue Room and the men went into the Green Room, where FDR chatted and joked with seven of the Supreme Court Justices — two members, Justice Louis Brandeis and Justice Harlan Stone, had been unable to attend.

When the party broke up and guests had left, FDR asked Sam Rosenman, by this time his chief speech writer, to stay and work on a message announcing the Court scheme. FDR had called a Cabinet meeting for the next morning and had invited key congressional leaders, including the chairmen of the Senate and House Judiciary Committees, along with Speaker of the House Bankhead, Democratic House Leader Sam Rayburn, and Joe Robinson, the Democratic Senate leader. A press conference where FDR intended to disclose the Court plan would follow the Cabinet gathering.

At the opening of the press conference, President Roosevelt read his prepared message about revising the Supreme Court. There was no discussion or further questioning then, but as soon as the plan became public, explosions began. Opposition came from the Congress, from the Court itself, and from almost the entire press of the nation. Congressional attacks were carried on more violently and bitterly by members of Roosevelt's own party than by the Republicans.

As soon as FDR's plan for reorganizing the judiciary reached Capitol Hill, supporters in both Senate and House dropped it into respective legislative hoppers. Seams in the New Deal coalition that had won victory in the preceding fall's election came apart so quickly that even FDR himself was surprised. Battle lines for the coming fight formed and hardened immediately.

Conservative politicians and newspapers gleefully jumped on the plan, and former President Hoover warned, "Hands off the Supreme Court!" The public was upset, for it had not been informed through previous planning and coordination. People needed time to consider an attack upon such a venerable institution as the Supreme Court.

The President had struck a tender nerve, sending shock waves everywhere. The stock market dropped; Chambers of Commerce, Daughters of the American Revolution, the Liberty League, American Legion, National Association of Manufacturers, civic clubs, and organizations of all sorts passed denunciatory resolutions. Ordinary voters flooded their elected representatives with pleas to save the country from "dictatorship."

FDR retaliated, and on March 4th, at a hundred-dollar-a-plate dinner celebrating his victory at the polls in the preceding November, he called upon Democrats to close ranks and preserve gains made over the past four years. Lashing out at the Supreme Court, he claimed that by electing him a second time American citizens wanted to throw off shackles of the past. Reform measures, however, were being continually frustrated in New Deal efforts to make democratic processes work. Major programs in response to present needs were being aborted by an antiquated Supreme Court.

A week later he gave a fireside chat in which he again offered reasons for his Court proposal. He hoped to quiet public clamor over the plot and to satisfy those who thought a constitutional amendment preferable. In this homey living room setting, FDR asserted:

> It would take months and years thereafter to get a two-thirds majority in favor of that amendment in both Houses of the Congress. Then would come the long course of ratification by three-fourths of all the States . . . Thirteen States which contain only five percent of the voting population can block ratification even though the thirty-five States with ninety-five percent of the population are in favor of it. . .

> And remember one thing more. . . An amendment, like the rest of the Constitution, is what the Justices say it is rather than what its framers or you might hope it is. 7

The U.S. Senate Judiciary Committee opened hearings on the President's proposal the second week in March, and the Administration's case was presented by Homer Cummings Attorney General, and his assistant Robert Jackson. Questioning of the two was vigorous and buttressed by a team of legal experts from the American Bar Association invited to the hearings by opposition leaders.

Twelve days later, Senator Burton Wheeler began the rebuttal by attacking the nub of the administration's argument: that lethargy from "overaged justices had created a logjam of unresolved cases." Drawing a letter from his pocket, Senator Wheeler dramatically announced, "I have here a letter from the Chief Justice of the Supreme Court, Mr. Charles Evans Hughes, dated March 21, 1937, written by him and approved by Mr. Justice Brandeis and Mr. Justice Van Devanter."

All were astonished! Not within memory had a Chief Justice taken part in a public controversy. Factually and unemotionally, Hughes's seven-page letter refuted the charge that the Court was unable to handle its workload or letting cases stack up.

"There is no congestion of cases upon our calendar," Justice Hughes had written, and he supported the contention by showing a statistical table. The addition of more judges, Hughes declared, would simply mean "more judges to hear, more judges to confer, more judges to discuss, more judges to be convinced and to decide." With consummate skill, the nation's highest judge had wiped out the President's plot to expand the Court.

Arguments by the public and within legislative halls continued, but the battle had been decided by the letter from Chief Justice Hughes. On July 22, 1937, the Supreme Court plan was finally and definitely rejected by the Congress. Roosevelt and New Deal diehards later would insist their arguments had swayed the Court so much that most goals had been achieved anyhow; more dispassionate observers wrote that the President had acted hastily and in anger, making the biggest single mistake thus far in his presidency.

# Chapter 9. Europe's War — 1939

"Today, September 1, 1939, Nazi Troops crossed Germany's eastern border and entered the sovereign state of Poland."

— *New York Times*, September 2, 1939

---

As the decade of the 1930s came to its end, the black horse of poverty and despair which had galloped across America — a land presumably protected by two oceans — was no longer front page news. Employment figures had risen, and the economy was rolling again. President Franklin Roosevelt's popularity reached 71% — the highest figure in the Gallup Poll Institute's seven-year "vote of confidence" index.

The gambit that set off World War II was taken on the first day of September, 1939, when Chancellor Adolf Hitler ordered Wehrmacht troops to cross Germany's eastern border and enter western Poland. That was the beginning of a debacle that would claim the lives of more than fourteen million men and women under arms as well as countless civilians killed either by deliberate intent or as innocent victims of modern warfare.

A tidal wave of German airplanes first swept into Poland, whose air force was destroyed in two days, its army in seven, and its capital city captured in sixteen. In fulfillment of pledges to Poland, England and France declared war on Germany, and then, worsening the crisis, came the Soviet Union's march into hapless Poland from the east.

For nearly a month after these happenings, except for scattered naval engagements there was almost no fighting by the Western Allies. The combatants were like wary boxers feeling out opponents in the opening rounds of a prize fight.

As soon as Poland was crushed, the German government put out peace feelers to Britain and France, but these were rejected. Conventional wisdom lay in believing that all sides were waiting for the coming of spring, and even in that season the Germans would not be able to pierce the Maginot Line, a defense arrangement extending from the border of Switzerland to Belgium.

Joseph Goebbels, Nazi Minister of Propaganda, instructed German soldiers facing the Maginot Line to shout friendly greetings across it, engaging the French in brotherly conversation. One careful chronicler of what historians would label the Phony War wrote:

> Propaganda teams blasted news and information over loudspeakers, aimed at proving that France and Germany were really not enemies. At night sentimental songs were broadcast . . . and before signing off the announcer would say something like: "Good night, dear enemy. We don't like this war any more than you do. Who is responsible? Not you nor I. So why shoot each other?" . . . In the daytime French troops were showered with leaflets showing a shivering *poilu* at the front in one picture and his wife in bed with an English soldier in another.[1]

Britain was expected to maintain control of the seas, so there would be no need for the United States to get involved. Except for the appearance of men and women in uniform, life in the European capitals was little changed from the prewar era.

In America, the mood was complacent and strongly isolationist. The forerunner of a world war was over; the dire event had come, but we were secure behind our sea bastions on east and west. Nevertheless, lives in the U.S. began changing.

On May 16, 1940, President Roosevelt had addressed a joint session of the U.S. Congress, his first appearance there since the beginning of the European war. For thousands of citizens in western Europe, it had been a dreadful week. The aroused Nazi Wehrmacht had traded the *sitzkrieg* (stalemate war) for a *blitzkrieg* (lightning war) in which ground forces overran armed defenses and crossed rivers and canals as if they were concrete roadways. In Holland thousands of citizens had been killed; the Belgian army was destroyed, and France was being overrun; its capital city was endangered, and indeed in another month it, too, would fall to the invaders.

With such knowledge as backdrop, President Roosevelt devoted nearly a third of this address to a description of the vulnerability of

American cities to airplane attacks from Greenland, the Azores, and islands in the Caribbean. In an age of air warfare, he declared, the Atlantic Ocean no longer gave the protection it had in the past.

The democratic nations in Western Europe standing in the path of Hitler's incursions continued to look toward the United States for help. Added to their eagerness was President Roosevelt's insistence that only this country possessed the necessary resources — an abundance of raw materials, oil fields, bauxite mines, assembly lines in factories, production equipment, engineering skills, and manpower sufficient to match those of Nazi Germany.

In his address to Congress in that May, 1940, President Roosevelt startled the citizenry by asking for appropriations to increase the number of men in the army, to purchase guns and equipment, to build modern tanks, and to construct naval ships. Then he announced a dramatic call for production of fifty thousand airplanes per year — a figure so high most Americans thought impossible.

When he needed money, FDR chose to act independently, sending personal emissaries to London rather than using regular diplomatic channels, and as the U.S. moved ever closer to actual involvement, his secret moves increased. For example, Congress did not learn until after the war that from January 1941 until March of the same year, when the United States was not an official belligerent, British military staffs had flown to Washington to conduct secret strategy talks with American Chiefs of Staff.

The year of 1940 saw air battles intensifying over the skies of Europe. At first, German strategy was to bomb Britain into submission. Cities like London, Coventry, and Birmingham suffered massive destruction. In the second week of May, 1940, the reins of government were passed from the faltering hands of Neville Chamberlain into the iron grip of Winston Churchill, who grimly announced he had little to offer but "blood, sweat, toil, and tears." Throughout the world, Britishers and all who supported their cause responded to his call. Gallant defenses by Hurricane and Spitfire pilots exacted an unsupportable toll from Hermann Goering's *Luftwaffe*, and by September, 1940, the German air force had to admit its bombing campaign had failed.

On the ground, however, Nazi forces were more successful in 1940. Eastward along the French cost toward Belgium thirty-nine sea miles from Dover, England lay Dunkirk. The community there had begun in the early Middle Ages around a church or kirk on the dunes, and in May, 1940, it had become the last point of retreat for British and French forces fleeing from the overwhelming forces of the Wehrmacht. British Expeditionary Forces together with more than 110,000 French soldiers were trapped — it would be surrender or drown in the sea. Back in London, the new Churchill government debated whether to continue the war or offer indirect peace gestures to the Nazis. Churchill and his hard-liners prevailed.

A valiant rescue effort was mounted by British civilians who amassed yachts, barges, steamers, nearly every private craft that could be found. In Germany, der Fuhrer hailed the end of "the greatest battle in world history" and decreed that throughout the Third *Reich* church bells should toll for three days in celebration. Meanwhile, the jerrybuilt fleet from Britain crossed the waters to Dunkirk and picked up more than 340,000 British soldiers along with 110,000 French. It might have been the most brilliant rescue in world history; nevertheless, soon afterwards in the House of Commons, Churchill growled, "Wars are not won by evacuations."[2]

After Dunkirk, the German army swung south and began decimating remnants of the French army. In two weeks, French forces collapsed. From Rome, Benito Mussolini watching the scenario and wanting to be in on the spoils, on June 10, 1940, declared war on France. Five days later, Paris fell to the invaders, and a hastily formed French government under the aged Marshal Pétain sued for peace. Hitler was not generous; he occupied more than half of France, leaving only a southern portion to be administered by Pétain and Pierre Laval, who agreed to collaborate and even to recruit workers for German war industries.

The fall of France raised the distinct possibility of the fall of England, too, for Germany already was amassing troops and supplies on French ports along the English Channel. An overwhelming number of Americans wanted to see the defeat of Hitler and his satellites, but an even larger number wanted to keep out of the war.

Eyes of diplomats in Washington looked toward Europe, but trouble also was brewing far west in the Pacific. In September, 1940, Japan formally joined the European Axis in a Tripartite Pact which stipulated that in the event any of the three members — Japan, Germany, and Italy — got into war with the U.S. the other two members of the Pact would pitch in.

President Roosevelt , a political calculating machine in his head, assessing the citizenry mood adopted an everything "short of war" policy. FDR's strategy was: 1) to help keep England fighting in Europe, 2) to gain time for American rearmament, and 3) to restrain Japan by diplomacy and naval "deterrence."[3]

His lieutenants engineered a compromise bill passed by a support-
ive Congress, and this legislation permitted belligerents to obtain war
materials from the U.S. on a "cash and carry" basis. Britain and France
promptly took advantage of the opportunity, but it would be months
and even years before tanks, planes, and armaments sufficient to match
German armaments could roll off assembly lines in America.

President Roosevelt took other significant actions in 1940. In mid-
September under his urging Congress passed the first peacetime conscription bill in U.S. history. The law, named the Burke–Wadsworth
Act after its congressional sponsors, provided for registration of all men
between the ages of 21 and 35, and the induction into the armed services
of 800,000 draftees.

In the same month, FDR announced an arrangement for transfer to
Britain of fifty destroyers, which Prime Minister Churchill explained just
happened to be in British ports by the "long arm of coincidence." The
deal did not arouse much public disapproval, certainly not as much as
it might have done under a different leader and at another time. Some
critics did charge that when coupled with other measures taken by the
Administration it was dragging the U.S. inexorably into the European
war; supporters rebutted that only by helping Britain and France defeat
Hitler could the U.S. be saved from similar attacks.

Lines were formed, committees created, and arguments between isolationists and interventionists dominated newspapers, radio, and meetings of all sorts. The day after revelation of the destroyer deal, isolationists announced formation of the America First Committee. This Committee, an outgrowth of an earlier student organization at Yale University,
caught national leaders such as General Robert E. Wood, chairman of
the board of Sears, Roebuck and Company, and soon had chapters established across the land.

Chicago was chosen as the Committee's headquarters, and Wood
along with six others formed an executive committee that supervised
America First Committee's strategy and policies. Among prominent
members drawn into the America First Committee were General Hugh
Johnson (former NRA administrator), Alice Longworth Roosevelt, Mrs.
Burton K. Wheeler, Mrs. Bennett Champ Clark (wives of two well-
known U.S. Senators), World War I air ace Eddie Rickenbacker, Hanford MacNider, writer Kathleen Norris, and actress Lillian Gish. Indus-
trialist Henry Ford was a member for a time but was dropped in order
to refute the charge of anti-Semitism thrown at the Committee. Charles
Lindbergh was not an initial member but joined the national committee

in April, 1941.[4] Before its demise after December 7, 1941, the America First Committee had more than 450 chapters in the U.S. and a national membership of more than 850,000 persons.

One month before France surrendered to Germany, William Allen White, combative editor of the *Emporia Gazette* in Kansas, announced formation a Committee to Defend America by Aiding the Allies. This interventionist group opposed the isolationists, supported Administration moves, and formed its own chapters across the nation. White's Committee had its own notables, including John J. McCloy, writer Elizabeth Cutter Morrow (Lindbergh's mother-in-law), and the intellectual community led by playwright and part time speech writer for FDR, Robert Sherwood. This Committee's efforts were indefatigable in gathering signatures, mailing pamphlets, and distributing handbills arguing its case. The Committee to Defend America by Aiding the Allies had lots of financial backing after winning support from most newspapers except for the *Chicago Tribune* and the *Washington Times-Herald*. By early summer of 1940, the pendulum marking arguments between isolationists and interventionists swung back and forth. Some observers noted that the upper classes tended to be interventionist with more than two-thirds of America's business and intellectual leadership favoring increased shipments to Britain.

# Chapter 10. Third Term

> "I struggled as hard as I could to beat Franklin Roosevelt,
> and I tried to keep from pulling my punches. He was elected
> president. He is my president now."
>
> — Willkie to Senate Foreign Relations Committee, Feb.
> 8, 1941.

---

At the beginning of 1940 the political strength of the Democratic Party had fallen below its peaks of 1932 and 1936. Depression and unemployment problems so overwhelming in earlier years of the decade were disappearing, and now criticisms of the New Deal were increasing. FDR's attempt to purge nonconformists from the Democratic Party had floundered, and his court-packing scheme of 1937 had burst the enchantment of many supporters. Even some stalwarts were saying that given the resurgence of business, a Republican victory in the approaching presidential election was possible. Ballots in the 1936 election had hardly been counted before speculation about a successor to FDR began sprouting.

Within the Democratic Party, isolationists teamed with conservatives to form a coalition to block more of the hated New Deal measures. There was no dearth of aspirants in line for FDR's job. Possible candidates like Cordell Hull, James Farley, and John Nance Garner were foremost, but they were not sympathetic New Dealers and could not be counted upon to continue enacting reform measures like ones in the past eight years. If domestic issues could be kept in the forefront, conservatives held hopes; but those hopes wilted whenever questions of foreign policy arose.

Despite the best attempts by the coalition to capitalize on domestic issues, it was foreign policies which captured citizen attention; undeniably voters and party members looked to FDR for leadership in that realm. Elevated by his eight years in office, President Roosevelt personified an ever-growing role for the Chief Executive and a lesser one for the Congress. None of the leading isolationists opposing him wanted a totalitarian dictatorship patterned on either of the ones set up by Hitler or Mussolini, but even some Democrats were alarmed by the growing power of FDR — that Man in the White House.

"That Man in the White House," or often simply "That Man," were epithets coming from haters of FDR and his policies. It's often impossible to document where a particular phrase originates, and "That Man" referring to FDR is a case in point. Some writers attribute its impetus to a note from Walter White, Executive Director of the NAACP during the time FDR was Governor of New York. White then referred to President Hoover as "the man in the lily-White House," later adding that his "phrase gained considerable currency, particularly in the Negro world." Robert Jackson, a favorite of FDR's during the latter's first two terms as President, chose the phrase when he started to work on his own memoirs. Another Roosevelt biographer, Geoffrey Ward, points out that by birth and upbringing, Franklin Roosevelt was a member of the ruling class, but he jumped the fold and in the country's highest elective office brought in large numbers of minorities — Catholics, blacks, Jews, and all the rest.

Ward continued his explanation:

> In doing so, (i.e., bringing in minorities) he (FDR) had made bitter enemies of the wealthy Protestants among whom he had lived most of his life. He had raised their taxes, regulated their business practices, threatened their dominance; he was, they said, a hypocrite, untrustworthy, demagogic, a "traitor to his class," and many of them, hating his name too much even to utter it, simply called him "That Man in the White House."[1]

As the year of 1940 began, the world was in disarray. Happenings from abroad dominated the front pages of every American newspaper. At the end of the Phony War, Nazis legions had moved fast, first invading Denmark, Norway, and Holland. Then in early June they swept around the Maginot Line, and France fell soon thereafter. A new British Prime Minister, Winston Churchill, warned: "I expect the Battle of Britain is about to begin. . . If we fail, then the whole world, including the United States, will sink into the abyss of a new Dark Age."

Although it is not written in the Constitution — at least it was not until 1951 — in that year of 1940 it was an established tradition that presidents would not run for a third term. Americans and most citizens in Western Europe considered Franklin Roosevelt an international leader who would stand up to Hitler; they were unsure of all others. Yet Roosevelt was coy, declaring in June that he would not actively seek the nomination. Nevertheless, at the beginning of the next month he summoned his chief speech writer, Sam Rosenman, from New York and kept him in Washington working on various drafts of statements and an acceptance speech intended to be delivered to the Democratic National Convention.

FDR told several friends and associates that he was ready to retire. He was fifty-eight years old, and the strain of the presidency had taken a toll. Unknown to all but his most intimate circle he had suffered a minor heart attack the preceding February, and his physician, Dr. Ross McIntire, warned him his life was far too sedentary — not at all good for blood circulation.[2]

Besides Hull, Farley, and Garner there were other potential candidates. One was Senator Burton K. Wheeler of Montana, a formidable Democrat with good credentials as a progressive. Wheeler savored the nomination and did all he could to bolster his chances to win it.

Wheeler's battle against the court-packing scheme had drawn conservative support within the party, and in the summer of 1940 he had the backing of several mainline Republicans including the 1936 nominee Alf Landon as well as isolationists like Amos R. E. Pinchot and Hiram Johnson. During the 1930s, Senator Wheeler had not been as prominent in foreign affairs as such colleagues as Johnson, Nye, Borah, or Vandenberg, but in votes during that decade he generally went with the isolationist side. Yet FDR never forgave Wheeler for his attacks upon the court-packing plan, and in June, Wheeler added to the enmity by broadcasting a major speech criticizing the President's policies toward the war in Europe and berating the "mad hysteria" emanating from Washington. By late summer, Wheeler was saying that FDR's policies would lead inevitably to war. Thereafter, Wheeler was not an acceptable candidate to FDR — not even to share the ticket if FDR himself chose to run.[3]

James Farley was considered by many to be a strong candidate. Farley had campaigned strenuously for Al Smith in 1928 and had been indefatigable in working to get out votes for FDR in 1932 and 1936. However, Farley was a Catholic, and FDR was convinced that Catholics or members of any other minority group would face overwhelming odds in a run for the U.S. Presidency. Furthermore, according to biographer Sam Rosenman, FDR did not consider Farley a bona fide New Dealer.[4]

Also in the wings and anxious for the nomination was Senator James F. Byrnes from South Carolina. He had risen with FDR's backing to several positions which encouraged newspapers to refer to him as an "assistant president." But Byrnes was a Southerner and for that reason would not appeal to the large black vote in Northern cities. In addition, Byrnes had antagonized labor to such an extent that support from that source was only lukewarm. Byrnes had been born a Catholic but had changed his religion later in life. That would be a double burden politically; not only would anti-Catholics oppose him, but Catholics themselves might resent his abandonment of the faith.

Cordell Hull had enormous prestige and was mentioned frequently, but Hull was getting old for the top job and probably would not be a vigorous campaigner. Moreover, there was considerable doubt as to whether he really wanted it.

Earlier, FDR had considered Harry Hopkins an acceptable successor, but by 1940 Hopkins had rankled numerous strong FDR supporters who resented the aide's intrusions and closeness to the President. Moreover, Hopkins' frequent illnesses and precarious health made it clear he could never garner much political backing.

No one then or now can be sure of what was in Roosevelt's mind when in June or before he chose to confront tradition and go for a third term. We have to surmise from recollections and memoirs of colleagues attesting to what he told them; we have FDR's memoranda with their various loopholes about the nomination, and we have the unmistakable fact of his summoning Rosenman and other speech assistants to come to Washington where under his guidance they could prepare messages to leaders in the Democratic Convention.

In June, FDR told Secretary Hull that he wanted him as his successor and gave no indication that he was considering a run himself. Two weeks later Hull for the first time noted a change in the President's words and attitude, leading him to conclude that FDR had made up his mind to run again. Hull wrote in a memorandum that Roosevelt thought "he could win unless the war should stop, but in that event Willkie might defeat him."[5]

Roosevelt had reason to be concerned about Wendell Willkie. Before either of the party conventions, Thomas E. Dewey from New York was clearly the frontrunner for the Republicans. He had strength in the West, but his largest following was in the Northeast where he had gained fame as a federal prosecutor rooting out such malefactors as Lucky Luciano and other gang leaders. Dewey was no isolationist, but his stands on foreign affairs were not drawn sharply enough to inspire great enthusiasm.

In addition to Dewey, there were isolationists hoping to get the nod: Gerald P. Nye, who continued to blame arms and munitions manufacturers for causing World War I, and Iowan Hanford MacNider — a decorated hero from World War I and an experienced diplomat afterwards, for examples. But MacNider won small support outside the Middle West. More likely possibilities among the prominent isolationists were Senator Robert A. Taft of Ohio and Senator Arthur H. Vandenberg of Michigan. Both were conservatives and non-interventionists.

When Republican delegates gathered in Philadelphia for their convention three weeks before Democrats would meet in Chicago, interventionists coalesced to block any isolationist. A well-financed drive began and then swelled rapidly for dark horse Wendell Willkie. Willkie had secured powerful endorsement from owners of *Fortune* magazine, Henry Luce and his Time-Life publications, and the prominent publishing family of Gardner Cowles in Iowa and Minnesota. Willkie had grown up in Indiana, had moved to New York, and had become head of the Commonwealth and Southern Corporation which had battled against FDR and the TVA when that vast project was being debated. At their convention, Republicans five times shunted aside other candidates. On the third ballot taken, Willkie moved ahead of Taft into second place, and on the fourth tied with Dewey. Packed with Willkie supporters, the galleries took over with resounding cries of "We Want Willkie!" He was nominated on the sixth ballot. As expected, the former Hoosier lawyer proved to be a powerful debater and mounted a vigorous campaign. Acerbic Harold Ickes would say Willkie was "nothing but a simple, barefoot Wall Street lawyer."

The Democratic Convention three weeks later in Chicago was confusing, uninspiring, and poorly-managed if compared with the Republican one. Roosevelt was so coy about seeking a third term that he failed to provide his usual leadership. Senator Alben Barkley of Kentucky was chairman of the Convention, and he read to the attendees FDR's statement that he did not wish to be a candidate; yet the wording in the message stressed that delegates were absolutely "free to vote for any candidate." FDR had chosen a back-handed way of saying he was available if nominated. That was done quickly by Senator Lester Hill of Alabama, and FDR won on the first ballot with an overwhelming 946 votes compared with only 146 for all other contenders.

The only genuine contentions at the Democratic Convention in 1940 came with selection of a running mate for FDR and in the preparation of the Party's platform. FDR already had informed a coterie of private advisors that he would decline the nomination if his choice of Wallace over Bankhead of Alabama or any other was not approved. His threat worked, and Wallace albeit with considerable opposition was chosen.

More fireworks exploded when the platform was written and adopted. Senator Robert Wagner of New York was chairman of the Resolutions Committee, and Wagner had been given a draft prepared and revised by writers at FDR's side in the White House. Bitter fighting among members of the Committee as well as among other delegates broke out about what should be said about foreign affairs. A well-organized group succeeded in putting in the statement: "We will not participate in foreign wars. We will not send our armed forces to fight in lands across the seas." A party's platform normally is written after collecting and assessing the presidential nominee's concerns and wishes; in this case, FDR would not tolerate such outright declarations as this first one presented to him. He knew, however, that his opponents could gain great advantage if he insisted that the plank be taken out entirely; they could lambaste him as being in favor of entering the on-going war in Europe.

Rosenman, FDR's chief collaborator by this time, suggested adding this proviso:

> . . . "except where necessary to defend and protect our own American interests." The President was not satisfied with that. After some phone talks with Byrnes in the presence of Hull and me, he finally substituted in his own hand: "except in case of attack."[6]

The summer of 1940 was a busy one for Roosevelt. Inspection trips to war plants and shipyards, and speeches in nearly every part of the country as well as the myriad of administrative details which come to every president. In accepting the nomination for his third term, he had told delegates and voters throughout the nation that presidential duties would keep him from personal campaigning. He would intervene only if confronted by "deliberate or unwitting falsifications of fact." Soon, however, opponent Willkie's successes began alarming the Democrats. Telegrams poured into the White House and phone calls from every state warned that the challenger was making headway, and the President had better do something about it.

FDR decided to go on the stump, and during the first week in September he wired Sam Rosenman vacationing in Oregon to come to Washington immediately. Rosenman obliged and was put to work drafting campaign speeches, including one to be delivered to the Teamster Union Convention on September 11, 1940.

In this address, President Roosevelt incorporated Rosenman's proviso and reiterated:

> I hate war. . . I stand with my party, and outside of my party as President of all the people, on the platform . . . that was adopted in Chicago less than two months ago. It said: "We will not participate in foreign wars, and we will not send our army, naval, or air forces to fight in foreign lands outside of the Americas, except in case of attack."[7]

The Willkie campaign gathered momentum, and the swap of the fifty destroyers to Britain helped fuel more public comment. A Gallup Poll in late August showed FDR and Willkie in a virtual dead heat, the president leading 51 to 49 percent. The challenge was great enough that FDR and advisors found it necessary to make public rebuttal. A major address was prepared for delivery to a huge crowd of the party faithful gathered in Madison Square Garden in New York City on October 28. In his talk there, FDR tried to refute Republican charges that he had allowed the army and navy to deteriorate and that under his administration needed defense measures had been ignored. He castigated Republican rivals for what he alleged was continued opposition to whatever he and the Democratic Party tried to do in strengthening our defenses. FDR did not mention Wendell Willkie by name in this address; instead he leveled his fire at Republicans in Congress — Senators Taft, Vandenberg, Nye, and Johnson, along with three Congressmen — Martin, Barton, and Fish — all of whom had been Willkie's law partners. It was the first time Roosevelt used the rhythmic phrase, which became watchwords for the rest of the campaign. Followers quickly seized upon them, and in FDR's future talks they would shout the three names out in unison as soon as he began with, "Martin — ."

Nomination of Willkie brought a new entry into the political arena, but the Hoosier's vigorous campaigning was plagued with small disasters. Willkie had no training for stump oratory — even with microphones — and in September after two days of almost continuous speaking, his voice literally gave out. In Rock Island, Illinois, he gamely croaked, "The spirit is — *unintelligible squawk* — but the voice is — *another unintelligible squawk*, is . . ."

Willkie was heckled by members of his own party, for only recently had he switched from the Democratic Party to the Republican. Blue-collar toughs hissed at him; one threw an egg which hit his wife standing beside him. In Detroit he was booed by watchers in factory windows, and a rock was hurled through his train window in Grand Rapids.

Many voters seemed to respond favorably to Willkie's openness, but his unpolished performances led to a lot of foot-in-mouth mistakes. For instance, to a labor audience in Pittsburgh he announced he would appoint a secretary of labor directly from the ranks of organized labor — a slam at Frances Perkins, FDR's appointee. Then Willkie added gratuitously, "And it will not be a woman, either."

When told of the incident, FDR, who relished such stories, chuckled. "Why didn't he leave well enough alone? He was going good. Why did he have to insult every woman in the United States? It will lose him many votes."[8]

When asked to support Willkie, an old time Republican, James E. Watson, snorted, "If a whore repented and wanted to join the church, I'd personally welcome her and lead her up the aisle to a pew, but by the Eternal, I'd not ask her to lead the choir the first night!"

Republican firebrands put out advertisements so rough they created sympathy for the President: When your boy is dying on some battlefield in Europe . . . and he's crying out, Mother! Mother! Don't blame Franklin Roosevelt because he sent your boy to war. Blame yourself because you voted to send Roosevelt back to the White House!

One of the lowest slurs came from the man FDR had chosen for the vice-presidency, Henry Wallace, who charged that Willkie was the Nazis' choice. Wallace though did not have a lot of support beyond that of the all-important Man in the White House. Countless Democrats figured Wallace was unstable, a man who in 1933 and 1934 had corresponded with Nicholas Roerich, a White Russian émigré. The letters to this cult leader had been addressed "Dear Guru," and the messages made it clear that Wallace had fallen under the mystic's spell.

A larger problem for the Democrats came from the alleged homosexuality of Undersecretary of State Sumner Welles. Rumors of the appointed official's sexuality preferences were widespread and when they reached the White House. FDR ordered J. Edgar Hoover to conduct "a full and thorough investigation." The FBI put its top agents on the assignment, and in January, 1941, two months after the election had been decided, Hoover reported to Roosevelt that the accusations were indeed true. Senior executives of the Southern Railroad supplied affidavits from Pullman car porters attesting to the undersecretary's overtures. Welles who had been drinking heavily, asked for oral sex with each of the porters working in his car; they refused and reported the incident to their employers. This incontrovertible evidence along with similar reports of other incidents forced Cordell Hull to demand Welles's resignation.

Republican leaders refused to make political capital out of these embarrassments of their opponents; perhaps fearing that Democrats would retaliate with damaging information about their own candidate. The problem was Willkie's extra-marital relationship with Irita Van Doren.

FDR doted on such stories and had amassed a file on the former Hoosier's long-standing romance with Van Doren, editor of the Book Review Section of the *New York Herald Tribune*, the former wife of Columbia University's renowned historian Carl Van Doren, and one of the nation's foremost literary figures in her own right.

Throughout the campaign, Irita Van Doren remained in the background, while Edith, Willkie's wife, traveled with her husband. Like Franklin's relationship with Eleanor, the Willkie marriage was one of residual affection and political expediency. For FDR and his coterie of advisors, the Willkie affair was an ace-in-the-hole in case Republicans got mean or personal in the campaign.[9]

Wendell Willkie shouted himself hoarse against FDR's defiance of tradition, and in doing so was able to garner more votes than any Republican in history up until that time; yet he could not overcome FDR's popularity. The popular vote that fall showed 22,304,755 for Willkie, while Roosevelt topped him with a total of 27,243,466. The electoral vote was even more favorable to Democrats; Roosevelt won 84.56 per cent (449 votes representing 38 states) and Willkie received only 15.44 per cent (82 votes representing 10 states.).

Foreign policy was never a real issue in the 1940 campaign. There was overwhelming predominance of antiwar sentiment among both Democrats and Republicans, and at no time did Roosevelt or Willkie or any other party leader openly propose that the U.S. should enter Europe's war. Contentions were over which leader was more likely to adopt measures that would maintain the neutrality and peace of the United States.

Emboldened by victory in the 1940 election and with Congress adjourned until the following year, FDR gave an epochal fireside chat on December 29. He called it a talk on national security and in it coined an expression that would permeate American debate for generations. Presidential scholars disagree over who originated the fortuitous wording, but certainly FDR gave it popularity and credence. The talk in which he uttered "arsenal of democracy" for the first time was one of his longest radio talks — lasting just under forty-five minutes.

Robert Sherwood reported that FDR enjoyed working with him on this particular talk. The writer added that the Germans and the Japanese feared the psychological impact of the President's rhetoric:

> On the night when Roosevelt gave this Fireside Chat, the Germans sub-
> jected London to one of the heaviest bombings of the war; this was the
> raid in which so large a part of the city was destroyed by fire, St. Paul's
> Cathedral escaping miraculously. The Germans used this psychological
> warfare tactic frequently on some major disturbance in the hope that it
> would blanket the speech in the morning's news and mitigate the effect
> that Roosevelt's words might produce on American and British morale.
> But they needed far more bombs and bombers than they possessed to nul-
> lify the lasting effect of those words, "the arsenal of democracy."[10]

By November, 1940, when the election was held, war in Europe was intense and Japanese incursions in the Far East were proceeding almost unimpeded. The Depression had run its course, and American voters weren't sure as to whether its end came from New Deal measures or from increased armament spending. Whatever the reason, they were reluctant to change horses with a world storm approaching, and they chose to retain Roosevelt — undeniably the nation's most articulate spokesman and revered leader.

# Chapter 11. Lend Lease

> "It [Lend Lease] is the most unsordid act in the history of any nation."
> — Winston Churchill

> "Lend Lease will plow under every fourth American boy."
> — Sen. Burton K. Wheeler, Montana

-------

In 1941 the population in the U.S. stood at 132,000,000 — a quarter of whom still lived on farms — a typical farm family earning an income of $1500 per year. The average citizen had left school after the eighth grade. Although the number was creeping up, fewer than 17% of American women were working outside the home. One of the most successful measures of the New Deal had been the Rural Electrification Act passed by Congress in May, 1935. An executive order made possible by this Act had brought electricity to thousands of farm families, yet six years later three out of every four were still lit by kerosene lamps. One out of every five Americans had an automobile, and one out of seven a telephone. Prices were still low: a hot dog cost a nickel; movie admission twenty cents, most magazines from the local drug store a dime, and a brand new automobile could be bought for $750.

Most travelers went by train, and the new diesels were fast and luxurious. Road beds were maintained so that passengers in sleeper berths could really rest, and during the night an attendant would shine whatever shoes were laid outside the berths. Meals on such trains were well-served and delicious; for those who could afford it in time and money; train travel was a pleasant adventure.

There were still pockets of unemployment although the number of jobless men was going down every month. The Works Project Administration begun in 1935 with a primary purpose of employing manual labor had cut more than a third of the jobless from its high of 3,400,000 persons. Pundits weren't sure whether the rosy reduction was due to New Deal measures or the armament race that had gotten underway.

In the last month of 1940 the position of the Allies was at its most desperate low. British armed forces were being defeated on all fronts, and the United Kingdom's homeland was suffering terrible damage from Hitler's bombers.

In America upon the heels of his success in the presidential election, FDR enjoyed a respite and was relaxing aboard the cruiser *Tuscaloosa* in the Caribbean when on December 9, 1940, a sea plane delivered a personal letter from Winston Churchill. The dire message told him Britain was running out of supplies and lacked money enough to buy more; its treasury was down to two billion dollars. The United States was the greatest industrial nation on earth — the last bastion. Wasn't there some way the American President under his constitutional powers could save a sister nation from complete subjugation?

The actual conception of the gargantuan Lend Lease program which this letter generated is clouded in secrecy. Churchill wrote that Harry Hopkins told him FDR read and reread Churchill's letter for two days without being sure of what to do. FDR talked with no one about it, but after this two-day contemplation period, he himself came up with the basic idea.

One of FDR's most sympathetic biographers, Robert Sherwood, gives the entire credit to FDR. According to Sherwood, four or five days after receiving Churchill's letter, the *Tuscaloosa* headed back to port. President Roosevelt held a brief press conference with three correspondents and talked only of sites he had visited, giving no indication of the radical plan in his mind. He gave the impression of having spent two weeks in relaxation and away from the prospects of world calamity. Sherwood wrote:

> Hopkins said later, "I didn't know for quite awhile what he was thinking about, if anything. But then — I began to get the idea that he was refueling, the way he so often does when he seems to be resting and carefree. So I didn't ask him any questions. Then one evening, he suddenly came out with it — the whole program. He didn't seem to have any clear idea how it

could be done legally. But there wasn't a doubt in his mind that he'd find a way to do it."[1]

FDR needed little convincing that it was in America's best interests to help the Allies; indeed, this had been the major tenet underlying the nation's foreign policy throughout most of his second term.

Weather across America on New Year's Day 1941 was unusually pleasant. A bundle of low pressure air had passed into the northeast, and only vestiges of it remained over Eastern Maine. Temperatures reported from several major cities were: San Francisco 53, Los Angeles 62, Chicago 37, Miami 72, New York 41. A front page story in the *New York Times* reported, "Adolf Hitler in a New Year's proclamation to Germany's National Socialist Armed Forces declared, 'The year 1941 will bring consummation of the greatest victory in our history.' "[2]

In the same issue, a high ranking British Air Officer reviewed the air war to date and prophesied, "The production of American planes will greatly influence the war . . ." Other stories that day printed accounts of RAF bombers striking heavy blows on defenses in Italy — Taranto, Crotone, Naples, and Palermo in Sicily, and on a besieged town in Libya. In battles on the ground in North Africa, British patrol cars had advanced to within a few miles south of Tobruk.

Other news included a caption predicting "National Defense will Dominate 1941." Experts were saying that the Administration would spend as much as $17,000,000,000 on defense measures. Already there were record demands for steel, copper, and aluminum.[3]

Three and a half months earlier, September 16, 1940, the U.S. had passed the Selective Service Act. The law provided that "all male citizens and all male aliens in the United States who have declared their intention to become citizens, between the ages of 21 and 36, shall register under rules and regulations prescribed by the President."

Upon his return to Washington, FDR called a press conference on December 17, 1940, and used a simple analogy attempting to scuttle arguments of isolationists who argued against giving further financial or material aid to Britain:

> Well, let me give you an illustration: suppose my neighbor's home catches fire, and I have a length of garden hose four or five hundred feet away. If he can take my garden hose and connect it up with his hydrant I may help him put out the fire. Now, what do I do? I don't say to him before that operation, 'Neighbor, my garden hose cost me $15 dollars; you have to pay me $15 dollars for it.' What is the transaction that goes on? I don't want $15 — I want my garden hose back after the fire is out.[4]

In this instance, Roosevelt's parable was persuasive but deceptive. There were great differences between a simple garden hose and war planes, ships, tanks, small and large arms as well as tons of ammunition and millions of dollars. The President was ready to offer not only a garden hose, but hydrant, water, expensive plumbing — perhaps even the manor itself. Nevertheless, White House aides quickly moved FDR's proposal to lieutenants in Congress where the idea was drafted into a bill and given the symbolic number of 1776.

With the wheels in motion, President Roosevelt went before a joint session of Congress on January 6th 1941 to deliver his State of the Union Message. In it he enunciated "Four Freedoms," stressing that the U.S. would not be deterred from giving assistance to the Allies by claims from dictators that such assistance would be an act of war. In ringing tones and sublime phrasing he declared:

> They did not wait for Norway or Belgium or the Netherlands to commit an act of war... Victory over dictators would bring a world founded upon four essential freedoms — freedom of speech, freedom of religion, freedom from want, and freedom from fear — everywhere in the world.[5]

Robert Sherwood later wrote that the Four Freedoms were Roosevelt's own idea. In going over the third draft of the address two nights before it was to be delivered, FDR told Sherwood, Rosenman, and Hopkins he had no idea for a peroration; the fortuitous phrase came from his pen alone.

Not long after the State of the Union Address, Wendell Willkie preparatory to a planned trip to England paid a courtesy call on FDR at the White House. On this occasion, Roosevelt and Willkie spent more than an hour together, and when he left, Willkie had in hand letters of introduction to European leaders and a penned note from FDR to Churchill reading:

> Dear Churchill,
>
> Wendell Willkie will give you this. He is truly helping to keep politics out over here.

Roosevelt had enclosed a handwritten note of a Longfellow passage he remembered from school days at Groton:

> Thou, too, sail on, O Ship of State!
> Sail on, O union, strong and great!
> Humanity with all its fears,
> With all the hope of future years
> Is hanging breathless on thy fate.[6]

A few days after receiving Willkie and the note from FDR, Prime Minister Churchill in a radio message to British citizens told them of the exchange and that the American President had asked what were Britain's most urgent needs. "What answer shall I send to our ally across the Atlantic?" Churchill asked before declaring: "Here is the message I will give to President Roosevelt . . . Give us the tools, and we will finish the job.[7]

Controversy over defense measures continued to spread across America throughout all of 1941. At first isolationists prevailed, but as more citizens saw pictures of Nazi bombers and the resultant burnings in London and adjoining communities, interventionist sentiment started swelling. On June 1940, a Gallup Poll reported that public opinion on the conscription bill then being debated in Congress was fifty-fifty. After the fall of France in that same month, conscription was favored by 67% and soon rose to 71%.

In November of that same year, registered voters were asked, "If it appears that England will be defeated by Germany and Italy unless the United States supplies her with more food and war materials, would you be in favor of giving more help to England?"[8] The responses were:

YES   90%
NO    6%
UNDECIDED 4%

Throughout 1941 President Franklin Roosevelt did nearly everything possible to aid the British. In addition to sending them fifty "over-aged destroyers" he had begun assigning to Europe all production of P-40 fighter planes.

When he needed money, FDR chose to act independently, sending personal emissaries to London rather than using regular diplomatic channels, and as the U.S. moved ever closer to actual involvement, his secret moves increased.

As soon as the text of the Lend-Lease proposal was out, isolationists attacked it. An army of critics ranging from the extreme right to the extreme left launched accusatory rhetoric. Another Great Debate was begun and would not end until the bombing of Pearl Harbor twelve months later.

Wendell Willkie, FDR's defeated opponent in the election held two months earlier, refused to heed backers' urging that he join the assault, but there were others quick to jump on the wagon: old-time progressives like Robert La Follette and Burt Wheeler, jingoists Martin Dies from the

House of Representatives, Communist supported pros like Vito Marcan-tonio, anti-war liberals Robert Hutchins (President of the University of Chicago), socialist Norman Thomas, historian Charles Beard, and labor leader John L. Lewis. All echoed a similar strain: international bankers were trying to drag America into war.

Isolationism flourished on college campuses. At prestigious Princeton, once headed by Woodrow Wilson, students drafted a letter to FDR asking him to appoint an Unknown Soldier immediately, "so we can know who he is before he gets killed."

Lend Lease was drawn up to offset the exhaustion of British credits for the purchase of war supplies, but it was not until the third month of 1941 that the Bill completed its passage through both Houses of Congress. The Senate passed the measure, 60 to 31, and the House followed suit three days later with a vote of 317-71. After Congress approved the patriotically numbered H.R. 1776 measure by an overwhelming margin, it was signed into law by the President on March 11, 1941. The new law gave the Chief Executive authority to aid "any country whose defense the President deems vital to the defense of the United States." Not since Andrew Jackson's Force bill in 1833 had an American President been given such power.

An initial appropriation of $7 billion was authorized, but at the conclusion of World War II when the program was ended abruptly by FDR's successor President Harry Truman, the total amount in goods and services provided to Allies expended under its provisions amounted to more than $50 billion. A triumphant Winston Churchill hailed Lend Lease as "the most unsordid act in the history of any nation."

Interventionist support, only lukewarm when the year 1941 began, built rapidly after passage of Lend Lease. The support was heightened by losses of Allied shipping in the Atlantic, some of which was dangerously close to American shores. A few weeks after passage of Lend Lease, the U.S. seized all Axis shipping into American ports and announced that the American navy would patrol the sea lanes in defense zones.

Throughout the first two months of 1941 while the Lend Lease proposal was being drafted by congressional committees, isolationists and interventionists battled it out in public forums, in the press, and over the radio. Yet despite the seriousness of the basic issue, the lives of many Americans went on pretty much as usual.

During the second month of 1941 when the Lend Lease proposal was debated in Congress, both isolationists and interventionists realized that if adopted, Lend Lease would be a point of no return. Approving it would change the status of the United States from being a cautious neutral to an active belligerent. Passage of Lend Lease in effect would set up a de facto alliance between the United States and Hitler's foes, but in 1941 the Allies were being defeated everywhere.

## CHAPTER 12. INTERVENTION OR ISOLATION

> "President Roosevelt's foreign policy is a sort of shooting craps with destiny."
>
> — General Hugh Johnson in 1940, former NRA Director

The years of 1940 and 1941 were anything but tranquil in the United States. Interventionists charged FDR was not doing enough to help the western Allies, and isolationists insisted he was rushing America into Europe's war.

Debates between interventionists and isolationists during the period is a complicated story and one involving important personages including not only FDR, his followers in Washington and in the U.S. Congress but others like Joseph Patrick Kennedy of Massachusetts and Charles A. Lindbergh, quintessential American hero of the 1920s.

Kennedy had amassed his fortune by using a vanguard of allies drawn from barons in Boston, Wall Street, Hollywood, and other power centers. In the spring of 1930, believing that drastic changes would have to be made in the nation's economic system, he had hitched his moneyed chariot to Franklin Roosevelt's run for the governorship of New York. In November of that year, citizens in the Empire State amassed a landslide vote to push FDR into the chair at Albany, and Joseph Kennedy told his wife that the new governor was the man who would save the country. His early assessment was not wrong.

Kennedy liked to think of himself as one of the few men who could talk to FDR on equal terms. Actually, both men were of the same type

— each believing he could sway the other to his own goals. When the presidential campaign got underway in 1932, the millionaire from Hyannis Port filled the Democratic Party's war chests for early primary races, wherever FDR was one of the candidates.

There is little doubt among historians that Joseph Kennedy on the heels of FDR's first election to the presidency expected to become the power behind Roosevelt's throne. Having donated such huge sums, the millionaire felt he was entitled to be named Secretary of the Treasury.

By inauguration day, however, Joseph Kennedy had received no offers of appointment. It was humiliating, and he threatened suit for repayment of his campaign "loans." Fulminating in private, he, nevertheless, sent a florid congratulatory note to FDR.

As late as 1935 when economic recovery was well underway, Kennedy continued to support Roosevelt. *Time* magazine devoted two cover stories to Kennedy; *Life* magazine gave him special attention, and an important piece in Fortune detailed his financial wizardry and his rise as a Washington insider.

Later in that year of 1935 while Kennedy was preparing for an extended European trip, Roosevelt asked him to serve as an unofficial emissary, and he supplied Kennedy with letters of introduction to government leaders in Great Britain, France, Italy, Switzerland, and the Netherlands. Kennedy returned and told FDR that he had found European governments unsettled and confused. Kennedy then went to his retreat at Palm Beach where he intended to spend the winter, but from there he reported to White House staffers that isolationist Liberty Leaguers were very active in Florida, even filling local churches.

At the beginning of 1937 when he learned that the American ambassador to the Court of St. James in England was mortally ill, Kennedy opted for the post and relayed his desire to friends in Congress. He also privately told James Roosevelt, FDR's son, that he was intrigued at the thought of being the first Irishman to serve as ambassador from the U.S. to the English Court. Roosevelt's son agreed that would be quite a "precedent" and said he would report the request to his father.[1]

In weighing the idea, FDR considered advantages and disadvantages of having Kennedy in the London spot. First, Kennedy was wealthy enough to entertain influential Britons in the expected grand manner. Also, the past had shown him to be candid enough that he probably would submit honest reports of British and European opinions. Furthermore, he had demonstrated uncanny bargaining abilities in previous assignments — the Securities role and Maritime commission. That ability might be valuable in promoting Anglo-American trade agreements. And there was that tasty irony in having an Irishman at the Court of St. James!

On the negative side, FDR wanted appointees who would carry out his own goals. He didn't want persons who might have different beliefs and values. FDR couldn't be sure about Kennedy; he was a man with an independent mind who might be a loose cannon rolling on deck if the ship of state entered troubled waters. Yet getting him out of Washington and away from the influencing of financial and conservative barons in America who opposed New Deal measures would be smart politics. In the end, FDR decided the positives outweighed the negatives, and the story of Kennedy's appointment as Ambassador to the Court of St. James was leaked to Arthur Krock of the *New York Times*.[2]

In the next two years, Ambassador Kennedy interpreted worsening relations among European nations as economic imbalances rather than political rivalries. Hitler's annexations of Austria and Czechoslovakia failed to shake Kennedy's conviction that solving the continent's economic problems would erase threats to European security. He approved Neville Chamberlain's policy of appeasement and shared that Prime Minister's fear of war and communism. From interviews and articles as well as public and private statements, it was evident Kennedy believed American policy ought to veer away from involvement in Europe's internal struggles. Expressing such views, thrust him into the mainstream of isolationism and put him at odds with his chief in Washington — a chief who by this time was determined to help western Allies withstand Hitler's onslaughts.

By the summer of 1938 speculation among Washington insiders was rife that Joseph Kennedy was preparing to run for the presidency two years later. Rumors abounded that he and Arthur Krock of the *New York Times* had agreed to advance the ambitions of each; Kennedy would throw heavy weight in helping Krock become managing editor of the newspaper that "printed all the news fit to print," and Krock would do all he could to support Kennedy's aspirations for the White House.

FDR learned of the two's maneuverings, and his confidence in Ambassador Kennedy began to erode. By the first week in September, 1938, as Europe moved more rapidly toward war, FDR had reduced Kennedy's duties to figurehead size and was relying on Harry Hopkins and other confidants for information which helped him reinforce his decisions about increasing aid to threatened Britain.

After Austria and Czechoslovakia had fallen to Hitler, Kennedy in interviews with representatives chosen from the Hearst press urged that we Americans should "not lose our heads" over Europe's struggles, and in preparing a speech scheduled for later delivery, he sent an advance copy to President Roosevelt. One passage in the scheduled address included the wording, ". . . but for the life of me, I cannot see anything involved which would be worth shedding blood for." Roosevelt struck out the offending utterance and said to Henry Morgenthau, "The young man needs his wrists slapped rather hard."[3]

It must have been some time in 1940 that subtle pressures emanating from FDR led Kennedy to retire from his ambassadorship. Kennedy by this time was convinced that American claims of staying completely clear of the European conflict were pipe dreams. However, in his letter of resignation he gave as a reason his need to retire to private business.

In the following February, the President replaced him with John G. Winant, a person most openly in sympathy with his own foreign policy views. Winant came from a wealthy New England family, was the liberal Republican Governor of New Hampshire, and former head of the first Social Security Board.

Isolationism continued to spread across America, and the biggest catch drawn into the net of the America First Committee was Charles A. Lindbergh. Thirteen years earlier, Lindbergh had taken off in a small monoplane named *The Spirit of St. Louis*, piloting the craft from New York to Paris in a solo, nonstop, trans-Atlantic passage. The feat captivated the world, and upon his return to tumultuous crowds in America, he was promoted to colonel. Then he embarked on a nation-wide tour meant to spark more interest in aviation. Everywhere he went he was met by cheering crowds; there was no doubt, his epoch-making flight across the Atlantic established him, *the Lone Eagle*, as the most idolized American of the 1920s, and his reputation remained impeccable until 1940 when some of the luster began to tarnish.

In early 1940 Lindbergh made an extended tour of Germany visiting airfields and military installations, and before returning to America he stopped in London to talk with Joseph Kennedy. The aviator told the Ambassador that his tour had convinced him the *Luftwaffe* was the strongest air power in the world and would be invincible in any war with democracies. Back in America, Lindbergh soon joined the chorus of isolationists attacking those who advocated closer support of Britain and western Allies, and to a rally of America Firsters, he asserted that we could not win the war for England regardless of how much assistance we sent.

Lindbergh continued to speak out against Roosevelt's foreign policy maneuverings calling such actions subterfuges and charging that deception was the antithesis of democracy; duplicity would lead inexorably to war.

America Firsters were delighted with having another champion and quickly scheduled Lindbergh to speak at a massive rally to be held in Boston on December 12, 1941. Lindbergh already had drafted the address he intended to give, but with the Japanese bombing of Pearl Harbor on December 7, 1941, the rally was immediately canceled.[4]

Throughout 1940 and for eleven months of 1941 FDR and his lieutenants fought it out with isolationists in newspapers, halls of Congress, press conferences, and over the politically powerful medium of radio. At some times, it seemed the isolationists were winning the arguments, but the Man in the White House was a shrewd and determined opponent.

After 1937, as war clouds thickened over Europe Roosevelt's rhetoric focused more on international matters. In 1935, a Gallup Poll reported that "keeping out of war" was the third most important issue in the minds of voters. In December, four years later, the question was asked, "What do you think is the most important problem before the American people today?" To the question 47% answered, "Keeping out of war." Unemployment, the subject that had been ranked first in 1935, was now the first concern of only 24%. Three months after Prime Minister Neville Chamberlain had conferred with Hitler in Munich, another survey disclosed that half the people replying believed that war was likely by the end of 1939. In the same survey, 94% named Germany and Hitler as the probable starters, and to add more ground to war fears, 57% believed that if war came the United States would be drawn in.

Masterful as he was in reading manuscripts before the microphone and upon the dais, FDR did not rely upon those performances alone for communicating with the American public. In press conferences, he was equally adept if not even more so. Few presidents would match his success in establishing favorable, lasting relationships with working members of the press. At the outset of his presidency, the press usually referred just to newspapers and magazines, but soon radio, photography, and newsreels were added to media he could use for persuading the citizenry. He seemed to enjoy his twice-weekly meetings with the Washington press corps. In all he held 998 press conferences, most of which he conducted like a friendly, informal schoolmaster presiding over a seminar of attentive students. He was able to influence the news gathering by the very exclusiveness of attendees, for the gatherings were limited in attendance to correspondents who had credentials from either the House or Senate Press Galleries or from the White House Correspondents Association. Moreover, only accredited correspondents could ask questions or make comments.

A legislature, be it state or federal, speaks with many voices, an able executive with one. Few could dispute that FDR was one of the most eloquent spokesmen in the nation's history; not only persuasive at the rostrum, he was unsurpassed when it came to using press conferences as forums to advance his own interpretations of news events or the goals of his administration. His talents in this regard were abetted by radio, which had grown tremendously since the beginning of the century. During that time political power in the U.S. had tilted away from legislatures to executives. Radio reduced the effectiveness of multiple voices in an assembly and enhanced the persuasiveness of the single-voiced strong executive. FDR most certainly was one of the latter.

Most of FDR's press conferences yielded live news for an avid public, and for that was reason enough for an unusually high standing with a subservient press. Some journalists agreed with Heywood Broun who wrote that "Franklin Roosevelt is the best newspaperman who has ever been President of the United States." Reporters admired him for his political skills and craftsmanship. Leo Rosten, chronicler and analyst of the Washington press corps of the 1930s, saw it differently and observed that Roosevelt was not so much trying to help reporters get their stories, but rather to get them to frame stories in ways that were favorable to him.[5]

House Majority Leader John McCormack, dominating Irishman and powerful Democrat from a south Boston constituency, at first was troubled by any legislation authorizing FDR's concept of Lend Lease. Aware that most bills are named after their sponsors, he knew voters in his home district would be incensed if any aid-to-Britain bill carried his name. With advice and connivance with the parliamentarian, the aid bill was numbered 1776 with its backers fully conscious of that number's implicit appeal to patriotism. When McCormack introduced it in the House on January 10, 1941, he described it as "a bill further to support the defense of the United States and for other purposes."

As soon as the measure was presented, isolationists arose in force. *The Chicago Tribune* called it "a dictator bill" which would destroy the Republic. Thomas E. Dewey, emerging as national leader for Republicans, alleged the bill would bring "an end to free government in the United States," and in a line which rankled FDR more than any other, Senator Burton K. Wheeler of Montana asserted that HR 1776 "will plough under every fourth American boy." Roosevelt himself brought up this allegation at a press conference on January 14, claiming the comment was "the most untruthful, the most dastardly, unpatriotic thing. . . that has been said in public life in my generation."[6]

Senator Arthur Vandenberg of Ohio claimed the bill would give FDR the authority "to make war on any country he chooses any time he pleases." The best line came from Republican Senator Robert Taft of Ohio, who said, "Lending war equipment is a good deal like lending chewing gum. You don't want it back." [7]

In September 1940, while political campaigning was underway, an enterprising twenty-four-year-old Yale student, R. Douglas Stuart, Jr., headed a campus organization with a declared purpose of opposing policies which would lead to involvement in Europe's war. The Yale group blossomed into the American First Committee and won notice and support from prominent Middle West business and industrial leaders. With General Robert E. Wood as Chairman, Stuart and five others from the Middle West formed an executive committee which would direct the Committee's policies. By November, 1941, the America First Committee had approximately 450 chapters and subchapters with a total membership of around 800,000 to 850,000.[8]

The America First Committee (AFC) was silent about Roosevelt's swap of the fifty destroyers to Britain; it took no stand on the call for selective service and attempted to be non-partisan in the 1940 presidential election. Announcing as its principal goals, the AFC declared:

1. The U.S. must build an impregnable defense for America.

2 No foreign power, nor group powers, can successfully attack a prepared America.

3. American democracy can be preserved only by keeping out of the European war.

4. "Aid short of war" weakens national defense at home and threatens to involve America in war abroad.[9]

Spokesmen from AFC, notably General Wood, joined others in trying to persuade President Roosevelt to pressure the European belligerents for a negotiated peace. Senator Wheeler said that before we lend or lease arms to England, we should know whether it is possible to have a negotiated peace, and Wood on several occasions insisted that if the U.S. made it clear to Britain that we would *not* enter the war, peace was almost certain to be ensue. FDR ridiculed such thoughts, and in a moving fireside chat laying groundwork for approval of Lend Lease, he declared the "Nazi masters" of Germany meant to dominate not only life and thought in their own country but to enslave all Europe before using its resources to dominate the rest of the world.

Charles A. Lindbergh was the biggest catch drawn into the net of the America First Committee. His emergence as a factor in debates between isolationists and interventionists during the period the U.S. was moving inexorably toward armed conflict is a complicated story.

On September 11, 1941, at an America First rally in Des Moines, Lindbergh delivered his most controversial and most damaging address. The speech was entitled, "Who Are the War Agitators?", and in it the famed aviator named three groups he considered most responsible for pushing the U.S. toward Europe's war: the British, the Jews, and the Roosevelt Administration. In naming Jews as one of the principal agitators in the on-going European war, the American hero wiped out considerable of his great prestige. He declared respect for both Jews and the British, before adding:

> Their [the Jews] greatest danger to this country lies in their large owner-ship and influence in our motion pictures, our press, our radio, and our Government. I am not attacking either the Jewish or the British.

> Both races I admire. But I am saying that the leaders of both the British and the Jewish races, for reasons which are as understandable from their viewpoint as they are inadvisable from ours, for reasons which are not American, wish to involve us in war.[10]

Radio and newspaper reports of this address focused on Lindbergh's reference to Jews; it was his only reference to them in any of his subsequent talks. In these he was most critical, least sympathetic, and most persistent in his criticism of the Roosevelt administration.[11]

It was Lindbergh's most controversial and damaging address. The pronouncement from one so famous gained enormous publicity and encouraged many well-meaning and patriotic citizens to join the America Firsters or similar isolationist groups.

Against such critics, an army of organizations arose to back the Lend Lease proposal. Most prominent and influential among these backers was the Committee to Defend America by Aiding the Allies. Led by William Allen White, this faction was the first organization to combat isolationism on a national scale. With hunger for publicity and knowledge of how to achieve it, White's committee used newspaper and radio ads extensively to refute Lend Lease attackers and to acquaint private citizens with the linkage between the Allies, particularly between Great Britain and the United States. If the British navy could be preserved, the Committee argued, America would have at least two years to prepare for the assault which inevitably would come to it.

A month after the German invasion of Poland, American voters had been asked, "Do you think the United States will get into the war in Europe sometime before it is over, or do you think we will stay out of the war?" [12]

|  | STAY OUT | GO IN |
|---|---|---|
| Oct. 1939 (outbreak of war) | 46% | 54% |
| Feb. 1940 (war's quiet phase) | 32% | 68% |
| May 1940 (invasion of France) | 62% | 38% |
| June 1940 | 65% | 35% |
| Sept. 1940 | 67% | 33% |
| Dec. 1940 (Greek-British successes) | 59% | 41% |
| Jan. 1941 | 72% | 28% |
| Feb. 1941 | 74% | 26% |
| Mar. 1941 | 80% | 20% |
| Apr. 1941 (Balkan Invasion) | 82% | 18% |
| May 1941 | 85% | 15% |

In June, 1941, pollsters asked Americans, "Do you think President Roosevelt has gone too far in his policies of helping Britain or not far enough?" The responses were: [13]

| Too Far | About Right | Not Far Enough |
|---|---|---|
| 23% | 55% | 22% |

Prior to Pearl Harbor both General Wood and Lindbergh argued that the U.S. should try to pressure the belligerents into seeking a negotiated peace, but the America First Committee never conducted a major drive on this option, perhaps fearing that such declarations would bring down upon them the damaging charge of appeasement. The Committee took the position that a negotiated peace was a matter for the belligerents; the Committee's concern was to serve American interests by opposing intervention in Europe's ongoing war.

Much of the bitter fighting between the Roosevelt Administration and isolationists in that crucial year of 1941 concerned practices of informing and influencing public opinion — practices which included mailing lists, the franking privilege, motion pictures, radio, newspapers, and propaganda agencies. The use and abuse of these media brought charges and countercharges from both sides as the furor grew more emotional, more vicious, and more distorted.

As months passed, FDR's standing with the press on foreign policy issues was much stronger than it had been on domestic issues throughout the thirties. Colonel Robert McCormick's *Chicago Tribune* and the Hearst newspapers headed the isolationist factions, but other influential news publications, notably the *New York Times*, the *New York Herald Tribune*, the *Chicago Daily News*, and Henry Luce's *Time* Magazine strongly supported the President on foreign affairs. Splinter groups in sympathy with William Allen White's organization and in general backing Roosevelt's actions were the Committee to Defend America, Fight for Freedom Committee, and Friends of Democracy; none of these smaller offshoots attained the prominence of America Firsters, however.

Both Roosevelt and isolationists followed public opinion polls closely, filtering them for segments to reinforce their own preferences in the foreign policy debate. Throughout most of 1941, the polls moved steadily toward showing that a majority of Americans thought it more essential for the U.S. to help bring defeat of the Axis than it was for the United States to stay out of the war. In 1941 Roosevelt marshaled enough congressional majorities to pass his desired legislation, yet until the Japanese attack on Pearl Harbor he was unable to achieve national unity behind every one of the foreign measures he spooned to underlings.

As soon as the Lend Lease proposal was unveiled, Roosevelt's lieutenants in Congress aligned Republican moderates to support it. Wendell Willkie, FDR's opponent in the preceding November, refused to join critics of the measure or those who claimed the President was going beyond his authority. The defeated Republican in testifying before a U.S. Senate Investigating Committee declared, "It is the history of democracy that under such dire circumstances, extraordinary powers must be granted to the elected executive." One senator hostile to Lend Lease pretended not to understand Willkie's position and reminded the former candidate of charges he himself had made against FDR during the political campaign. In rebuttal, Willkie answered that he had struggled as hard as possible to beat Franklin Roosevelt but had lost. The people had cast their votes, and FDR had been elected — was now his President and leader of all Americans. Such testimony from the de facto head of the Republican Party almost assured passage of Lend Lease.

Emotions in proponents and opponents mounted though. On the second day in February, more than 1,000 men and women carrying placards denouncing FDR's proposal paraded in front of the White House. The visitors were members of the American Peace Mobilization, and this time marchers had come by train or auto from Boston, Bridgeport, New York City, Newark, and Baltimore.

Almost at the same time a mass meeting was being held by the Washington chapter of the America First Committee. This conclave was to express by resolution the organization's opinion that while aid to Britain under existing laws might be permitted and advisable, the proposed lend lease action was unacceptable, war mongering, and would confer dictatorial power upon the President while stripping American defenses.

On several other occasions thousands amassed outside congressional halls to protest the bill. Protesters were drawn from America Firsters, Mothers Against Mobilization, the Liberty League, and groups sharing similar goals. Both Houses of Congress established investigating committees to explore the arguments, and throughout the month of February newspapers devoted their front pages to accounts of witnesses appearing before the committees — who they were, what they said, and what testimony was likely to influence the final vote.

General Hugh Johnson, whom FDR once had appointed as head of the ill-fated NRA program, pounded the table belligerently as he told the Senate committee he thought no man should be given the power that HR 1776 would grant the President. Charles Lindbergh with his reserve military rank as colonel declared to the same committee that the foreign policy of the Administration would lead to America's entrance into the war — a war that could not be won.

On another day, a woman was able to sneak into the House of Representatives. Once inside, she donned a Halloween mask, and clad in an overflowing black dress rushed past guards and down the aisles shouting, "Don't lead us to war! Avoid giving more aid!"

The leading newspaper in Washington, D.C. ran an account of polls taken by Dr. George Gallup, Director of the Institute of Public Opinion. The account was detailed under a caption reading: "Aid to Britain Helps Keep Us Out of War, U.S. Voters Believe." The account reported that back of a widespread desire to help England, the nationwide study showed most voters believed such aid was more likely to keep war from U.S. shores in the long run than remaining entirely neutral would do.

Seventy per cent of those interviewed in the national cross section chose the statement: "Sending war materials to England is helping to keep us out of war, because if Britain can keep Germany in check, there is less chance that we will have to fight the Germans later on."

Twenty-three per cent believed: "Sending war materials to England is bringing us closer to getting into the war, because once we start helping we won't be able to stop short of war."

The remaining three per cent said they were undecided or without a definite opinion on the question.

Observers also noted that by and large, the same people who said, "Let's give the British what they need" were ones who also said, "Sending war materials to England is helping keep us out of war."

Non-interventionists challenging the President's proposal argued that the more desperate the British became the more the U.S. would have to underwrite them with the consequence of increasing danger to America of being drawn into the conflict. Before September, 1939, when the European war first broke out few U.S. citizens had given much thought to the question, and even in December, 1940 — a month before FDR launched his proposal — 85% of voters surveyed declared the country should stay out of Europe's war.

By February 1941, however, the desire to aid Britain had shown a steady increase, and results of various polls and surveys made it obvious that American thinking on aid to Britain would be an increasingly strong factor unless public opinion was reversed.

FDR and supporters were doing all they could to further the favorable tide. In his fireside chat, he had boldly stated, "The nub of the whole purpose of your President is to keep us now — and your children later, and your grandchildren much later — out of the last ditch war for the preservation of American independence."

As the month of February approached its end, opinion polls made it unmistakable: the idea of lend lease had won a significant majority of voters. Most of them were unimpressed by allegations that the legislation gave the President too much authority. Republican leaders on Capitol Hill struck a responsive chord, however, when they attacked the lack of time limits on the proposal. One survey asked voters, "If Congress does pass the proposed lend lease bill, should the power it grants to the President be given him for as long as the war lasts or should it be for a limited period of time, perhaps two years? [14]

The aid promised by Roosevelt was slow to develop, and as more months passed it was clear the President's rhetoric had moved ahead of the country's production capacity. A year earlier his call for production of an impressive fifty thousand airplanes a year had intended to put the

U.S. ahead of Germany thus creating an air armada second to none in the world. Although airplane production had moved up, the big auto makers were still turning out new cars in record numbers and in doing so gobbling up 80% of all available rubber, 49% of strip steel, 44% of sheet metal, and 34% of lead. Opinions reported in this survey varied somewhat according to region.

|  | Central | New England & Mid-Atlantic |
|---|---|---|
| As long as war lasts | 31% | 35% |
| Limited Period | 59% | 56% |
| No Opinion | 710% | 9% |

In America, movements towards ever deeper involvement in the European war accelerated. Government regulatory agencies were set up, and top notch executive talents were lured to Washington. Heavy industry swelled with the hiring of three million new workers, while in factories red, white, and blue flags waved over assembly lines warning: *Time is Short*. President Roosevelt declared "an unlimited national emergency," and froze German and Italian assets in the U.S. Axis ships and ships from countries which had been overrun by the Germans were seized "to prevent their sabotage." The move included custody of the luxurious French liner *Normandie*, convoyed to a New York port and berthed there until destroyed by a mysterious fire the next year. On February 9, 1942, a spark from an acetylene torch landed on a pile of kapok life jackets piled on the deck, and soon the entire ship was ablaze. Whether the incident was from carelessness or deliberation was never fully determined. The conflagration was so great as to destroy the vessel; it could not be salvaged, and thirteen months after the war ended, the former pride of France was sold as scrap for a mere $160,000.

## Chapter 13. Barbarossa

"History shows there are no invincible armies."

— Russian Premier Joseph Stalin, Radio Broadcast, July 3, 1941.

---

Not only did 1939 mark the year in which Nazi Germany invaded Poland, setting off World War II; it also was the year in which Joseph Stalin, General Secretary of the Soviet Union, decided that a buffer zone was needed for the important city of Leningrad, only 32 kilometers from the Finnish border. Just north of Leningrad lay the Mannerheim fortification line extending across the Karelian Isthmus. When negotiations between the Soviet Union and Finland broke down, the Soviets immediately attacked, confident they would be able to defeat the Finns within a couple of weeks.

Russian confidence was shaken by the fierce resistance put up by Finland, who quickly set aside political differences in order to defend their country. World sympathy lay with little Finland in the brief struggle known as the Winter War. Sweden and Norway sent volunteers and supplies to the out-matched Finns, and more materiel came from Britain and France, but the American arsenal yielded neither equipment nor supplies.

Despite international sympathy, small Finland could not withstand the giant USSR. The Soviets had four times as many troops, 100 times as many tanks, and 30 times as many aircraft as the Finns. The Winter War

ended when Finnish diplomats signed a peace treaty with Soviet coun-
terparts on March 12, 1940, and in the treaty Finland ceded part of the
disputed Karelian Isthmus and several border territories to the Soviets..
The conflict had been brief, but from it Russian military officers gained
experiences which would be of value later in resistance to the Germans.

Russo-Finnish relations remained relatively peaceful until June, 1941,
when the Russians broke the treaty and attacked Finland again. The Soviets claimed the Finns were really continuing the war, and that Nazi
Germany was providing them aid. By this time Great Britain was allied
with the Soviet Union, and the British government under leadership of
Winston Churchill found it necessary to declare war on Finland, marking hostilities which lasted until September 19, 1944.

In that year of 1941, offensives by German and Italian forces under
the command of General Erwin Rommel in North Africa had compelled
the British to evacuate Bengazi and withdraw to Egypt. British strength
in North Africa had been drained by sending 60,000 troops to help embattled Greece, yet troops of the United Kingdom managed to hold out
at Tobruk.

In March and April of 1941 more countries fell to German domination.
Nazi troops invaded Greece and Yugoslavia, and the Yugoslavian army
surrendered in the middle of April.

The Greek campaign, basically different from earlier ones Germany
had waged in Poland and France, also ended in a complete Nazi victory.
The following factors seemed to have had the greatest significance in
Greece when despite British intervention the fighting was over in twenty-four days: 1) Germany's superiority in ground forces and equipment,
2) the *Luftwaffe's* supremacy in the air, 3) inadequacy of the British expeditionary force, 4) poor condition of the Greek army and its shortage of
modern equipment, and 5) lack of cooperation between British, Greek,
and Yugoslavian forces.

After British soldiers withdrew from the Greek mainland, German
airborne troops landed in Crete, and that island, too, was captured in
slightly more than a week Nazi troops were being successful everywhere
in Europe. Yet despite claims of *Luftwaffe* invincibility, Germans were
unable to dominate the air space over the English Channel; hence Nazi
strategists switched plans for invasion of Britain to attempts to sever
her Atlantic lifeline. Submarine wolf packs were increasingly successful,
sinking 756 merchantmen bound for British ports and damaging another
1450 vessels during the first half of 1941.[1]

Advisers urged President Roosevelt to order the U.S. Navy to escort convoys crossing the Atlantic, but he hesitated, giving domestic and international restraints as his rationale. He was not certain American voters were ready to accept actions that would push the nation to the brink of war.

During this critical period, Roosevelt's focus was almost entirely on Europe. In the main he conducted foreign affairs himself. He did relegate relations with Vichy France to Secretary of State Cordell Hull, and the resulting U.S. policy enabled French forces under command of General Maxime Weygand to join Allied troops in the North African campaign against Germany.

Throughout the spring of 1941, Prime Minister Churchill continued to send frequent messages to FDR hoping to increase American war support and to warn that German U-boats were operating almost within sight of the U.S. coast. Moreover, two thirds of American voters seemed to accept President Roosevelt's speech to Congress as a noble and inspiring commitment that the United States was going to increase its efforts in supplying war materials to the Western Allies.

During the spring months of 1941 while opposing troops slugged it out on the western front of Europe, farther east on borders between occupied Poland and its hungry Soviet neighbor, diplomatic machinations were edging toward open warfare.

As early as 1925 Adolf Hitler had written in *Mein Kampf* [My Struggle] that the Soviet Union would have to be invaded. In his rambling tome he asserted that raw materials needed by the German people lay in lands to the east. After he rose to power as *der Fuhrer*, it became standard Nazi policy to kill, deport, or enslave Russians and other Slavic populations. Therefore, a peace pact signed in 1939 between Germany and Russia had surprised most of the world because mutual hostilities and competing economic philosophies between the two countries had been so long recognized.

Peace between Russia and Germany was broken in the second summer of the European war when Nazi troops moved east beyond Poland. The code name for Nazi Germany's invasion of the Soviet Union was *Unternehmen Barbarossa* [Operation Barbarossa]. Barbarossa [Red Beard] was named after Frederick I, the Holy Roman Emperor who with his legions had marched east in 1190 to take the Holy Land.

Secret plans for Germany's incursion into the Soviet Union had been accepted by Chancellor Hitler and Wehrmacht generals in December, 1940. On March 30, 1941, Hitler summoned field commanders and more than two hundred leading staff officers to reveal his reasons for the maneuver. War with Russia, he said, was inevitable, and now was the time to undertake it. The United States could not reach the peak of production and military power for four more years. Germany would enter the U.S.S.R. with the most powerful armed force in the world. German might would destroy the Soviet Union and annihilate the Red Army. More Lebensraum (living space) for Germans would be attained and needed resources obtained. Victory over the Soviets would be quick and overwhelming. War with the Soviets, he maintained, would have to be harsh and unrelenting; it would be no "knightly crusade." The single problem, he admitted, would be how to treat prisoners of war and non-combatants. A very few of his listeners saw through the charade to realize his real concerns: destruction of Bolshevism and complete annihilation of Jews.

The generals acquiesced, and the initial assault began on June 22, 1941. As the conflict developed, the German war with the U.S.S.R. became the largest military offensive in history until that time involving 4.5 million troops of the Axis powers. At 6:00 A.M. on June 22, loudspeakers in Berlin and many other cities of the *Reich* relayed Hitler's announcement telling of machinations by Russia and England to crush Germany with the aid of American supplies. Then with his voice rising in pitch *der Fuhrer* shouted:

> People of Germany! National Socialists! The hour has come! Oppressed by grave cares, doomed to months of silence, I can now speak to you frankly. I have decided today to lay the fate and future of the German *Reich* in the hands of our soldiers. May God help us in this fight![2]

Two days after Germans invaded Russia, President Roosevelt in Washington promised aid to the Soviet Union. Moreover, within the month, Great Britain and Russia signed a mutual assistance pact at Moscow barring a separate peace with Germany. Later that summer, U.S. and British missions conferred in Moscow to determine Russian needs, and FDR announced America was prepared to grant Russian requests for materiel. It would be November, however, before such aid actually came about, and before FDR revealed that under Lend Lease the U.S. would grant credit of $1 billion to the Soviet Union.[3]

War on the eastern front went on for four years. The death toll may never be established with any degree of certainty. Most authoritative western estimates of Soviet deaths are put at around seven million who lost their lives either in combat or in Axis captivity. Soviet civilian deaths remain under contention, although roughly 20 million is a frequently cited figure. German military deaths are also to a large extent unclear. One estimate concluded that about 4.3 million Germans and a further 900,000 Axis forces died either in combat or in Soviet captivity. Barbarossa would be recorded as one of the most lethal battles in the world's history.[4]

Germany's intrusion into the U.S.S.R. had not come without dissension. Marshal Hermann Goering, Commander of the *Luftwaffe*, and Admiral Erich Raeder, Commander of the Fleet, tried to dissuade der Fuhrer from an eastern campaign and to convince him that first Great Britain ought to be subdued by air and submarine assaults. Hitler could not be swayed, and instructed his generals to go full speed ahead with plans for invasion of Russia. His convoluted thinking can be seen in a passage taken from one of his conferences:

> Stalin must be regarded as a cold-blooded blackmailer; he would, if expedient, repudiate any written treaty at any time. Britain's aim for some time to come will be to set Russian strength in motion against us. If the U.S.A. and Russia should enter the war against Germany, the situation would become very complicated. Hence any possibility for such a threat to develop must be eliminated at the very beginning. If the Russian threat were non-existent, we could wage war on Britain indefinitely. If Russia collapsed, Japan would be greatly relieved; this in turn would mean increased danger to the U.S.A.[5]

The U.S. State Department was not uninformed of the Nazi invasion. In January, 1941, an American intermediary in Berlin was given a top-secret document issued by Hitler to his armed forces the preceding month. The document, headed Operation Barbarossa, warned, "German armed forces must be prepared to crush Soviet Russia in a quick campaign before the end of the war against England . . ." The directive further admonished, "Preparations are to be completed by May 15, 1941."

Secretary of State Cordell Hull at first doubted the authenticity of the document, believing it must have been a "plant" intended to mislead American policy. Would Hitler, who seemed on the verge of delivering a knock-out punch to beleaguered Britain, be crazy enough to open a two-front war? It didn't make sense. Nevertheless, intelligence reports from all quarters soon confirmed the Nazi attack; the document was exactly what it had purported to be.

The German–Soviet war seemed to provide a glimmer of sunshine through darkened clouds for the western Allies, yet both London and Washington held out slim hopes of Russia's ability to withstand for long the Nazi assault. Military experts held low opinions of the Soviets' capacity to wage war against the mighty Wehrmacht, and the dismal performance of Red Armies against tiny Finland bolstered beliefs that Soviet purges of the 1930s had destroyed the effectiveness of Stalin's troops.

Germany's assault upon the U.S.S.R. reinforced views of American isolationists and non-interventionists who still were maintaining that U.S. policies should aim to keep the country apart from European battles. The day after Germany launched its invasion of the USSR, the executive committee of America First approved a statement saying, "the entry of Communist Russia into the war certainly should settle once and for all the intervention issue here at home." Senator Arthur Clapper of Kansas wrote: "I am against Hitler and hope he will finally be crushed. I have no sympathy for Stalin." Harry S. Truman, just into his second term in the U.S. Senate, seemed to reflect the attitude of most Americans in his comment, "If we see that Germany is winning the war, we ought to help Russia, and if Russia is winning we ought to help Germany — in that way kill as many as possible."[6]

Together with captured Finnish and Romanian troops, German forces were able to penetrate Russia along a 2,000-mile front extending from the Arctic to the Ukraine. By mid-August Hitler's minions had overrun most of the Ukraine; by early September they reached Leningrad, and two months later they were holding Sevastopol under siege and had reached the outskirts of Moscow. Rostov fell, the last of November, but was retaken by Russians a week later.

Battle lines stretched an unprecedented 1800 miles, from the Baltic to the Black Sea. Along these lines, more than 3,000,000 well-led German troops armed with 3,000 tanks, 2,000 planes, and 7,200 guns hurled themselves against limitless Russian armies. When one Red Army was defeated, another appeared on the horizon from somewhere in the east. An early objective of German forces was capture of the city of Minsk, and after Nazi success there, small pockets of Russian troops were surrounded and blasted into submission by German artillery. By July 2, 1941, Nazi generals were claiming capture of more than 1,500,000 Soviet troops along with 1,200 tanks and 600 big guns.

The situation was so grave that Soviet leader Josef Stalin took to air waves and gave one of his rare public speeches. In it, he announced to his people and the world that Latvia, Lithuania, and considerable portions of Byelorussia as well as large parts of the Ukraine already were in the enemy's bloody hands. Then in an attempt to rally all Soviet citizens, he said:

> In this great war, we shall have true allies in the peoples of Europe and America... Our war for the freedom of our country will merge with the struggle of the peoples of Europe for their independence, for democratic

> liberties [*sic*]. . . In this connection, the historic statement of the British Prime Minister, Mr. Churchill . . . and the declaration of the United States Government signifying readiness to render aid to our country, which can only evoke a feeling of gratitude in the hearts of the people of the Soviet Union, are fully comprehensible and symptomatic. [7]

Immediately after the German invasion of the U.S.S.R. had begun, President Roosevelt's published words and deeds were hesitant and cautious. Then he ordered unfrozen some $40 million of Soviet funds held in the U.S. along with others from European Axis powers. Three days later in a press conference, he said he favored giving the Russians whatever aid it was possible for the U.S. to provide but that Britain would continue to have first call on American resources. He added that he had received no aid request from the U.S.S.R. and had no idea as to what they might need.

Secretary of War Stimson along with Chief of Staff George Marshall advised him that the German-Soviet combat would delay any possible Nazi invasion of Britain; hence, there would be a "breathing spell" in which U.S. policy should be to push with utmost vigor all efforts in protecting Atlantic shipping and in building military defenses at home. FDR listened but was not fully persuaded. Others, chiefly former Ambassador to Russia, multi-millionaire Joseph E. Davies, were telling him that forces behind the Ural Mountains could be amassed in numbers that would be almost invincible if convinced the U.S.S.R. was not being used to pull chestnuts of the western Allies out of the fire.

Early victories in the war with the Soviets seemed to justify Hitler's high hopes. German tanks burst through enemy lines and roamed at will. One gloating Nazi, General Franz Halder, wrote in his diary: "It is no exaggeration to say that the campaign against Russia has been won in fourteen days."[8]

By September, the important city of Kiev had fallen to invading Nazis, and Hitler glowed with satisfaction as he told of capturing more than 145,000 prisoners. The rich Ukraine valley was the granary for all Europe and now he could concentrate his energy and the *Wehrmacht's* might for an all-out assault on Moscow itself.

That assault began on the last day of September, 1941. Soviet high commanders were caught by surprise, believing that, given the severe Russian winters, no responsible military leader would begin such a campaign so late in the year. Initially, Nazi Panzers had easy going, racing more than fifty miles in the first twenty-four hours; German infantrymen then rushed into the vacuum to mop up pockets of disintegrating Russian resisters.

Soon Berlin newspapers were boasting of victory at Moscow. Two entire Soviet armies had been encircled; the capital city was ready to fall at any time. German citizens were ecstatic, and in beer-restaurants throughout the *Reich* patrons stood and saluted when radios played "Horst Wessel" or "Deutschland über Alles."

In October, 1941, Hitler traveled to Berlin in his special train and from the *Sportpalast* there with loudspeakers throughout the Third *Reich* relaying his words he proclaimed the Bolsheviks were "already beaten and would never rise again." He recounted some of the statistics: German soldiers had advanced more than 1,000 kilometers into former Soviet territory, taken 2,500,000 prisoners, destroyed or captured 22,000 artillery pieces, 18,000 tanks, and more than 14,500 airplanes. Listeners broke into wild acclaim.

In November, Soviet defenders of Moscow stiffened, and Nazis spearheads which had advanced to within forty miles of the capital city were driven back. Rains and snows began, and the powerful German Mark IV tanks which comprised the Panzer divisions were mired in the mud while the more maneuverable Soviet T-34 tanks rolled free.

As 1941 drew to a close, Soviet armies having forestalled the best of Hitler's troops at Moscow and elsewhere began to take the offensive. The Soviets recaptured Mozhaisk in January, Dorogobuzh the next month, advanced to Kursk, and attacked near Kharkov in May. For five months the vaunted Sixth Army of the Third *Reich*, victors in Belgium and Holland in 1940, was entrapped in savage fighting with Russians 600 miles south of Moscow around the vital industrial city of Stalingrad on the Volga River. Nazi bombers set fire to large areas within the city, and land forces succeeded in ramming their way into the city's northwestern portions. Yet the Soviets managed to hang on, and in late November, 1941, the Red Army began attacking the besiegers.

The Sixth Army rather than being a threat was cut in two, stranding more than three hundred thousand German soldiers without food, supplies, or ammunition. Roosevelt and Churchill meeting then in Casablanca, North Africa, learned that rations for Nazi soldiers facing Stalingrad had been reduced to a few ounces of bread each day; more than ninety thousand of them would die of starvation before that siege ended. It was only a matter of days before German Field Marshal Friedrich von Paulus, very recently promoted to his nation's highest military rank, would be forced to surrender despite telegrams from his Fuhrer that Germans at Stalingrad must "fight to the last man."

The Sixth Army under command of General von Paulus was unable to make any significant progress at Stalingrad; whatever advance was achieved was measured in yards, and the cost for each yard was incredibly high. By the end of November, 1941, the entire Sixth Army was surrounded by a gigantic pincer movement of the Soviets which in effect took out of action more than 200,000 of Germany's finest troops, along with 100 tanks, 1800 big guns, and at least 10,000 vehicles. Chancellor Hitler ignored pleas from embattled von Paulus for permission to "break out" of the encirclement and retreat southwest; der Fuhrer only reinforced his order to "stand fast," promising to send help as soon as possible.

But sending help was not possible, and on February 1, 1942, Moscow announced that Marshal von Paulus had surrendered the Sixth Army at Stalingrad. It was a momentous victory for the Soviets and marked the end of Hitler's ill-fated Barbarossa venture. The Soviet Union claimed capture of 91,000 prisoners, including 24 generals and 2500 officers; only a very few of them would ever return to Germany. One was von Paulus, who when in Soviet hands publicly condemned Hitler and Nazi tyrannies.

After German troops were in Soviet territory, President Roosevelt in Washington promised aid to the Soviet Union. Moreover, within a month of the outbreak, Great Britain and the USSR signed a mutual assistance pact at Moscow, barring a separate peace with Germany. Later that summer, U.S. and British missions conferred in Moscow to determine Russian needs, and FDR announced America was prepared to grant Soviet requests for materiel. It would be November, however, before such aid actually came about, and before FDR revealed that under Lend Lease the U.S. would grant credit of $1 billion to the Soviet Union.[9]

## Chapter 14. Troubled Waters

"Sending ships out to be sunk by submarine wolf packs is like pouring water into a leaky bathtub."

— Secretary of War Henry Stimson

As the year 1941 began, the war overseas was at its darkest for the West. France had fallen in the previous summer, and the fate of Great Britain appeared hopeless. British cities were subjected to ever heavier bombings from the *Luftwaffe*, and German U-boats using "wolf-pack" tactics were exacting grim tolls everywhere in the Atlantic. Henry L. Stimson, Roosevelt's Secretary of War observed, "sending ships out to be sunk by submarine wolf packs is like pouring water into a leaky bathtub."

Nazis planes had been unable to win control of skies over Britain, and in 1941, Adolf Hitler switched plans for the invasion of that island to attempts in cutting its Atlantic lifeline. In retrospect and fairness, it might be realized that it made no sense for Germany to bomb or destroy munitions, railroads, factories, and industries in the British homeland if those same military supplies were permitted to be imported by an ally from abroad. Accordingly, U-boat attacks increased, and American ships were further endangered. During the first six months of 1941, U-boats sank 756 merchantmen bound for English ports and damaged another 1,450 vessels.

In a two-month period, the *Scharnhorst* and the *Gneisenau* — two German surface warships — sank or captured 22 Allied vessels (115,000 tons). In slightly more than twelve months, Allied losses on the Atlantic amounted to 2,314,000 gross tons.[1]

Such tolls if allowed to continue would be twice the replacement capacity of both British and American shipyards.

Encounters with Nazi U-boats in the Atlantic continued throughout 1941 and in fact mounted in seriousness. On different occasions during those hectic, dangerous months Allied, neutral, and American ships were increasingly endangered. Yet Churchill pressed for stepped-up U.S. naval support, and yielding to it in part, FDR agreed to provide American escorts for all fast convoys between Newfoundland and Iceland. Churchill then disclosed that Britain planned to occupy the Canary Islands — a move that probably would lead to Spain's counterattack with aid from the Nazis. The British later canceled their plans for seizure of the Canary Islands, but Roosevelt's willingness to support the Azores is an indication of how far even then he was ready to stretch neutrality interpretations.

In the early spring of 1941, few persons were aware that high level talks between British and American strategists were taking place in Washington. One of the first recommendations coming from this cabal was the withdrawal of all U.S. forces in the Pacific Ocean east of 180 degrees. Luckily, the recommendation was never implemented, for doing so would have meant sacrificing not only the Philippines but U.S. posts on Guam and Wake Island as well as forfeiting Manila Bay, the finest anchorage under the American flag in the western Pacific.

One agreement of the talks, however, was adopted and would guide American foreign policy throughout the twelve months of 1941. Named the United States-British Commonwealth Joint Basic War Plan, known more commonly as Rainbow Five, the document's basic premise was that in the event of hostilities between the United States and the Axis, the Allies would conquer Italy and Germany first. Concerning Japan, conferees agreed that Allied "strategy in the Far East will be defensive" because the U.S. had no plans to add to its present military strength there. An upshot of this lapse was virtual abandonment of the Philippines.

Beyond public debate, confrontations in the Atlantic Ocean continued to grow. In November of 1940 sea battles in those waters had been grim enough, Germans sinking or capturing 22 ships (115,000 tons). By the opening of 1941 the Allies were being defeated everywhere. From Britain, Churchill weighed in with simple eloquence, "Give us the tools, and we will finish the job."[2]

The aid promised by Roosevelt was slow to develop, and as more months passed it was clear that his rhetoric had moved ahead of the country's production capacity. A year earlier his call for production of an impressive fifty thousand airplanes annually had intended to put the U.S. ahead of Germany thus creating an air armada second to none in the world. Although airplane production had moved up, the big auto makers were still turning out new cars in record numbers and in doing so gobbling up 80% of all available rubber, 49% of strip steel, 44% of sheet metal, and 34% of lead.

April, 1941, was a particularly dire month for Allied forces. Germany had crushed Yugoslavia before going into Greece where Mussolini's troops had been given a bad drubbing. By midsummer, the Wehrmacht controlled all of the Balkan Peninsula and Crete. Axis armies also had recaptured earlier losses in Libya, advanced eastward and were threatening the Suez Canal. Farther west, British sea power in the eastern portion of the Mediterranean was stymied.

In that same month of April 1941 the U.S. signed an agreement with Greenland winning the right to establish weather stations there. Included in the agreement was a pledge that the U.S. would defend Greenland if that huge island were attacked. The President declared that the defense of Greenland was essential to the security of the western hemisphere.

Security meant providing safe escorts for Allied ships in the western hemisphere, but how far east did the hemisphere extend? That's what isolationists and FDR's opponents in Congress wanted to know. A private poll of U.S. Senators disclosed that forty-five of them would approve of U.S. warships escorting freighters halfway across the Atlantic, but forty were against even that.[3]

Losses from German raiders and "wolf packs" of submarines continued to rise, and FDR cabled Churchill that the U.S. would extend its security zone to west longitude 26 degrees. The President asked that the British Admiralty notify American naval units in "great secrecy" of its convoy dates and destinations. With that information, American patrol units would be able to seek out ships or planes of aggressor nations operating west of the designated line.

By June, the mounting losses in the Atlantic had helped push popular support for U.S. convoys up to 52 per cent, with 75 per cent approving it if appeared that Britain would lose the war without convoys.

The first incident happened on April 10th when the *U.S.S. Niblack*, a destroyer picking up survivors from a torpedoed Dutch freighter, made sonar contact with a U-boat before driving it away with depth charges.

President Roosevelt decried the attack and told the press, "It would be suicide to wait until they are in our front yard." Then by definition he extended the "security zone in the western hemisphere" to the North Sea, for all practical purposes the eastern shoreline of the United Kingdom.

Iceland lay along the North Atlantic shipping lanes between the U.S. and Britain. Occupation and Allied control of Iceland would promote the effectiveness of American supply lines. In the first week of July, President Roosevelt sent a battalion of U.S. Marines to Reykjavik, Iceland's capital, to relieve British troops stationed there. His message to Congress informing that body of his action explained that as commander-in-chief he had ordered the Navy to take "all necessary steps . . . to insure to insure the safety of communications in the approaches between Iceland and the United States, as well as on the seas between the United States and all other strategic outposts."[4]

Roosevelt's unilateral action in this instance provoked less uproar than might have been expected; nevertheless, isolationists responded. The chairman of the American First chapter in New York called it "an audacious act," and "possibly the beginning of the end of Constitutional Government in the United States." This isolationist group went further to allege that next FDR might make similar moves in dispatching troops to Norway, Ireland, or Scotland to protect Iceland and the supply lines. Former President Hoover and Republican Senator Robert Taft of Ohio weighed in by exploring the possibility that sending military forces to Iceland put U.S. troops and ships squarely into the Battle of the Atlantic. James MacGregor Burns, one of Roosevelt's most distinguished biographers, asserted, "If there was a point when Roosevelt knowingly crossed some threshold between aiding Britain in order to stay out of war and aiding Britain by joining in the war, July 1941 was probably the time."[5]

The Atlantic Ocean was anything but peaceful throughout the summer of 1941. Another happening to add to rising tensions over submarine attacks in the shipping lanes was the *Robin Moor* incident.

The *U.S.S. Robin Moor* was a 5,000-ton merchant steamship sailing under the American flag when it was attacked and sunk by a German submarine in the tropical Atlantic 750 miles west of the British-controlled port of Freetown, Sierra Leone. The ship, sailing without a protective convoy, carried a crew of nine officers, twenty-nine crewmen, and seven passengers. A German submarine with U-69 clearly marked on its hull, rose to the surface and called to the mate of the *Robin Moor* that the ship was about to be sunk.

The U-boat's captain allowed a brief period during which all aboard the *Robin Moor* could scramble into four life boats and row away from their targeted vessel. The U-boat first torpedoed the *Robin Moor* before shelling the vacated ship to make certain it sank with all its cargo. Once that vessel disappeared beneath the waves, the U-boat's captain sent a life boat of his own to one of the four stricken life boats from the *Robin Moor*, and gave its occupants four tins of ersatz bread and two tins of butter, explaining that the ship had been sunk because it had been carrying supplies to Germany's enemy.

The captain of the U-boat promised he would radio the position of the ship just destroyed, yet it would be eighteen days before any of the survivors in the four lifeboats were rescued. Eventually, however, all were saved and taken to Brazil, the nearest neutral country.

On June 20, 1941 President Roosevelt sent a written message to Congress in which he asserted:

> I am under the necessity of bringing to the attention of the Congress the ruthless sinking by a German submarine on May 21 of an American ship, the *Robin Moor* . . .

> According to the formal depositions of survivors the vessel was sunk within thirty minutes from the time of the first warning given by the Commander of the submarine to an officer of the *Robin Moor*. . .

> The *Robin Moor* was sunk without provision for the safety of the passengers and crew. It was sunk despite the fact that its American nationality was admittedly known to the Commander of the submarine and that its nationality was likewise clearly indicated by the flag and other markings.[6]

In the final draft of the message, President Roosevelt in his own handwriting, penciled in the warning: "We are not yielding, and we do not propose to yield."[7]

Most Americans seemed ready to accept FDR's disingenuous explanation, but some, notably those opposing further entanglements in the European war, disagreed. Isolationists charged the President was playing fast and loose with the truth. Senator Wheeler took issue with FDR's statements that the ship's load was for civilian purposes only. The senator asserted that contrary to what FDR said or implied, more than 70% of the *Robin Moor*'s cargo consisted of the kind of materiel that fell under German and British standards for contraband. And defending the legality of Germany's right to destroy the vessel, Wheeler further charged that with this message, President Roosevelt was trying again to drag the United States into the war.

In America, movements towards ever deeper involvement in the European war accelerated. Government regulatory agencies were set up, and top notch executive talents were lured to Washington. Heavy industry swelled with the hiring of three million new workers, while in factories red, white, and blue flags waved over assembly lines warning: Time is Short. President Roosevelt declared "an unlimited national emergency," and froze German and Italian assets in the U.S. Axis ships and ships from countries which had been overrun by the Germans were seized "to prevent their sabotage."

President Roosevelt and his lieutenants continued to maintain that attacks in the Atlantic were unprovoked, and an influential columnist, Arthur Krock of the *New York Times*, went to the dictionary for a reasonable meaning of the term "attack." He found it defined as "an onset, an aggressive initiation of combat, a move which is the antithesis of 'defense.'" The columnist went on to say that under such a definition, of our ships in recent engagements — the *Robin Moor*, the Kearney, and the *Greer* — all three attacked the German submarines.[8]

Encounters between merchant vessels and submarines continued during the summer of 1941, and as fall approached there was open conflict involving a ship of the U.S. Navy. U.S. ships as non-belligerents could not attack Axis submarines, but as more Allied vessels attempted to deliver supplies for the ground forces fighting on the continent, the German high command stepped up wolf pack attacks. Among American ships operating in the North Atlantic was a destroyer named the U.S.S. *Greer*, and its involvement with a German sub made America's entry into the war very imminent.

On the morning of September 4, 1941, the *Greer*, carrying mail and passengers, was en route to Iceland when it received a signal from a British airplane that a German submarine had crash dived ten miles ahead. The British plane, running low on fuel, had to leave the area, but before doing so dropped four depth charges on the underwater enemy. The *Greer* continued to trail the submarine, broadcasting its position so that other British naval ships could target it. The cat and mouse game went on for about two hours before lookouts from the *Greer* warned of a torpedo heading toward it. The destroyer ran up flank speed, and the torpedo passed 100 yards behind it. The *Greer* than charged for an attack, laying down a pattern of eight depth charges — all of which apparently missed the sub. Then from it came a second torpedo which missed the destroyer by 300 yards to port.

The *Greer* continued maneuvering and searching the area for about two hours, dropping eleven more depth charges, but apparently not damaging the submarine. The *Greer* had held the underwater raider in sound contact for three and a half hours, and with nineteen depth charges had become the first American ship in World War II to attack the *Kriegsmarine*.

President Roosevelt lost no time in calling the U-boat and *Greer* encounter an act of piracy, and in making that charge he also announced a radical change in rules for U.S. engagements. Wearing a black mourning band on his sleeve — his mother Sara had died four days earlier — he addressed the nation on September 11, asserting:

> We have sought no shooting war with Hitler; we do not seek it now... but we will keep open the line of legitimate commerce... When you see a rattlesnake poised to strike, you do not wait until he has struck before you crush him. These Nazi submarines are the rattlesnakes of the Atlantic.[9]

Going further, the President added:

> ... in the waters which we deem necessary for our defense, American naval vessels and American planes will no longer wait until Axis submarines lurking under the water, or Axis raiders on the surface of the sea, strike their deadly blow — first.[10]

Roosevelt's attempts to portray the encounter as an unprovoked attack did not satisfy everyone. Allegations arose that his statements were misleading, "if not false." The U.S. Senate Committee on Naval Affairs called upon Admiral Harold R. Stark to give more details of the incident, and in doing so, the Admiral's report to the Committee opined "the President's statements ... appear in some respects inadequate, and, in others, incorrect."

Following the *Greer* affair two more American destroyers tangled with U-boats during the undeclared naval war. In slightly more than a month the *U.S.S. Kearney* was ripped by a tornado while on escort duty and eleven of her crew killed. Within that same week the *U.S.S. Reuben James*, an old four-piper, became the first American naval to be sunk by a U-boat; of the entire ship's company of 160 men, only 45, including no officers, were rescued by other escorts.

In early October, a convoy of 50 merchant ships left Iceland and ran into a concentration of U-boats 400 miles south. Three ships in the convoy were immediately torpedoed, and in response to radio appeals, five U.S. destroyers (*Plunkett, Livermore, Kearney, Greer,* and *Decatur*) rushed to the scene. The destroyers were not yet equipped with radar, and torpedo attacks on the convoy continued for more than a day. Then on 17

October, a corvette from the merchant fleet crossed the bow of the *Kearney* forcing her to stop. Before she could resume speed a torpedo from one of the U-boats struck her on the starboard side. The *Kearney* lost eleven Americans but under escort of the U.S.S. *Greer* was able to limp back to Iceland. The U.S. Congress was in the midst of heated debate over revisions of Neutrality legislation, and the Kearney incident helped push FDR's desired changes through the House the following day by a margin of almost two to one.

Administration spokesmen quickly asserted the *Kearney* disaster was clear evidence of the German menace; isolationists responded that the attack showed why Neutrality legislation should not be revised in the direction sought by the White House. FDR, well aware of the split in public reaction, took no immediate action but waited for another incident.

A more serious one came on 31 October when the U.S.S. *Reuben James*, a destroyer, was escorting a fast-moving convoy from Iceland. The convoy was 600 miles west of Iceland and the destroyer had just turned to investigate a direction-finding bearing when a torpedo struck her port side. The blast ignited the forward magazine, and the entire fore part of the ship was blown off. The aft part went down as several depth charges exploded, killing survivors who had been thrown into the water. Of the ship's company of 160 men, only 45, including no officers, were rescued by other escorts.

Again, Democratic supporters argued the incident was further proof of German intentions, and opponents countered that sending merchant ships escorted by U.S. Navy vessels was drawing us inexorably closer to actual war. Republican Senator Gerald Nye of North Dakota put it bluntly: "You can't expect to walk into a barroom brawl and hope to stay out of the fight."[11]

FDR's administration had taken on gargantuan responsibilities for protecting wide expanses of the North Atlantic, and the *Niblack*, *Robin Moor*, *Greer*, *Kearny*, *Reuben James*, and other disasters resulting from submarine attacks meant the U.S. was engaged in a de facto naval war with Germany. Many Americans trusted in the "short of war" concept, holding to the hope that Britain and Russia, if we gave them enough help through Lend-Lease, would be able to stave off the Hitler onslaught. Isolationists remained undaunted, however, stepping up their opposition with increased numbers and presenting them with deeper emotions.

# CHAPTER 15. AMERICANA 1941

"There are three things I will never forget about America:
Niagara Falls, the Rocky Mountains, and Amos 'n Andy."

— George Bernard Shaw

Franklin Roosevelt began his third term in office on January 20, 1941. By that time social and personal lives had been transformed into modes unimaginable to the nation's forefathers. Among the most dramatic of the changes were vastly improved communications.

Radio, only experimental when the twentieth century began, by 1941 had swollen fantastically since the first commercial stations opened in the century's second decade; the comparative new medium was at the height of its popularity. Comedies, dramas, audience participation programs, variety shows, sports, crime drama, or musical presentations — radio offered them all and at small direct cost to listeners.

Daytime programming was geared to housewives — avid followers of fifteen-minute offerings like "Portia Faces Life", 'Our Gal Sunday", "Stella Dallas", "John's Other Wife", and "Life Can Be Beautiful". Listeners reported they liked the shows because they were "so true to life." The programs featured marital difficulties, chronic illnesses, alcoholism, or missing persons, and because the productions were sponsored mainly by soap producers like Duz, Chipso, or Oxydol, they were dubbed "soap operas."

Night time variety shows garnered radio audiences even larger than soap operas. The "Chase and Sanborn Hour" starring ventriloquist Edgar Bergen and his brash wooden dummy, Charlie McCarthy, was an example. Other popular evening productions helping to make up radio's top ten evening programs for 1941 were: "Jack Benny", "Fibber McGee and Molly", "Lux Radio Theatre", Bob Hope", "The Kate Smith Hour", "The Aldrich Family", "Major Bowes' Amateur Hour", "Kay Kyser and His College of Musical Knowledge", and "One Man's Family".

Diplomacy and war overseas gave prominence to radio news reporters. Names of newsmen Lowell Thomas, Bob Trout, Gabriel Heater, William L. Shirer, and H.V. Kaltenborn were joined by younger reporters soon to become household names themselves: Edward R, Murrow, Eric Sevareid, and Winston Burdette.

The Jazz Age of Scott Fitzgerald and Sophie Tucker had ended and was replaced by big bands: Paul Whiteman, Glenn Miller, Woody Herman, Benny Goodman, Duke Ellington, Tommy Dorsey, Harry James, Les Brown, and Louis Armstrong to name a few. Beyond radio and Hollywood, jukeboxes in restaurants and cafes across the land added more coin to recordings made by the famous orchestras.

Radio brought reports of sporting events into every home with a set. Listeners could hear the roar of racing engines from the Indianapolis 500, an announcer at ringside describing another win for boxing champion Joe Louis, a bugler calling the horses to the starting gate at Churchill Downs for the Kentucky Derby, or a New Years Day football broadcast from the Rose Bowl in Pasadena. There were followers for every sport; baseball was still the national pastime, and 1941 was a bonanza season for it.

A host of players who would become famous were just appearing in the major leagues: Stan Musial, Red Schoendist, Hank Greenberg, Pewee Reese, Bob Feller, Phil Rizzuto, and Ted Williams of the Boston Red Sox, whose incredible batting average of .406 for the season gave promise of being unequaled.

The climax of the baseball season in 1941 came in the fourth game of the World Series — a contest between the New York Yankees and the Brooklyn Dodgers. The Yankees already had won two games, the Dodgers one. In the ninth inning, the Dodgers were ahead 4–3, and the Yankees were at bat with two out and two strikes on the third batter. One more strike and the Series would be tied at two games each. The Dodger pitcher threw a huge, sharp breaking curve which fooled Yankee batter Tommy Henrich. Henrich swung and missed, but the missed ball bounced off Dodger catcher Mickey Owen's mitt and careened toward the Dodgers' dugout. Henrich raced to first safely. The next Yankee batter hit a single to left field, and the following one a double off the screen in center field, scoring two runs. The Yankees won the game which had seemed like a sure thing for the Dodgers, and then went on to win the Series.

Crime, no newcomer to America — it had existed in colonial days when ducking stools, public lashing, and pillories were acceptable punishments — also changed during the Depression of the 1930s and its immediate aftermath. Notable was an increase in the number of kidnappings. By far the most sensational kidnapping of the era was that of Charles Lindbergh's 19-month-old son. Lindbergh was still a preeminent American hero in 1930; Baltimore scribe H. L Mencken called seizure of his son "the biggest story since the Resurrection."

A nurse had tucked the infant in bed at the regular time, but when she went to check on her charge two hours later, she discovered the tot was missing. She immediately informed Mrs. Anne Morrow Lindbergh, the aviator's wife and mother of the baby. A handwritten letter, riddled with spelling errors and grammatical irregularities, was discovered on the nursery window sill, and outside a shoddy, homemade ladder had been placed reaching from the ground to the second floor window.

Word of the kidnapping spread quickly. Persons ranging from Chicago gangster Al Capone then in prison and Herbert Hoover in the White House offered to help. The Bureau of Investigation, not yet named the FBI, was authorized to investigate the case, and the U.S. Customs Service, the Coast Guard, the Immigration Service, and the Washington, D.C. police were alerted and told their assistance might be required. Despite numerous false leads and complications, for an agonizingly long time no real progress was made toward finding the child or the culprits.

Following instructions contained in mysterious letters, a ransom of $100,000 was paid in gold certificates which at the time were being withdrawn from circulation. It was hoped that anyone passing large amounts of gold certificates would attract attention and thus aid in identifying perpetrators of the crime. Two and a half months later, a corpse identified as the missing baby, was found. The body, decomposed, its skull fractured, and with one leg and both hands missing, was discovered within 4.5 miles from the Lindbergh home.

A $10 gold certificate from the ransom money was discovered on September 18, 1934, more than two years later. A gas station attendant had received the certificate as payment. The puzzled station attendant turned it over to the police, remembering that it had been given him by a man driving a dark blue Dodge sedan bearing a New York license plate. The car was owned by Richard B. Hauptmann, who was arrested the next day and charged with the baby's murder.

In the trial that followed, all the evidence was circumstantial, but Hauptmann was a German with a criminal record, and the public sympathy for the Lindberghs ran high. Hauptmann was found guilty and sentenced to death. Despite intercession by the Governor of New Jersey, on April 3, 1936, nearly four years after the crime had been committed, Richard Bruno Hauptmann was executed in Old Smoky, the electric chair at New Jersey State Prison.[1]

# Chapter 16. The Labor Front

> "Politics is the science of how who gets what, when, and why."
>
> — Sidney Hillman, President of the CIO

_____

No one could be sure whether it was due to demands of the war in Europe or to programs of the New Deal, but throughout 1940 the U.S. the economy was on the upswing. Reports in the second week of February, 1941, revealed that 1940 earnings of the five biggest U.S. steelmakers had made a dizzy surge. U.S. Steel, biggest of the five, earned $102 million — its highest since 1930. Bethlehem Steel, number two company with earnings of $48 million, set an all-time record with income well over its 1929 high water mark. Republic Steel's earnings of $21 million was twice as high as its best previous year. Jones and Laughlin with an income of more than $10 million was at its highest since 1929. National Steel — the only steel company to have shown a profit in 1932 — gained a healthy 12% in 1940 over its 1939 earnings.

The year of 1940 had been relatively quiet on the labor front, but in the year that followed strikes broke out like freckles under a Kansan sun. In 1941 one out of every twelve workers would go out on strike — a percentage exceeded only in the years of 1919 and 1937. Disputes were not only over wages, but over work conditions, work loads, hours, and jurisdictional authority as well.

The War Department seized on the strikes as products of unpatriotic propaganda, issuing bulletins showing how many man days had been lost through stoppages at Allis Chalmers, Vultee Aircraft, American Car and Foundry, and Motor Wheel. Production of critical items such as tanks, P-40 fighter wheels, ammunition, generators, blankets, bombs, and zinc was almost halted. The public was aroused, and in theaters across the land, patrons booed whenever newsreels showed pictures of strikers. [1]

Labor unions by 1941 had won recognition and contracts from two of the country's major auto makers — General Motors and Chrysler — but the Ford Motor Company refused to recognize the UAW (United Auto Workers) or any union as a bargaining agent for workers. Founder and magnate Henry Ford was adamant in opposition to unionization.

At the River Rouge plant of Ford Motors near Dearborn, Michigan, workers went out on strike — the first such action taken in that corporation's history. The gigantic Ford factory stood on more than twelve-hundred acres, generated enough power to light all of Chicago, and used more water than Detroit, Washington, D.C., and Chicago combined.

Ford was a complex individual with a contradictory personality, having a wide range of interests and strongly held opinions. At the opening of the twentieth century he had built and driven race cars and had begun demonstrating that his engineering designs produced reliable vehicles. For more than a decade his Model T Tin Lizzie became the symbol for middle class prosperity. A strong pacifist, he arranged and paid for a ship to sail to Europe during World War I in the hope of persuading governments there to end the conflict. The effort failed, and he returned home to build a larger factory for production of more automobiles. Extremely successful in developing assembly line techniques for parts and vehicles faster and cheaper, he was the epitome of an American success story.

In some ways progressive, Ford built village industries and small factories in rural Michigan where people could work and farm during different seasons, thereby bridging urban and rural experiences. He sought ways to use agricultural products in industrial outputs, such as soybean-based plastic components in automobiles. He established schools in several areas where education was built around a "one-room school" concept, and students learned "through doing." A strong traditionalist, he financed a large, excellent museum to preserve historical items that illustrated the American experience and American ingenuity.

When America entered World War II, Henry Ford swung into action, changing his gargantuan auto enterprises into military factories, turning out bombers, Jeeps, and tanks for the war efforts. Yet despite his patriotism and foresights, Ford throughout the 1930s had remained one of the nation's foremost opponents of labor unionization and was last of the Big Three auto-makers to recognize unions as bargaining agents for workers.

In April, 1941, the Ford Company's head of security fired eight union members. Immediately the company's entire labor force walked out in a wildcat strike, blockading the huge plant. A few, mostly black workers loyal to Henry Ford, remained inside the plant. They were paid $1.00 per hour for their time although no work was done. Racial conflict complicated the Ford strike, for while an overwhelming majority of workers stood with the union, nearly two thousand non-union Negroes stayed in the plant, hurling insults and objects on the marching or picketing strikers outside the gates.

In Washington, President Roosevelt was surrounded with advice: 1) he should issue an injunction and send in federal troops to quell the disturbance; 2) he should cancel all defense contracts with industries which failed to recognize labor unions; 3) he should remain on the sideline and regard it as the concern of the state where it occurred.

At the time when the Ford strike of 1941 was most intense, Eleanor was at Hyde Park and from there she sent her husband in Washington a long memorandum she had received from civil rights leader Mary McCleod Bethune. The essence of the memo was that Henry Ford was hiring semi-skilled and unskilled Negroes not as bona fide workers but as guards against union workers.

Intensity was eased when Walter White, head of the NAACP (National Association for Advancement of Colored People) went to Detroit and standing on a union car urged black workers to forgo their role as strikebreakers, to evacuate the plant, and stand shoulder to shoulder with their fellow workers.

Blacks heeded his plea and a day or two later came out of the plant. Civil rights leaders did not give up easily though, and Eleanor Roosevelt endorsed most of their goals as well as some of their strategies. Allied with Harold Ickes, she kept relentless pressure on her husband to be more vigorous in supporting rights for minorities. Eleanor insisted that as President her husband should intervene. FDR's opponents in Congress also railed against his inaction, but he refused to be drawn into the strike, saying he meant to give the mediation machinery a full chance to work it out. He would adopt a policy of "watching, waiting, and watching."

In March, 1941, two of the nation's most prominent black leaders, Philip Randolph head of the American Railway Union and Civil Rights Leader Bayard Rustin started organizing a march in Washington to protest against racial discrimination in defense industries. In May, Randolph issued a "Call to Negro America to March in Washington on July 1, 1941, for jobs and Equal Employment in National Defense." Within a month estimates of the number preparing to participate reached 100,000.

President Roosevelt invited the two leaders to the White House where he attempted to persuade them to call off the march. His efforts failed; the two were adamant and urged him to issue an executive order barring such discrimination in defense industries. He maintained he couldn't do that, saying that every other minority group would ask for similar action. Nevertheless, when attitudes hardened and the threat of a march loomed more imminent, Roosevelt issued Executive Order 8802 barring discrimination in defense industries and federal bureaus (the Fair Employment Act). As a result of this Order, Randolph called off the proposed march.[2]

Henry Ford continued to believe that he could win over the two competing unions (CIO — Congress of Industrial Organizations and the AFL — American Federation of Labor). Edsel, Henry's son, had replaced him as president of the company, however, and insisted that times had changed — now, according to Edsel, negotiating with elected labor officials was the only path for successful manufacturing.

Edsel's arguments won out, and preparations began for a company-wide election to determine which union Ford workers wanted to represent them. Ballots from this election showed that the CIO had won a smashing victory, 70% of the votes compared with 27% for the AFL. A minuscule 2.6% had voted to keep Ford a non-union shop.

The union kept up the pressure for ten days, at the end of which Henry Ford capitulated, making concessions even beyond union demands. He and his son agreed that Ford Motor Co. would become a closed shop, meaning all employees had to be union members, and that it would initiate a "dues check-off" provision, allowing union dues to be deducted from payrolls and sent directly to the union. The final settlement granted the union virtually everything it had sought, including the highest wages in the industry and reinstatement of all workers dismissed previously for union activities. CIO leaders trumpeted the settlement as the greatest victory for labor in their generation.[3]

Auto manufacturing was not the only industry with labor troubles in that year of 1941. Coal miners in America had united in anger over the horrendous conditions of their labor. Most of the miners belonged to the CIO, whose founder and head was the lion-maned, beetle-browed John L. Lewis — able, fervent, stubborn isolationist and implacable foe of FDR.

Even with the best of conditions, the miners' work underground was always hazardous. Their jobs that prevailed in 1941 was as dangerous as a soldier's in combat. More than 1300 miners had been killed on the job in 1940 and thousands more permanently injured. There was no national safety law protecting miners, and whatever laws were adopted by the several states were usually flouted by mine owners and operators powerful enough to have their way with state and local governments. The fatal accident rate in American coal mines was three times that in England, four times that in France, and six times that in Holland. [4]

In the late summer of the preceding year when it had been time for the signing of new labor contracts, Lewis, whose CIO union by this time had enrolled 95% of the mine labor force, promised union peace if steel management would agree to a union shop, i.e., union membership would be a condition of initial employment. Steel management refused the offer, believing uninterrupted steel production was essential to the nation and that it would have immense support from public opinion as well as that from a business-dominated defense bureaucracy. In mid-September, therefore, Lewis called fifty-three thousand mine workers out on strike.

In principle, Roosevelt was not opposed to the principle of a closed shop, but he maintained such agreements ought to come about through negotiations between management and labor, not through government interdiction. President Roosevelt held several White House conferences over which he presided, and members of the National Defense Mediation Board, steel executives, and labor leaders attended. Minimal progress was made, and as fall approached, the two major labor leaders resigned from the Mediation Board along with five CIO members. This meant that no labor representatives were any longer on the National Defense Mediation Board.

An exasperated Roosevelt summoned mine union officials and steel executives to a meeting in the White House the second week of November and in that gathering he stressed national defense and the absolute necessity of uninterrupted coal production. He said he was not threatening but currently was under "constant and heavy pressure" to ask the Congress for restraining legislature. He said that he did not think the Congress would order a closed shop, but in an unmistakable thrust at Lewis he concluded by stating:

> I never threaten. I am asking you to resume collective bargaining immediately following this meeting, and if you cannot agree today, please keep on conferring tomorrow and Sunday. [5]

Following this meeting there were days of fruitless wrangling between steel executives and labor leaders. The steel executives agreed to submit the question of closed shop to arbitration, but Lewis held out, insisting he would have to consult the membership. After having done that, he reported that the United Mine Workers' membership had voted unanimously to accept the offer of binding arbitration. There was more bickering and delay, and it was the last of November, 1941, before Benjamin Fairless, President of U.S. Steel, could inform the President that his board, too, had voted in favor of the closed shop for mines that already had signed with the union.

Fairless delivered this final report on the morning of Sunday, December 7, 1941, but his otherwise worthy announcement was eclipsed by news of a far greater event. Nevertheless, records would show that John L. Lewis, combative leader and in the eyes of many citizens at the time the most hated man in America, through an unyielding stance and indefatigable efforts had won a significant victory.

## CHAPTER 17. FROM MARRIAGE TO ALLIANCE

"Veneer: an outward show that enhances but misrepresents what lies beneath."

— American Heritage Dictionary of the English Language

During this period of turmoil, President Roosevelt sought escape in fiddling with his stamp collections, taking supper in bed, perhaps reading a detective story, or spending a weekend at Hyde Park where he would have tea with his spinster cousins. He enjoyed gossip, small talk of gardens and weather, pets, and relatives.

He was fifty years old when he began his first term in the White House. He had been married for twenty-eight years then, but he and Eleanor were no longer living together as man and wife. They had agreed to change their marriage into a political alliance, and each was following a different living pattern; their marriage was a veneer presented to the public. The arrangement was carefully guarded and unknown to most people until after FDR's death in 1945.[1]

Causes for the estrangement can be traced back to World War I when Franklin was Assistant Secretary of the Navy. In the winter of 1914, his wife Eleanor, pregnant with Franklin Jr., decided to employ someone to come in to help her three mornings a week. Upon a recommendation from Auntie Bye, she hired Lucy Page Mercer.

Twenty-two-year old Lucy Mercer seemed an excellent choice. She was pretty, had a ready smile, was lively, and charming to all who met her. Lucy had an enviable heritage; even acid-tongued Alice Roosevelt Longworth years later would say that Lucy was very "well-bred." Indeed, she was; her family background was as distinguished as the Roosevelts', but her fortune had been spent by her alcoholic father. The Mercers were leaders in the high society circles of Washington, and Lucy's mother Minnie was described as "the most beautiful woman in the city." After divorcing her besotted husband, Minnie became an interior decorator moving to New York, where it was said she found rich patrons on whom to bestow her favors. She sent young daughter Lucy to Austria to attend a strict convent school.

Lucy inherited her mother's good looks but little of her flair and ostentations. At first, Eleanor and Franklin treated Lucy precisely as a governess should be treated. Not only did she help with the children, but soon she was Eleanor's social secretary, answering letters, filing bills, and running errands when necessary. Trust deepened, and from time to time when at the last moment an extra woman was needed to fill out a dinner party, Lucy was asked to substitute. Gradually, she became part of Franklin Roosevelt's household, impressing everyone in the family. Sara, ever the watchful mother, praised Lucy in a letter to her daughter-in-law when Eleanor and FDR were in San Francisco. Sara wrote, "Miss Mercer is here. She is so sweet and attractive, and she adores you, Eleanor."[2]

It was the custom for wives and children of Washington officials to spend the summer in cooler places, and for Eleanor and the children that meant Campobello, a slender rockbound island off the coast of Maine. Sara and Franklin's father James had been so taken with the invigorating sea air and the congenial social life that in 1883, a year and a half after Franklin's birth, they bought four acres and built a summer home on the island.

It is likely that Franklin and Lucy's love affair began during the summer of 1915 when Eleanor was with the children at Campobello while Franklin remained in Washington, with only Lucy and servants in the household. In his early thirties at the time, Franklin was blessed with great vitality and physical attractiveness; a newspaper described him as a matinee idol. Naturally enough, the Adonis was attractive to ladies — a talent he exploited. Eleanor knew of her husband's flirtatious habits, but she could put those aside as long as she believed she was his only true love.

In that summer of 1915 Eleanor and the children stayed at Campobello longer than usual because of an infantile paralysis scare, and the period gave Franklin three months of bachelor life. His wife was away; he was young and in the prime of young manhood. Lucy was beautiful and nearby; the opportunity was irresistible.

The situation worsened when Lucy joined the Navy as a female yeoman third class, and in that position she saw the Navy's Assistant Secretary daily. Lucy's naval records described her as five feet nine, blue-eyed, brown-haired, with a small scar on her left arm and another small one on her right leg.

When Eleanor returned in the fall from Campobello, if she sensed anything was going on between Franklin and Lucy, she withheld comment. A year later, she could no longer ignore signals that another woman might be pulling her husband from her.

Ordinarily, Eleanor left for Campobello in mid-July, but that year she had resisted going, accusing Franklin of wanting to get rid of her so that he could stay in Washington alone. Franklin protested, saying she was a "goosey girl" even to think such thoughts. A summer in Washington would be hell on his nerves, he said. She could go to Campobello, but because of the press of duties he could not.

Lucy Mercer had qualities of femininity that Eleanor lacked. Pretty enough to be genuinely admired, she attracted men in social gatherings like summer flowers attract honey bees, winning gentlemen in soft spoken words with her knowledge and repartee. A representative from the British Embassy once said her voice reminded him of dark velvet.[3]

Franklin and Lucy were together often throughout the summer of 1915. He was debonair, fun-loving, full of energy, and the life of every party he attended; Lucy matched his zest and vitality. They made a handsome couple moving about in Washington society where they were accepted by friends who believed association of the two was with Eleanor's approval.

Alice Roosevelt, Theodore's daughter, who had married Nicholas Longworth, once telephoned Franklin to say that she had seen the two of them in a car. "I saw you twenty miles out in the country," Alice said. "You didn't see me. Your hands were on the steering wheel, but your eyes were on the perfectly lovely lady by your side." Franklin replied, "Isn't she lovely?"[4]

In October of 1917, Lucy's father died, and she was discharged from her Navy assignment upon orders from her superior, the Assistant Secretary of the Navy, who tried to console her while he himself was being torn between his duties as father and husband and the pull of passion for his paramour.

Eleanor may have sensed that an affair was developing between Franklin and Lucy. Whatever the circumstances were, she and Franklin must have talked about its possibilities, and as a result Lucy was let go. It was an amicable parting, and Franklin promised his wife that he would not see nor get in contact with the former governess again.

By 1918, America had been at war for two years and had sent the AEF (American Expeditionary Force) to Europe. Other Washington officials, Herbert Hoover the U.S. Food Administrator, Edward Stettinius in charge of Army purchasing, and Edward Hurley, chairman of the U.S. Shipping Board were examples of ranking officials sent abroad. Franklin did not want to be left behind and had implored his boss, Secretary of the Navy Joseph Daniels, to send him to Europe where he could gather information that would give the Nave Department a new perspective. Daniels, perhaps aware of his underling's ambitions, had turned down such requests, but in July, 1918, the pressure from Congressional members was too strong to ignore, and Daniels relented enough to issue orders sending FDR on an inspection trip to Europe. The orders were "to look into our Naval administration and help coordinate its efforts with those of other American agencies." FDR also was authorized "for such other purposes as may be deemed expedient by you on your arrival."

With such latitude, FDR seems to have had a uniformly grand time during his eight weeks in Europe. He met and talked with important persons and rode through the streets in London and Paris he had known as a young adult. Only near the end of his stay did he make a cursory visit to an actual battlefield — a site about which he had been excited and on which other Roosevelts were distinguishing themselves.[5]

During his European stay, Franklin made a trip by private railroad car to Rome. There he met with senior Italian officials including Prime Minister Vittorio Orlando. The trip was not a total success, for Franklin acted well beyond his assigned purposes. He reported to Secretary Daniels that he had persuaded Italy to agree to "a commander-in-chief for all the naval forces in the Mediterranean," but Orlando disclosed that he had agreed to that provision only after being promised by Roosevelt that Italy would have the final authority over all operations in the Adriatic. French officials complained that Franklin was making high level strategic statements that undercut objectives of the Western Allies. Secretary Daniels had to assure President Wilson and the U.S. Secretary of State that he had never authorized his impetuous assistant to say "who should command" in the region. Franklin's venture into diplomacy had been an embarrassment, and he received a guarded reprimand from Daniels, his superior in Washington.

Back in Paris by the end of August, 1918, Franklin began to fall ill. He shook with fever, and his temperature reached 102 degrees. Nevertheless, he attended several parties with family, friends, or officials before pushing on to London. He boarded the *U.S.S. Leviathan* in Brest and set sail for New York on September 12. Spanish influenza, the pandemic that would claim a million lives worldwide that year, swept over the ship. Several officers and men died during the five-day voyage home and were buried at sea. Franklin collapsed in his cabin and was diagnosed as suffering from double pneumonia.

He had written Eleanor several times each week, and from Brest before boarding the *Leviathan* he had wired her he was coming home. For Eleanor the marriage balloon already had burst. She had gone to Hyde Park to unpack effects Franklin had sent home, and while going through those articles had come upon a bundle of love letters Lucy had sent to Franklin.

The correspondence showed unmistakably that the affair had not been broken up as Franklin had promised. The letters raised again Eleanor's childhood fears and loneliness. Later she would confide to a friend, "The bottom dropped out of my own particular world, and I faced myself, my surroundings, my world, honestly for the first time."

Franklin had lied when he told her he would break all contacts with Lucy Mercer; the two of them had kept up a correspondence which clearly showed the intimacy she had suspected. Everyone she trusted had betrayed her — her adored father, her handsome husband, and even her social secretary. Such thoughts tortured Eleanor. She had borne her husband six children and now was being discarded for a younger and prettier woman.

Eleanor confronted Franklin with the evidence, and according to her account, she offered him a divorce if that was what he wanted.[6]

In those days divorce was a very grave matter, and in New York State then the only legal grounds for it was adultery. Adultery, if charged and accepted, carried a stigma not only for the couple but for everyone in the family, including Sara and the children. When the contretemps reached Sara, she stressed to Franklin that a divorce would mean the end of all his hopes for a political career — voters would never accept a divorced candidate — especially one known as an adulterer. If her son chose to leave his wife for another woman, she could not stop him, but she held the purse strings, and she was adamant. Franklin must understand: if he and Eleanor divorced, he would not inherit the estate at Hyde Park, and she would "not give him another dollar."[7]

Added to those drawn into making a decision was Louis Howe, FDR's political mentor and guardian. Howe helped convince his ambitious protégé that there would be no future for him in politics with a divorce on his record. Moreover, Lucy was an ardent Catholic, and Howe doubted if she would ever agree to marry a divorced man. Also there is little doubt that both Franklin and Eleanor loved their children, and both were concerned about the effect a divorce would have on them.

All of the arguments given Franklin and Eleanor against divorce are as yet unknown. Long afterwards, Eleanor asserted that the threat to his political ambitions had been the compelling reason, but no one can be certain. At any rate, FDR was persuaded, and he and Eleanor worked out a solution. They vowed that for the public they would present an appearance of marriage, but its old intimacy was gone, never to be resumed; they would never again live together as man and wife.

The odd arrangement began and was followed for twenty-seven years. It meant a strange household, for each retained a passionless affection for the other. When Franklin fell ill with paralysis in 1921, no one could have been more attentive and caring than Eleanor, who watched over him constantly, giving reassurance and encouragement for him to remain active with political contacts.

Franklin worked extremely hard in rehabilitation; he got advice from numerous sources — much of which was unscientific and unproductive. He purchased different kinds of leg braces and bravely undertook crutch-walking. It was slow and clumsy; the braces were heavy, painful, and did nothing to build up his legs. With constant exercise and experimentation, however, very slowly and with pain he responded enough to stand with great difficulty. With perseverance and magnificence determination, he was able to stand holding on to the lectern and deliver his celebrated Happy Warrior speech at the Democratic National Convention in 1924 nominating Alfred Smith for the Presidency.

In the years between 1925 and 1928 when Franklin was in the South, either on the Larooco or at Warm Springs, Georgia, hoping to regain the use of his legs, Eleanor taught at Todhunter, a private school for girls in New York City, and it was there that she first met Nancy Cook and Marion Dickerman. The three women found a lot in common, sharing beliefs in Democratic politics and social values. Often away on his own, Franklin didn't object to their association and even took on the role of a paterfamilias to the threesome, calling them "our gang."

Not long after the convention in 1924, FDR, Eleanor and her two friends accompanied FDR for a relaxing picnic on the wooded banks of Val Kill, two miles east of the Roosevelt estate at Hyde Park. It was on that outing that Franklin suggested the idea of a home for the three women at Val Kill. The land was not a part of Sara's Hyde Park property; Franklin had bought the land himself, and he told his three companions there was no reason they shouldn't have a cottage for themselves on it. "You can build a shack here and live in it. I'll deed the land to you. The three of you can come and go as you please, and I'll deed the land to you with the understanding that it will revert to me upon the death of the last survivor." (FDR must not have entertained the thought that he might die before any one of them.)

The women were delighted with the idea, and construction was started soon afterwards. The project would be far from a shack, for the stream was dug out to form an old-fashioned swimming pool, and the cottage was built of fieldstone in the traditional Hudson River Dutch style. In the rear of the living quarters was a big gray stucco building which Eleanor and her friends hoped to use as a furniture shop.

The "cottage" became the focus of the three women's lives. Initially, Eleanor, Nancy, and Marion slept together in a single, loftlike dormitory bedroom. Nancy and Marion maintained their apartment in Greenwich Village, but it was merely a place to stay during the week until they could go home to Val Kill.

The first venture at Val Kill was to build furniture for the new home, but soon that venture expanded into establishing a furniture factory — an enterprise which produced authentic copies of early American furniture. Although Eleanor put up most of the capital out of her growing income from radio and writings along with her small inheritance, it was Nancy Cook who was the moving spirit behind what was called the Roosevelt Industries. Nancy diligently collected and guarded bottles and jars of stains of the exact color and viscosity she wanted. Only after every piece of choice wood was polished and rubbed until it had a texture like velvet was she satisfied.

After leaving employment in the Roosevelt household, Lucy Mercer accepted a position offered her by Winthrop Rutherfurd and lived in his spacious estate called Tranquility, situated in northern New Jersey near the small Erie Railroad station at Allamuchy.

Winthrop Rutherfurd was a wealthy man already old; his wife was chronically ill and his children were growing. Lucy was an ideal governess and chatelaine for this country gentleman and his dependents. In the winter, when Winthrop and his family moved to another estate among the horsy set around Aiken, South Carolina, Lucy went with them.

Winthrop Rutherfurd's wife died soon after this move to the South, and not long after her passing he asked the tall, demure governess to take her place. Winthrop was thirty-one years Lucy's senior, but she accepted his proposal, and they were married in February, 1920. The marriage restored Lucy's fortunes and awarded her a permanent place in the highest levels of Southern society.

In Washington, Eleanor, upon learning of the wedding, wrote Sara, "Did you see where Lucy Mercer married old Wintie?"[8]

But the evidence is incontrovertible; FDR did not honor the vow he gave Eleanor to break off all contact with Lucy. When he was elected President the first time, he secretly arranged for a limousine to bring Lucy to the inaugural ceremony. And there were times when Eleanor was away that FDR invited Lucy to the White House, where the two of them could meet privately. Occasionally, Lucy would stay for an informal dinner at which FDR's daughter Anna served as hostess. Once in a while, he telephoned Lucy from the White House — not often during his first two terms, but the calls became more frequent in the latter stages of his life. There were instances, too, when either going to Warm Springs or coming back to Washington from there, FDR ordered his private train sidetracked to Allamuchy, where a car would be waiting to take him to Lucy, and they would spend a day together. FDR had found little solace at home during the hectic years of the New Deal and its aftermath.

By this time FDR was untroubled by any lies or subterfuges he might or might not pass on to Eleanor. Lucy offered him warmth and companionship — two marital amenities his wife had not given.

## CHAPTER 18. EMPIRE OF THE RISING SUN

"Japan never declares war before attacking."

— General Billy Mitchell in 1932.

---

Europe was not the only continent darkened by war in the year of 1941. Americans interested in international diplomacy kept watching the events in Europe, but on the other side of the globe other ominous happenings were happening. Militarists in control of the Japanese government were well along in plans to bring India, Burma, Indonesia, Indo-China, and the Philippines into the Japanese Empire.

Not many Americans were bothered in the late thirties when Japan had denounced all naval agreements made in 1921 and 1930. By 1937, administration officials in Washington, D.C. were looking toward Europe where infections were bubbling into a genuine boil.

In 1931 only a few U.S. citizens took notice of the aggressive actions of Japan, who since 1915 had been vying with the United States for influence and access to China, which was struggling with revolution and civil war. Japan needed resources, and it sought to relieve a population boom by sending people to Manchuria. Battles raged. Japanese leaders sent troops into the Chinese cities of Mukden, Ch'ang-chi'un, and Kirin. In an opening move six years afterwards, which in reality set the stage for the beginning of World War II in the Far East, Japanese soldiers in July 1937 took over the cities of Peking and Tientsin, called their assault the "China Incident." Tokyo was furious that this struggle was taking so long, as they were strangling for lack of resources. The Japanese launched a massive attack on the newly established capital of the Republic of China, Shanghai, and when that city fell, Nipponese troops moved west to Hankow. Tens of thousands of young men were rounded up and herded to outer areas of cities or villages, where they were mowed down by machine guns, used for bayonet practice, or soaked with gasoline and burned alive. Experts at the International Military Tribunal of the Far (IMTFE) estimated that at Nanking alone in 1937 and early 1938 more than 260,000 noncombatants died at the hands of Japanese soldiers. Other experts placed the figure at well over 350,000.[1]

Near the end of 1940, Joseph C. Grew, America's ambassador to Japan, returned to the U.S. to meet with President Roosevelt and to express concern over what Japanese troops were doing. FDR in response spoke confidently of intercepting the Japanese fleet if it moved southward, of reinforcing U.S. troops stationed in Manila and Pearl Harbor, and of impressive naval maneuvers soon to be displayed in the Pacific. He reiterated that it would continue to be U.S. policy to avoid confronting the Japanese while setting in place machinery to assist the British in Europe.

Ambassador Grew returned to Tokyo and told a Japanese audience that American public opinion resented Japan's aggression in China and that his government favored economic retaliation against further violations of American rights in the region and disregard of international law. The U.S. went ahead with ongoing economic sanctions. The ambassador's remarks received enthusiastic editorial endorsements in America, but there was no legislative nor executive support for his assertions. Oil, gasoline, and finished steel continued to be sent to Japan. The Japanese, who depended on imports for 90% of their gasoline, were known to be stockpiling petroleum products, but throughout 1940 and the first half of 1941, when their intentions became clearly evident, American oil continued to be sold to them. The arsenal of democracy was the service station for fascism.

At the opening of 1941, Ambassador Grew sent Roosevelt a somber report obtained from the Peruvian minister in Tokyo: "There is a lot of talk around town to the effect that the Japanese, in case of a break with the United States, are planning to go all out in a surprise mass attack on Pearl Harbor. I rather guess that the boys in Hawaii are not precisely asleep." The State Department simply filed Grew's message away with similar ones. There were other warnings from American officials, including a memo from the Chief of the Navy War Plans Division, who speculated that Hawaii might be a "probable" target. Moreover, Secretary of the Navy Frank Knox, reiterating Ambassador Grew's and other warnings, wrote Secretary of War Henry Stimson that "hostilities would be initiated by a surprise attack on Pearl Harbor."[2]

In China some warlords attempted to resist the Japanese, and one faction led by Chiang Kai-shek garnered considerable support in the U.S. The Generalissimo's glamorous wife, Madame Chiang Kai-shek, traveled America raising sympathy and funds for her husband's army.

On one occasion Madame Chiang spoke to an audience of 50,000 persons gathered around the reception stand at City Hall in New York State's largest metropolis. Highly lauded there by the city's mayor, she asked for American citizens to help supply guns, vehicles, planes, and continued monetary support for troops under Chiang Kai-shek's command.

The week following her appearance in New York City, Madame Chiang went to her alma mater, Wellesley College in Massachusetts. She had graduated from there twenty-five years earlier, and now in a fur coat adorned with brown orchids and wearing a gown of Wellesley blue along with earrings of diamonds and sapphires, she arose to address the throng.

At the lectern, however, as soon as Madame Chiang uttered her second sentence she swayed and seemed about to faint. Her nurse was ready nearby with smelling salts. After a whiff the speaker was revived enough to finish her speech in which she told the undergraduate girls it would be their responsibility to build a "saner world." Enthusiastic receptions followed Madame Chiang across the country, and a fulsome editorial in the *New York Times* praised the Chinese visitor for her language, culture, and indefatigable efforts.

Within Japan, rival parties continued battling for supremacy, and in the summer of 1941 militarists won out and replaced the prime minister, Prince Konoye, with General Hideki Togo. Togo had commanded the Kwantung Army, the legion that enforced Japan's occupation in the puppet state of Manchukuo, and was a leading proponent for Japanese alliance with Germany. His elevation to the premiership was unmistakable evidence that the military would control Japanese foreign policy.

From London, Churchill wrote Roosevelt that the coup in Tokyo had made Japan a menace "much sharper in the last few days" and reiterated the advice he had given FDR earlier: "The stronger the action of the United States towards Japan, the greater will be the chance of preserving peace." Prime Minister Churchill further assured the American President that if peace with Japan should be broken, there would follow a British declaration of war against the Nipponese "within the hour."

Ambassador Joseph Grew was alarmed enough on one occasion to write State Department officials that Japanese news media were whipping up war hysteria. The situation was so grave he thought the Japanese would not yield to any economic embargoes; they would commit national hara-kiri rather than submit to any foreign pressures.[3]

While Lend Lease was being debated publicly and in Congress, secret U.S. and British staff talks were being held in Washington, D.C. From these talks, came the plan setting forth strategy for the war. In the event of Anglo-U.S. involvements in war with both Germany and Japan, the concentration of force would be on Germany first.

Early in February, 1941, Ambassador Haideki Nomura from Japan arrived in Washington to take up his new duties. Radiating confidence, he told reporters he was certain Japan and the U.S. would remain at peace, and he repeatedly said "no" to all questions as to whether he believed Japan would ever wage war against the United States. Going further, he said that his country was ready to act as a mediator to end all fighting between forces in Europe and in Asia. In the latter continent, Japanese troops had invaded and already were in control of large areas in China and Southeast Asia.

Relations with Japan were further strained when in Britain doughty Prime Minister Churchill announced his administration's inflexible stance. Churchill informed Japan's minister in London that "there can be no compromise or parley in Britain's war with the Axis." His pronouncement came after Churchill had informed Parliament that six days earlier the Undersecretary of Foreign Affairs had received a message from the Japanese Ambassador saying that Japan was fully prepared to act as a mediator or to take whatever action was calculated to restore peace and normal conditions, not only in greater East Asia but anywhere in the world.[4] It was almost the identical assurance Nomura had given in Washington.

Yet in Tokyo, Foreign Minister Yosuke Matsuoka was lambasting U.S. Secretary of State Cordell Hull for statements made to the effect that the Japanese invasion of Manchuria had been the first step in the destruction of peace. "The Manchurian Affair," said the talkative U.S.-educated Matsuoka, "was the result of U.S. interference in the Far East."[5]

Encouraged by German conquests of the Netherlands and France as well as by Nazi filtered reports of successes in the Battle for Britain, militarists in the Japanese administration turned eyes on outposts in Southeast Asia: oil fields of the Dutch East Indies, rubber plantations in British Malaya, and tin and rice paddies in French Indo-China. General Tojo, the new Minister of War, advised: "We should not miss the present opportunity or we shall be blamed by posterity."[6]

In July, 1941, Roosevelt persuaded U.S. congressional leaders to pass an embargo banning the export of high octane aviation gasoline and premium grades of iron and steel scrap to Japan, but the limited embargo produced an effect opposite to what had been intended. Convinced that American supply lines were in jeopardy, Japanese war leaders immediately moved troops into the northern portion of Indo-China, adjacent to the Chinese province of Yunnan. Within days Washington responded with a complete embargo of all types of iron and steel intended for Japan and announced a $100 million loan to China. In the months to follow, the U.S. and Japan undertook further moves that escalated tensions, each nation gambling that none of the moves would lead to outright war. With his eyes and mind trained on Europe, Roosevelt believed he could apply economic pressures without driving the Japanese into war, and militarists in Tokyo acted boldly, convinced that European matters would continue to dominate American foreign policy.

# Chapter 19. Atlantic Charter

"No society of the world organized under the announced principles could survive without these freedoms which are a part of the whole freedom for which we strive."

— President Roosevelt's Report to Congress on Atlantic Charter, August 21, 1941.

---

By 1941 Winston Churchill and Franklin Roosevelt were two of the most prominent newsmakers in the world, and as the frequency of messages between them increased, so did the cordiality of their exchanges. Roosevelt regarded himself as a smart Yankee horse trader. Always certain he was managing the best deal, he was matched with Churchill, one of the wiliest statesmen in all British history.

The two had not met since casual encounters twenty-eight years earlier — encounters so insignificant that in 1941 when the two came face-to-face off the coast of Newfoundland, Churchill, to FDR's chagrin, said he did not recall the prior meetings.

Those meetings had occurred in December, 1914, when Roosevelt as Assistant Secretary of the Navy had gone to London to study the workings of the British Admiralty. Churchill at the time was first Lord of the Admiralty, a position equivalent to the U.S. Secretary of the Navy, who then was Josephus Daniels, Roosevelt's superior. Churchill, perhaps piqued because America had not yet entered World War I, brushed off a formal request to help the visitor, giving an explanation that the Admiralty was far too busy to offer much assistance. The two men met again briefly four years later at a dinner for the British war cabinet given by Lloyd George. No one then could have foretold the world impact of their later relationship. "I always disliked him [Churchill]. At a dinner I thought he acted like a stinker," FDR remarked to Joseph Kennedy in 1939.[1]

In September 1939, two weeks after Germany invaded Poland, President Roosevelt wrote the Brit a warm note congratulating him upon being returned to the Admiralty. FDR invited further confidential correspondence. In January 1941, with the arms embargo repealed and relations with Britain growing ever closer, FDR told aide Harry Hopkins that many of the problems in supplying the Western Allies could be settled if only he and Churchill could meet privately. Hopkins in London set about arranging the details.

The date chosen was in the coming August and the place would be remote Placentia Bay, lying at the tip of Newfoundland, about 800 miles northeast of Boston. It would be the first face-to-face meeting between the two men since becoming President and Prime Minister and would establish a pattern of wartime get-togethers for Allied leaders.

In the first week of August, 1941, Prime Minister Churchill set off aboard *HMS Prince of Wales* to cross the Atlantic. Though the ship lost her escorts due to bad weather and had to make multiple changes in course in order to avoid U-boats, Churchill found the voyage restful, reading novels, watching films, and playing backgammon with Roosevelt's agent Harry Hopkins.

President Roosevelt used a cover story and told the press he was going on a ten-day fishing trip, but on the morning of Saturday, August 9, he was on deck of the *U.S.S. Augusta* in Placentia Bay anchored behind an impressive honor guard of naval vessels arranged in a line to welcome the visitors at the Naval Station Argentia, created earlier that year.

After Churchill's party came aboard the *Augusta*, both leaders were silent for a moment; then the Prime Minister spoke first, "At long last, Mr. President," to which Roosevelt replied, "Glad to have you aboard, Mr. Churchill." The two men had been eager for a meeting in which they could discuss respective war aims and outline a postwar international system. No doubt, too, each was anxious to take a measure of the other. Judged from those perspectives, the meeting was successful, for this conference started a friendship which would direct the war and mold a pattern for subsequent peace structures.

Sir Alexander Cadogan, one of Churchill's advisors, reported that at dinner on August 9, the American President had entertained all with descriptions of his Hyde Park estate where he hoped to grow Christmas trees for the market. Privately, Churchill first described FDR as a "charming country gentleman," — a description suggesting something of a lightweight. On his part, Roosevelt returned to Washington impressed by Churchill's qualities of mind, his easy banter, and his command of language.

Churchill had come to Placentia Bay as a suitor, using all his powers of persuasion to get a reluctant American bride to the altar. His aim was to draw the American navy across the Atlantic so that a clash with Germany was bound to come. Hitler would have to hold back U-boat attacks for fear of sinking American ships and precipitating a direct clash, or he could opt to take the direct risk of bringing America into the war. FDR responded with the same arrogance he had shown when warned about Soviet Russia, "But of course, you know, Grandpa's pretty good at trading, too."[2]

Out of the conference off the coast of Newfoundland came the Atlantic Charter, one of the most compelling statements of the war. Although wording in the broad postwar principles the U.S. and Britain laid down was idealistic and sentencious, the effect was inspiring and proffered guidance for future collaborations. After the conference, reports would show that among the premises agreed upon were: 1) renunciation of territorial or other aggrandizement, 2) opposition to territorial changes contrary to the wishes of the people immediately concerned, 3) support of the right of peoples to choose their own form of government, 4) support, with due respect for existing obligations, of easing restrictions on trade, and access to raw materials on equal terms, 5) support of cooperative efforts to improve the economic position and social security of the peoples of the world, 6) freedom from want and fear, 7) freedom of the seas, and 8) disarmament of aggressor nations pending the establishment of a permanent peace structure.[3]

In addition to these broad goals were significant strategic decisions and military commitments. The British believed that bombing, blockading, and wearing down Germany could win the war; American military leaders, particularly George Marshall, contended that before Germany could be defeated it would be necessary for Allied ground forces to invade the Continent and close with the enemy.

Churchill pressed for stepped-up American action in the Atlantic Ocean, and FDR agreed to provide American escorts for all fast convoys between Newfoundland and Iceland. Churchill disclosed that Britain planned to seize and occupy the Canary Islands lying off the coast of northwestern Africa — a move that no doubt would lead to Spain's counterattack with aid from the Nazis. The British later scrapped plans for seizure of the Canary Islands, but Roosevelt's willingness to support the Azores shows how far even then he was ready to stretch neutrality interpretations.

No formal document was released at the conclusion of this meeting between Roosevelt and Churchill, but after the former had returned to Washington and the latter to London, photographs were distributed to the press and the principles agreed upon were given out in the form of a diplomatic communiqué. The agreements approved the rights of free people to choose their own leaders, to regain land taken from them by force, to trade freely with one another, to have access to raw materials on equal terms, to upgrade the lot of backward countries, to disarm aggressor nations, and to enjoy freedom of the seas.

Drawn from FDR's State of the Union speech the preceding January, the charter also included freedoms from want and fear. The term "Atlantic Charter" was coined by the *Daily Herald*, a London newspaper, and in the following month of September, fifteen nations, including the Soviet Union, accepted its tenets.

The eight points expressed in the Charter were so popular that two years later the U.S. Office of War Information printed 240,000 leaflets recounting them. But despite the acclaim given the Charter by Americans and citizens of the United Kingdom, the meeting failed to produce the main objective of either leader. There is little doubt that Churchill came to the conference hoping to get America into the war; indeed, he admitted in memoirs that his fondest hope had been to get the U.S. into active conflict.[4]

Barring that, he would try to persuade the U.S. to increase its supply of military equipment to Great Britain and to warn Japan against taking aggressive actions in the Pacific. The Prime Minister was concerned that Japan might take advantage of the war in Europe by seizing British, Dutch, and French territories in Southeast Asia.

Churchill was disappointed when FDR brushed aside discussions of American entry into the war. Moreover, he was concerned that several aspects of the proposed declaration might be politically damaging to his own position as Prime Minister. In the agreements, both the United States and Great Britain committed themselves to supporting the restoration of self-governments for countries that had been occupied during the war and allowing all peoples to choose their own form of government. This clause acknowledged the right of colonial subjects to agitate for decolonization, including those of the far-flung British Empire. On his part, Roosevelt hoped the meeting would boost American support for increased intervention in the European war; however, upon his return to Washington numerous surveys warned him that sizable segments of public opinion remained adamantly opposed to such measures. Secondly, he wanted to arrange terms on which Great Britain would repay the U.S. for the assistance and supplies America was sending under the Lend Lease Act.

FDR also went to the meeting hoping to demolish British trade policies set up following World War I — policies which encouraged trade within the British Empire by lowering tariff rates between members of the Empire, while maintaining discriminatory tariff rates against outsiders. The fourth point in the agreements concerned international trade and emphasized that both "victor" and "vanquished" would be given market access "on equal terms." This provision repudiated the punitive measures Allied victors had established on the heels of the First World War. At Placentia Bay, FDR and his American advisors were unwilling to warn Japan about further military actions in Southeast Asia, fearing such threats might drive the Empire of the Rising Sun into the Dutch East Indies and bring on war in the Pacific.

Earlier in January, 1941, when Harry Hopkins arrived in London and initiated the plans for the Churchill–Roosevelt meeting, he had conferred with Edward R. Murrow, Columbia Broadcasting reporter, in an attempt to secure more information about the personality of Winston Churchill. At the time, Hopkins thought the formidable egos of Roosevelt and Churchill were certain to clash, and he saw himself as a "catalytic agent between two prima donnas." Hopkins disclosed to Murrow that a conference between the two leaders was in the works, but he was circumspect about its purposes and aims. His only role, he told Murrow, was "to try to get an understanding of Churchill and of the men he sees after midnight."[5]

By the time of the conference at Placentia Bay, FDR's announcements of fighting the attacks on Allied shipping in the Atlantic had won solid support from the American citizenry. Sixty-two per cent of a national poll approved of his "shoot on sight" directive, and although a congressional inquiry later revealed large distortions in his account of the *Greer* episode, no national majority asked for a change in the policy. Yet most of the country continued to hope that giving aid short of war to Hitler's enemies would bring about a Nazi defeat. According to Lord Halifax, Britain's Foreign Secretary at the time, "His [Roosevelt's] perpetual problem was to steer a course between . . . (1) the wish of 70% of Americans to keep out of war, and (2) the wish of 70% of Americans to do everything to break Hitler, even if it means war."[6]

At the close of the conference, an impressive religious service was held on the quarter deck of the British battleship *Prince of Wales*. American and British flags draped the altar, and the rites were led by two chaplains — one American and one British. Uniformed servicemen from the two nations intermingled and participated in the singing of three traditional hymns. Roosevelt returned to Washington, and in a news conference three days later commented that the "country hadn't yet waked up to the fact they had a war to win." He was disappointed that the conference and its "Charter" had not sparked a surge of public willingness to take up arms. Rather than changing public attitudes, the meeting and its reports seemed only to have hardened existing opinions: interventionists gave it enthusiastic approval, and isolationists warned of secret commitments to war and complained that the Charter had included nothing about freedom of religion or speech.

Churchill returned to London convinced that FDR was ready to bring the USA into the war but was restrained by awareness that voter opinion was not yet with him. The Prime Minister told his War Cabinet that Roosevelt had responded to an appeal to come into the war by saying he was "skating on pretty thin ice in his relations with Congress." However, he did not think congressional beliefs were truly representative of the citizenry and would have to look for an "incident" which would warrant his opening actual hostilities.[7]

Roosevelt had ample reason to believe the ice was thin, for even while he and Churchill were meeting, the U.S. House of Representatives was debating a bill which would extend the term of men drafted into the army beyond the twelve months authorized under the Selective Service Act of 1940. On the final day of the FDR–Churchill meeting, the U.S. House passed the extension bill by a single vote — 203 in favor and 202 against. The closeness of that vote helps explain FDR's reluctance to level with the press and the American public; it also encouraged him to take further steps to prepare citizens for conflict.

The conference off the coast of Newfoundland did not produce any new war plans or military strategies. There was not even a formal document coming from it, yet several agreements reached there were settled by FDR's subsequent executive orders. For example, there was the question of Atlantic convoys. From Washington, the President announced that henceforth American warships would accompany merchant vessels west of Iceland.

U.S. ships were to darken their lights at sea and be ready for combat at all times. Although freighters in the convoy were presumed to be American, orders for the U.S. Navy stipulated that "shipping of any nationality" could attach itself to the convoy. The new "shoot-on-sight" policy made "incidents," such as the U.S.S. *Greer*, the *Reuben James*, and the U.S.S. *Niblick*, inevitable. A gigantic stride toward U.S. involvement, one that could not be undone, had been taken by executive order. The most enduring result of the Argentia conference was the Atlantic Charter — a stirring declaration of broad principles for world peace. Language and symbols coming from that conference gave encouragement more binding than any formal treaty could. The words of the two leaders, each a master of public persuasion, heartened citizens of the western Allies as well as the embattled Russians on the eastern front.

# Chapter 20. Enter the Scientists

> "There is another way to truth: by minute examination of facts. That is the way of the scientist, a hard and noble and thankless way."
>
> — John Masefield, Poet Laureate of England

War, despite its horrors, usually speeds up scientific discoveries and their uses. The First World War gave impetus to gigantic improvements of motors and engines. Early tanks, considered behemoths at the time, were introduced and had clanked across the battlefields of Western Europe. Although field artillery during that war to save democracy was still drawn by horses, mules, and men, mounted horsemen were no longer practical and mobile operations were replaced by trench warfare. From front lines, motorized ambulances marked with huge red crosses and carrying maimed men bounced their way backwards toward hospitals. Air power, despite stirring accounts of deeds by aces like Eddie Rickenbacker and Manfred Richthofen, was not a pivotal factor in World War I. That debacle had hardly ended, however, before militarists in former belligerent nations turned their attention to air power. In America, pioneers like William "Billy" Mitchell, Henry "Hap" Arnold, and Curtis LeMay gave demonstrations to officials and politicians of what bombs dropped from airplanes could do.

Italy and France expanded their air power, and experts, noting Germany's *Luftwaffe*, predicted that a nation's armed might would be invincible. Along with German rearmament came political and social actions which brought radical changes throughout the world — none more cat-astrophic than Nazi treatment of Jews, Gypsies and other people who came to be painted as less than human. As Germany undertook its purg-es, many Jews emigrated to safer countries. Among those who would come to America to escape the tyranny of Hitler were scientists such as Albert Einstein from Austria, Leo Szilard from Hungary, and Enrico Fermi (whose wife was Jewish) from Italy.

These three men are among those most often mentioned by historians who trace the development of the atomic bomb, but like most scientific discoveries the bomb did not spring from a single group or collection of minds; its roots were many. As early as the seventeenth century, physi-cists theorized about the existence of atoms. At first, theorists specu-lated that atoms were very tiny elements much like the physical world visible to the naked eye. Gradually, the debate shifted to other kinds of an atomic world, and in 1873 a Scottish physicist, James Clerk Maxwell, introduced the idea of an electromagnetic field surrounding the atom. This field, according to Maxwell, permitted electric and magnetic energy to pass through it with the speed of light. Thus Maxwell's experiments demonstrated a form of electromagnetic radiation.

Ten years later Max Planck in his Ph.D. dissertation at the Univer-sity of Munich argued that if atoms did exist, they could not be purely mechanical. He wrote that the concept of atoms existing in a purely me-chanical sense violated the second law of thermodynamics, i.e., that heat will not pass spontaneously from a colder to a hotter body without some change in the system. If the atomic world was purely mechanical, then elements in it would run equally well forward or backward. "Thus a tree could become a shoot and a seed again, the butterfly turn into a cater-pillar, and the old man into a child. . ." But every thinking person knew that reversal did not happen. Planck stated the impossibility succinctly: "The consistent implementation of the second law of thermodynamics is incompatible with the assumption of finite atoms."[1]

Another scientist of great importance who contributed seminal thinking to the development of the atomic bomb was Niels Bohr, born in Denmark in 1885. After completing doctoral studies, Niels Bohr taught at both Cambridge and Manchester in England, and had won distinction for his theories and work. In January, 1936, he gave a landmark lecture to the Danish Academy, explaining his concept of the nucleus of an atom as an entity made up of neutrons and protons closely packed together rather than a single particle. A neutron entering such a crowded field would not pass through; it would collide with the nearest nucleons (i.e., nuclear particles), surrender its kinetic energy much as a cue ball breaks the racked balls in billiards, and be captured by the strong force that holds the nucleus together. [2]

Bohr's lecture stimulated the Hungarian physicist Leo Szilard to link concepts of nuclear energy with world peace. He took the idea to his mentor, friend, and collaborator, Albert Einstein.

Born in Ulm, Germany in 1879, Einstein had grown up in Munich. In schools he consistently earned high marks, particularly in mathematics and Latin. He completed his Ph.D. at the University of Zurich and by 1907 the twenty-eight-year-old had published his first paper suggesting the theory of relativity. He was an associate professor at the University of Zurich before becoming a researcher in Berlin under the aegis of the Prussian Academy of Sciences. In Berlin, Einstein began working with Max Planck, and he also met Leo Szilard, a theoretical physicist from Hungary. Einstein and Szilard became partners in practical inventions, and in the years between 1924 and 1934 the two of them were awarded twenty-nine different patents, mostly dealing with refrigeration.

In 1921 Einstein was invited to visit the U.S. where he lectured at Columbia University, the City College of New York, and Princeton University. By this time he was wearing a mantle as one of the world's leading scientists. It would be twelve years (1933) before he came to the U.S. and established residency as a professor at the Institute for Advanced Study in Princeton, N.J.

During his years in Berlin, Einstein had begun raising funds for the Zionist cause of a Hebrew university in Palestine, and along with scientific accomplishments came his recognition as a spokesman for Jewish causes. Returning to Europe in 1923, he had found anti-Semitism rampant, particularly in Berlin and Munich; he considered both cities his home base.

Adolf Hitler, imprisoned at Landsberg after the Beer Hall Putsch of 1923, was writing *Mein Kampf* (My Struggle), and following his release from prison the Austrian continued his long-winded orations, giving vent to malevolence against Jews wherever he could capture listeners. Hitler's rantings were too much for Einstein and the physicists in his coterie — Max Planck, Edward Teller, Eugene Wigner, Leo Szilard, Hans Geiger, and Niels Bohr.

Leo Szilard was a survivor of devastated Hungary after World War I, and alongside his scientific record in physics he had developed a passionate concern for human lives. Szilard came to America where he met Enrico Fermi. Both attended a conference in Washington, D.C., in April,

1939, where Niels Bohr read a paper declaring that a small amount of pure Isotope U235 of uranium with slow neutron particles of atoms would start a "chain reaction" sufficiently great to blow up a laboratory and many miles of countryside surrounding it.[3]

Further research was needed, and any decision to weaponize this discovery, if made, would demand significant funds and support — both of which could only come from America's highest executive. The threat of nuclear bombs already had been planted in the minds of Szilard and Fermi, and Bohr's declaration confirmed its imminence. Szilard, Fermi, and Einstein prepared an early letter to Franklin Roosevelt. Their original petition went through several drafts with minor alterations suggested by Edward Teller and Wigner, but the main idea remained.[4]

The scientists agreed that the proposal could best be presented to President Roosevelt if it came from someone outside their group. The man selected was Dr. Alexander Sachs, an economist who had contributed knowledge and advice to FDR on several occasions. It was not until October, 1939, a month after war in Europe had started, that Sachs could get a private audience with the President, and in that meeting he orally explained the idea of nuclear bombs, stressing that the concept was endorsed by Albert Einstein, the world's leading physicist. Einstein, Fermi, Szilard, and other scientists warned that fellow scientists in their native countries were close to obtaining the lead in uranium fission. What would happen if Germany got the bomb first?

After listening to Sach's explanation, FDR remarked, "Alex, what you are up to is to see that the Nazis don't blow us up."

"Precisely," Sachs replied.[5]

In a quick outgrowth of this historic meeting, Roosevelt established a presidential Advisory Committee on Uranium consisting of three members: an army ordnance expert, a navy ordnance expert, and Dr. Lyman Briggs from the National Bureau of Standards as chairman. Neither ordnance expert knew anything about nuclear theory, and Briggs had begun his professional career forty years earlier as a soils physicist in the Department of Agriculture. As fundamental as this Advisory Committee proved to be, the major work in advancing nuclear study came from academicians in their university laboratories.

By that fall of 1939 Bohr and other physicists had theorized that it was only the rare light of isotope of uranium, U-235, that fissioned under slow neutron bombardment; slow neutrons did not fission the slightly heavier isotope U-238, which made up 99.3% of all natural uranium. Furthermore, scientists had demonstrated that when a slow neutron was captured by a U-238 atom, the atom, instead of fissioning, shot out two beta particles or rays in the process of becoming a new, heavier "transuranium" element. This new element, dubbed plutonium, was certain to be more unstable (i.e., radioactive), hence even more fissionable than U-235. The findings strongly indicated possibilities of more powerful plutonium bombs.

In retrospect, one has to give great credit not only to the scientists but also to Franklin Roosevelt, who set in motion government machinery creating the atomic bomb. It is unlikely that FDR understood much of what the scientists had written him. His formal education had included nothing of physical science, almost nothing of science of any kind, nor had he after his formal education ended ever evinced any active interest in scientific subjects. He probably knew less of physics and chemistry than the average graduate of a liberal arts college, and certainly less than the average graduate of a technical school. He had to rely on the advice of men he thought were competent and knew what they were talking about. Moreover, there was that gnawing fear that enemies might be advancing in science and technology faster than his own country.

In truth, most German scientists at the time were concentrating on development and production of ballistic missiles rather than atomic fission. Their research enabled Goring's *Luftwaffe* to send the first "buzz bombs" over London in June 1944. These comparatively slow, strange-looking machines making an unnerving buzzing sound would appear over a city; the machine would go silent before it pointed downwards to come tearing out of the clouds in a steep dive, crashing to earth and exploding. It was the pilotless plane — the V-1 "vengeance weapon" as Joseph Goebbels, Nazi Minister for Propaganda, dubbed it. The vehicle looked like a small, stubby airplane, jet-propelled, controlled by a gyro-pilot, and carried a one-ton payload. The V-1s were not precision weapons but were genuine threats when aimed at a concentration of troops and supplies or, as the Allies maintained, the morale of citizens in British cities.

Allied intelligence sources discovered the launching sites for these pilotless jets along the northern coast of France, and soon Allied bombers hammered out of commission the so-called "ski resorts" in the Pas de Calais and along the tip of the Cherbourg Peninsula. Then the Wehrmacht changed tactics and began sending the buzz-bombs from mobile, heavily camouflaged sites, almost impossible to locate. Also, German scientists had developed a new V-2 with larger and more destructive power than the V-1. Some sources also warned that German scientists under the direction of Werner von Braun were about to put a payload on a supersonic guided missile capable of crossing the Atlantic and reaching New York City; that report was not accurate. Nazi scientists had begun initial research into the possibilities of an atomic bomb, but their efforts were halted by the urgency of more immediate war needs. German scientists had abandoned hope of developing an atomic bomb in time to be useable in the war, but in June, 1944, American and British intelligence groups were not aware of that decision.

Within weeks after FDR's conference with Alexander Sachs, the Manhattan Project in the U.S. was launched, and President Roosevelt entrusted the matter to the Office of Scientific Research and Development, an agency created in the preceding May, 1941. Teams of physicists and chemists were chosen and contributing experiments undertaken at several prestigious universities. Before the year ended, Fermi and others had achieved a self-sustaining nuclear chain reaction, the first lap in the race to build an atomic bomb.

The project was put under direction of army engineers headed by General W. S. Groves. A small city was built at Oak Ridge, Tennessee, and later a special physics laboratory at Los Alamos, New Mexico. There was no public disclosure, and the work with its vast problems of coordination was known only to a few scattered scientists. Individual workers on the project had no knowledge of what it was about, and the Manhattan Project with its resultant atomic bomb would be the most successful secret of World War II.

# CHAPTER 21. UNDECLARED WAR 1941

> "I have said this before, but I shall say it again and again and
> again. Your boys are not going to be sent into any foreign wars."
>
> — Franklin Roosevelt, October 30, 1940

―――――――――

At no time during his presidencies, was Franklin Roosevelt under greater public pressures than during the long autumn of 1941. Yet irrespective of diplomatic problems and political infighting, the public must have entertainment; the fall of 1941 was no exception.

Changes on the economic front may have been even more dramatic than those in entertainment. In 1939 when the war in Europe had broken out, the gross product of goods and services in the United States totaled $91 billion. Small wonder that many thought FDR's call in May 1940 for production of 50,000 airplanes per year nothing a left-over pipe dream from the New Deal. Yet that goal, ridiculed by Thomas E. Dewey and Charles Lindbergh, was attained and in 1943 would reach 85,946 planes, an increase of 90% over 1940. The hard times of the Great Depression had disappeared by 1941, and along with the demise came changes in living patterns for most American citizens — changes slower than events on sporting fields but ones which would prove to be more lasting and consequential.

At the turn of the century, America had been primarily an agricultural nation with more than half the population residing on farms. During the Depression years, most farms (42.2% of those in America) were worked by tenants. In the South then, over 70% of all nonwhite farm operators were tenants, the majority being sharecroppers.[1] In those years the average farmer and each member of his family lived on a net annual income of about $375.

The New Deal had introduced several programs aimed at limiting crop and livestock production in order to raise prices; and contributing further to such harvest curtailment had been a severe drought in Prairie and Plains states. During that drought one third of the nation's grain crop was lost, and "Okies" abandoned their Oklahoma homesteads to seek work in California. In 1940, the nation had 6.35 million farms totaling 174 million acres. Thereafter, each year the number of farms would decrease while the average acre per farm increased.

Farm tenancy had begun to fall in 1941 as rosier economic opportunities appeared. Among the opportunities was a rise in American manufacturing, for as war clouds threatened, new plants were built and built fast. Older plants that originally made passenger cars shifted to trucks, tanks, and weapons.

Passage of Lend Lease undeniably undercut assertions of neutrality and the populace was slowly beginning to come around. By fall of 1941, 73% of American citizens said they believed an Axis victory would constitute, if not an immediate military threat, a "serious danger" to the U.S.[2] Shortly after Hitler's victories in the Balkans and North Africa, American public opinion sagged. Most Americans did not believe the Soviets could repel Nazi aggressions, and many who had thought Lend Lease would give an edge to Britain began to feel that the *Wehrmacht's* drives were not going to be defeated by the West. The number of Americans who believed it necessary to help Britain rose steadily and had reached 68% in May; yet most remained adamantly opposed to U.S. involvement in a shooting war.

President Roosevelt proclaimed a national emergency and took innumerable executive moves designed to arouse public awareness of Nazi dangers, but the public was slow to follow. Some progress was made in production of war materials, but the record was far from satisfactory. Total industrial production by that summer of 1941 had increased by a third over the previous year, and in certain areas was impressive: aircraft production up 158% and shipbuilding up 120% over the preceding twelve months. These achievements were miniscule, however, in view of the vast requirements of American defense, aid to Britain, and the promised help to Russia. The U.S. had yet to become the Arsenal of Democracy promised by Roosevelt.

Later that fall, Congress passed a revision of the Neutrality Act in the form proposed by the President, and FDR announced that "pursuant to the power conferred upon me by the Lend Lease Act," he had found defense of Russia vital to the defense of the United States. Therefore, he was authorizing and ordering delivery of Lend-Lease supplies to the Soviet Union.

Inherent to defense of the United States was the condition of the American Army. The Selective Service Act passed in September, 1940, had called for recruitment and training of 1,200,000 men who were expected to serve for one year. Since the law had gone into effect efforts had been made to build the military, but the task was enormous. Men of the Regular Army and National Guard had to be assigned to training draftees, and the best units necessarily were officered by ROTC graduates or newly-commissioned sixty-day-wonder second lieutenants. Lack of equipment made training exercises unreal, and without involvement in actual war, there was a widespread sense of futility. More worrisome to military strategists was the realization that when the year was up, draftees would be discharged and returned to their homes. Forces just beginning to move into place would disintegrate and the whole building process would have to begin anew.

The drafted men lived in tents or hastily constructed barracks still smelling of pine. After the nightly sounding of taps, cockroaches would invade and could be heard crowding the corners or clambering up barracks walls. In daytime, trainees fought brambles, cacti, sand hills and rough ground or crawled through swamps infested with mosquitoes, lizards, and snakes. Without weapons, the selectees drilled with wooden rifles and cardboard boxes marked "tank" or "pillbox." More and more of the men marked off months and then days on calendars in the barracks. Chalked signs reading OHIO appeared on buildings, boxcars, trucks, or vehicles — "OHIO", Over the Hill in October, a motto looking forward to what they'd be doing when the ordered year of service ended.

Most of the selectees did not follow debates about extending the draft then taking place among citizens or in the halls of Congress — daily drills and duties were too tiring for that — but through gossip and latrine rumors nearly all draftees learned of an incident involving one of the country's highest ranking army officers, Lieutenant General Ben Lear. Lear was playing golf on a hot Sunday in July just outside Memphis when a military convoy carrying troops that had completed maneuvers in central Tennessee passed by. The convoy moved slowly, and the soldiers waved and shouted what later were called "pleasantries" at the golfers.

Girls on the course were wearing shorts, and the soldiers hollered along with a variety of "wolf whistles," and similar salutations. General Lear, not in uniform, was on the tee at the first hole when a soldier yelled, "Hey, buddy! Want a caddie?"

Lear, commander of the Second Army and director of maneuvers the troops were coming from, was incensed by what he considered insults. He leapt over the fence, ran to the officer in the lead vehicle, and ordered him to halt the convoy. Then he proceeded to dress down the officers and men in the convoy. The troops were ordered to pitch tents in a grassy area near the Memphis airport, and the next morning were assembled in formation when Lear appeared again and really chewed them out, berating them for loose conduct, rowdyism, and breach of discipline. But that was not enough! The convoy was ordered to return to the camp it had just left. To reach it every man in the outfit except vehicle drivers had to trudge the fifteen miles clad in hot uniforms and carrying a forty-pound backpack.

The incident was meat on which newspapers feed. Lear, in actuality a distinguished leader with an excellent military record, was nicknamed the "Yoohoo General." Parents and relatives at home were home were upset; a "mothers' club" in Arkansas demanded his removal, and numerous citizens complained to congressional representatives. One U.S. Senator referred to him as a "superannuated old goat." The incident was trivial compared to the momentous happenings at the time; nevertheless, its wide circulation reflected the mood of countless citizens — despair over separations caused by the draft and frustrations with government or military authority.

In Washington, added to decisions in diplomacy President Roosevelt was faced with constraints on American power. Forbidden by the Selective Service Act to send draftees outside the Western Hemisphere, advisers warned him the military was hard pressed to find even enough troops for regular state-side duty. In June he ordered a Marine brigade of 4,000 men to sail to Iceland, telling Congress that he had done so to forestall a German move that would have threatened Greenland and the northern portion of North America, all shipping in the North Atlantic, and the steady flow of munitions to Britain. Presented as a defensive move, his decision won endorsement from Congress and the public. A national opinion poll, for example, showed 61% in favor and only 20% unequivocally opposed.[3]

Sending troops to Iceland brought into bold relief the question of extending the one-year commitment for draftees. Led by General George

Marshall, advisors from the War Department recommended that the President attempt to remove the restriction on sending troops outside the Western Hemisphere and more importantly to extend the one-year enlistment period for draftees. Vigorous opposition to the latter idea sprang up immediately. Opponents played on sentiments for keeping the boys at home and denounced the proposal as an outright violation of the pledge made when the Selective Service Act was passed.

Radio commentators and newspaper columnists predicted that the Administration proposal would set off a bitter controversy cutting across party lines, which it did indeed. In the U.S. House of Representatives, even stalwart Democrat leaders like Speaker Sam Rayburn and Floor Leader John McCormack were upset by the idea of removing restrictions on sending troops overseas.

General Marshall was assigned the chief burden of arguing the Administration proposal to Congress. In a closed session with the Senate Military Affairs Committee, he hit especially hard on lengthening the term of service, stressing that disbandment of two thirds of trained enlistment strength along with three quarters of officer personnel in the Army would imperil the nation's defenses. Two days later he gave the same views to House leaders. On the whole, his presentations and arguments were excellent, winning conviction from most listeners and even grudging acceptance from recalcitrants. Again and again, he appeared before congressional committees reviewing in detail the dangers of dismissing so much of the army in a time of peril.

On July 21, President Roosevelt took a public stand, announcing in a Fireside Chat that the wave of Nazi aggression was coming ever closer to U.S. shorelines, warning, "We Americans cannot afford to speculate with the security of America."[4]

In the middle of July, FDR held a White House conference with congressional leaders and from them won a promise to extend military service if he would defer the matter of sending draftees outside the Hemisphere. His appeals won endorsement from the *New York Times*, the *New York Herald Tribune*, the *Washington Post*, the *Boston Herald*, and other prestigious papers, but opinion in the country at large remained divided. A Gallup poll at the end of July indicated that a razor-thin majority of voters — 51% — were ready to accept extension of the draft, and further questioning suggested a greater percentage would agree to it once the question of ending men abroad was eliminated.[5]

The U.S. Senate during the first week of August, after beating down various debilitating amendments, approved Roosevelt's proposal for draft extension as well as providing a pay raise for the men after a year of service. In the House, the opposition was yet to be convinced. Newspapers across the land described the House debate the most important since Lend Lease. Supporters hammered on threats posed by Nazi–Vichy collaboration and subsequent danger to Dakar, an important African port under French control; opponents countered that the threat was no more serious than at the time Selective Service Act had been adopted. Critics charged that the Administration was attempting to involve the country in foreign wars "without the consent of Congress."

Acrimonious debates continued, and when the final vote was taken on August 12, 1941, the Administration's bill was passed by a majority of one. But for a single vote, the nation would have been left with an Army in absolute dissolution. In favor were 203 members (182 Democrats and 21 Republicans); opposed, 202 members (65 Democrats, 133 Republicans).[6]

Among Democrats in the Senate was Harry S Truman of Missouri, hitherto little known beyond his Missouri constituents. (Harry Truman said he had no middle name, just the letter S, and he insisted no period should be placed after it.)

Truman had a countryman's distrust of Wall Street and big business in general and was concerned over the government's failure to bring small businesses into the defense efforts being promoted. Ft. Leonard Wood in central Missouri, Truman's home base, was being enlarged, and when he toured it he was dismayed to find huge waste, gross inefficiencies, and wholesale profiteering. In consequence, he proposed establishment of a special U.S. Senate committee to investigate the awarding of defense contracts.

After a little political horse-trading, FDR agreed to support the idea of a Senate Committee to Investigate the War Effort, and in keeping with custom, the Senate named the member moving the resolution (Senator Truman) its chairman. Quickly dubbed the "Truman Committee," this group was extremely busy for the next three years. Its members came to see the seamy side of war efforts when they uncovered crooked contractors on military installations, manufacturers who made faulty engines or parts, factories that cheated by putting out inferior products, army and navy wastes in food and other supplies, and hundreds of similar examples. Newspapers and magazines gave frequent reports of the Committee, and its activities put its chairman very much in the public eye. More important, it made him an acceptable vice-presidential candidate to Franklin Roosevelt three years later.

# Chapter 22. Russia: the Enigma

> "I cannot forecast to you the action of Russia. It is a
> riddle wrapped in a mystery inside an enigma."
>
> — Winston Churchill, October 1, 1939

———————

The land commonly called Russia was in those days more formally the Union of Soviet Socialist Republics (USSR). The Soviet Union, inheritor of the Russian Empire, was a patchwork of heterogeneous republics and was the largest state on earth, covering more than one seventh of its land surface and consisting of a population somewhat in excess of 201,000,000 persons. While St. Petersburg (or Leningrad) had served as capital from 1712 to 1918, Moscow was once again the capital, and its rule extended from the Baltic and the Black Seas to the Pacific Ocean, and from the Arctic Ocean to the borders of China, Mongolia, Afghanistan, Iran, and Turkey. Western borders of the USSR touched on the frontiers of Finland, Norway, Poland, Czechoslovakia, Hungary, and Romania. In a broad sense, the USSR consisted of four distinct zones of climate and vegetation: the arctic zone being a tundra region, the central zone an area densely forested and having a humid continental climate, the southern zone consisting mostly of fertile steppes with rich black-earth soils, and the Central Asiatic republics mainly vast hot, arid deserts.

Serfdom was the nature of peasant labor for centuries throughout Europe and Asia. In the Middle Ages, it developed in France, Italy, and Spain, later spreading to Germany, before spreading into Slavic lands early in the 15th century. Serfdom in early Russia took different forms, and although coming into that area later than it had in more Western nations, the practice persisted much longer. By the sixteenth century a landholding aristocracy had taken root, and under this arrangement peasants were bound to the landowner and their rights diminished very slowly. The system was virtual slavery, for masters could punish their serfs, send them to Siberia, break up their families, or sell them at will. Not until the 1830s was the breaking up of servile families forbidden.

In the first half of the nineteenth century, Great Britain moved to bring the international slave trade to an end, and by later in the century the US and finally Russia dropped the arrangement. It would be a gross oversimplification to attribute the end of serfdom to the writings of Karl Marx, yet it is not possible either to ignore the influence of his contributions.

The German social philosopher Karl Marx was born in 1818. As a young adult he studied law and philosophy before serving a brief stint as editor of a liberal newspaper. Then he went to Paris, where he became a full-fledged socialist, met Friedrich Engels, and began with him a life-long association.

In 1848, Marx and Engels published the *Communist Manifesto*, a book which set forth the basic premises of Marxism. In the next year, repercussions from the revolutionary book helped persuade Marx to flee in exile to London where he remained until his death in 1883. In London, Marx spent most of his time studying reports and statistics of the British economy, and in the process he became familiar with recognized economic theories and thoughts. In 1867 he brought out his monumental *Das Kapital*, a work which has exerted incalculable influence on the modern world — some economists compare it with the Gospel, the Koran, or Newton's Principia.

No modern economic or political system can ignore entirely the tenets of Marxism, or dialectical materialism as it is often called. Primarily an economic-political doctrine, its proponents argue that it is a methodology that can be applied to any problem of human thought. Underlying all doctrines of Marxism is the fundamental assumption that "the history of all hitherto existing society is the history of class struggles." According to Marx and Engels, the bourgeoisie (i.e., capitalist class) had displaced the nobility of the feudal system; commercial and industrial revolutions had simplified class structures, and the struggle had become one between bourgeois and non-propertied "wage slaves," i.e., the proletariat. Marxist theory supposes that the value of a commodity is determined by the socially necessary labor (measured in time) required to produce it.

Thus the bourgeois class prospers from the unpaid portion of the labor of the proletariat, the trend growing more pronounced with each industrial advancement. Hence, the rich get richer and the poor get poorer.

According to the *Communist Manifesto*, revolutions would occur first in the more industrialized nations; the proletariat was "to wrest" by all possible means the capital held by the bourgeois.

The foregoing paragraphs do injustice to the circumlocutions and depths of analysis in Marx's writings, but even from such abbreviated accounts it is no small wonder that his theories shook industrial titans in Britain, France, and America.

On the heels of World War I, alarmists in America united to wipe out all vestiges of Marxism. A. Mitchell Palmer, Attorney-General of the United States, who liked to be called the "Fighting Quaker," obtained an injunction which suppressed a legal coal strike. With that injunction, Palmer led a series of raids in which Communist leaders or even those accused of being so were rounded up for deportation to Russia. His actions were taken under the war-time Alien and Sedition Acts permitting deportation of aliens who were anarchists or believers who advocated or affiliated with any who argued for overthrow of the government. Under Palmer and other zealots, Communists and suspected liberals were seized in their homes; more than six thousand men were arrested and put in jail, sometimes for weeks, without learning what was the specific charge against them.

One widely-quoted historian of the period summarized:

> Mr. Palmer was in full cry. In public statements he was reminding the twenty million owners of Liberty bonds and the nine million farm owners and the eleven million owners of savings accounts, that the Reds were aiming to take away all they had. He distributed boiler-plate propaganda to the press, containing pictures of horrid-looking Bolsheviks with bristling beards, and asking if such as these should rule over America. . . [1]

Most government leaders during Roosevelt's third administration and members of the Congress which served him had been youths during the 1920s; they remembered well the frenzied fears over Communists, Reds, and Industrial Workers of the World (IWW — lampooned as 'I Won't Work') that once had swept the country. Americans in 1941 were ready to bring down Hitler and his gang, but understandably, they viewed Russia as an unreliable ally.

In November, 1940, a few days after the Soviets invaded Finland, FDR sent word to the chairmen of the House Ways and Means Committee and the Appropriations Committee that he would like a bill to help Finland. Those two leaders responded by informing him that a poll of their faithful showed no inclination to sponsor any such an action. Lieutenants in the Senate reported the same sentiment. In January 1941, FDR complained to his Cabinet that the Senators were "a bunch of 'Uriah Heeps' who did not realize that what was going on in Europe would inevitably affect this country."

Two weeks later in an address to the pro-Soviet Youth Congress, his irritation rose higher as he castigated isolationists who were insisting that any aid to Finland would be an attempt to force America into an imperialistic war. Such charges, he said, were "unadulterated twaddle ... based on ninety per cent ignorance." Going further, he asserted:

> The hope that Russia would eventually become a peace-loving, popular government ... which would not interfere with the integrity of its neighbors was either shattered or put away in cold storage for some better day. The Soviet Union is run by a dictatorship as absolute as any other dictatorship in the world.[2]

After the outbreak of war between Germany and the Soviet Union, the Soviets became an ally of the West, and President Roosevelt's estimate of the totalitarianism in the Soviet Government abated. He grew indignant when shipments of armaments and equipment granted under Lend Lease to Russia were delayed. Yet not all of his supporters were enthusiastic about closer relations with the Soviets.

Secretary of State Hull was among those who were at best only lukewarm to a closer alliance. Born in a log cabin in 1871, Cordell Hull was a product of backwoods Tennessee. He became chairman of the Clay County Democrats when he was only nineteen and graduated from law school while still a teenager. As a practicing politician he served first in the Tennessee House of Representatives, and then eleven terms in the U.S. House of Representatives. Appointed Secretary of State by the incoming President Roosevelt in 1933, Hull remained in this federal role for eleven years, retiring in 1944 because of ill health.

As Secretary of State he often was bypassed by FDR, whose dealings with Russia were like his other approaches to international diplomacy. As FDR said to underlings, really important decisions could be worked out, if only he could talk to his opposite in the other country.

Hull, a veteran statesman, was against teaming up with a partner that spread hostile propaganda through the Communist International, a regime where religious freedom was denied, where foreign nationals were thrown in jail on slight pretexts, and a regime that did not pay its war debts. (The Soviet Union had refused to pay Russia's World War I debt,

saying it was not responsible for debts run up by the Kerensky government that originally had replaced the monarchy.)

At the turn of the century, Franklin Roosevelt had begun to form
opinions about Russia. Shortly after he had graduated from Harvard, his
cousin Theodore (then in the Presidency) won the Nobel Peace Prize
for intervention in the Sino–Russian War. Japanese naval forces had defeated those of Russia at the Battle of Tsushima Strait (May 27–29, 1905),
and the Japanese government in consequence formally asked President
Theodore Roosevelt to act as a mediator in settling disputes between
the two foes. Under his guidance and direction, Secretary of War William Howard Taft drafted a Peace Memorandum which was accepted by
both belligerents. A year afterward from Christiana, Norway, came the
announcement: Theodore Roosevelt had won the Nobel Prize, the first
American to do so; and in wiring his acceptance speech, Theodore from
his bully pulpit disclosed that the $40,000 prize money would be used to
establish a permanent Industrial Peace Committee in Washington.

When Hitler in 1941 ordered the Wehrmacht into Russia, he must
have considered that the move would find favor with a great many British and American citizens. Churchill, that arch foe of Bolshevism, however, immediately urged all-out support for the Soviet Union, declaring,
that "If Hitler invaded Hell, I would at least make a favorable reference to
the Devil in the House of Commons."

In the U.S., Senator Robert LaFollette, Wisconsin Progressive, didn't
identify Roosevelt by name but predicted that America soon would be
given "the greatest whitewash act in history." According to him, Russia
rather than being a former threat now would be transformed into an acceptable ally, and American citizens would be expected to overlook Russia's confiscation of property, its persecution of religion, the 1936 purges
by its brutal OGPU, the Finland invasion, and Stalin's rapacious role in
seizing half of prostrate Poland.

*Time Magazine* expressed the average American's attitude concerning
the German–Russian conflict with the comment: "Like two vast prehis-
toric monsters lifting themselves out of the swamp, half-blind and savage,
the two great totalitarian powers of the world now tore at each other's
throats."[3]

Senator Bennett Clark, a Democrat from Missouri, took up the issue
and declared, "It's a case of dog-eat-dog. Stalin is as bloody-handed as
Hitler. I don't think we should help either one. We should tend to our
own business, as we should have been doing so all along." His fellow
Democrat, Senator Harry Truman from the same state was more belli-

cose and amended such thinking, declaring that he hoped "the Nazis will kill a lot of Russians and vice versa."[4]

Eleanor Roosevelt, in June 1941, was at Campobello sitting by a portable radio listening to news of the latest Nazi invasion when friends persuaded her to call her husband for more information about the importance of Germany's incursion into Russia. When Eleanor asked Franklin if it would be good or bad for America, he replied, "It all depends." FDR told her Hitler expected to defeat the Russians in two months and that he did not plan to go on the radio with a Fireside Chat because the weather now was "too damn hot."

Within weeks, President Roosevelt dispatched Harry Hopkins, by this time his most trusted aide, on a double mission to London and Moscow. In London, Hopkins met with Churchill and informed him he was on his way to Moscow to meet Joseph Stalin. Churchill and Hopkins discussed the changed scenario made by Germany's attack on the Soviets, and Hopkins informed the Prime Minister that President Roosevelt was preparing to send supplies and armaments to the Russians as soon as possible. Churchill asked how British and Russian requests could be put together, and Hopkins responded that President Roosevelt wanted to assure him that Britain would have first call on all planes, tools, tanks, and munitions the U.S. could produce for Allies.

Even though under provisions of the Lend Lease Act assistance was authorized, in the late summer of 1941 a few recalcitrants still held out against aid to Russia Those opposed to sending such aid tried to remind FDR that he would be helping Joseph Stalin, whom many considered a cold-blooded dictator, a man who had worked as a trouble shooter for the revolutionary under Lenin — recognized enemy of capitalism. Stalin had organized a series of bank robberies to fill revolutionary coffers, and had been efficient (read ruthless) enough to rise to the top of the Communist Party. In his rise, he had countenanced the deaths of millions of his own countrymen, and through forced collectivization of Russian peasants in the 1920s and his infamous purge trials of the 1930s had arranged for execution of every rival Bolshevik figure. How could America deal with a man having such a blackened past?

FDR grew irritated and impatient with delays, but it was not until October, 1941, when Lend Lease protocols finally were signed with Soviet diplomats that U.S. freighters began their dangerous runs to Murmansk and other ports in the USSR.

Hopkins journeyed from London to Moscow, and in his first meeting with the Soviet leader, Stalin admitted that Germany's attack had taken his nation by surprise. He pointed out, however, the vast superiority in numbers of the Soviet population. No matter how many Soviets were killed, there were always more. Then he told Hopkins his nation's most immediate needs were for light anti-aircraft guns and aluminum. Putting these two in the highest priority convinced Hopkins that Russia was preparing for a long-range war, and among other items in a lengthy cable to President Roosevelt he reported:

> Stalin said his soldiers did not consider the battle lost merely because the Germans at one point or another broke through with mechanized forces. The Russian mechanized forces would attack at another point often moving many miles behind the German line. . .
>
> He [Stalin] stated that the pressure on his army in the last ten days had become considerably less, and . . . he thought the Germans had been unable to supply their mechanized divisions and air forces with adequate fuel because of transportation difficulties, the lack of good roads and more particularly the effective interference of the Russians . . .
>
> He [Stalin] told me the first need of the Russian Army was light anti-aircraft guns. . . The second great need was aluminum to be used in the construction of airplanes. The third was machine guns of approximately 50 calibre . . .[5]

## Chapter 23. Japan: Expansion and Perfidy

> "It is now clear that Japan's claims cannot be attained through diplomatic means. . . At this moment, our Empire stands on the threshold of glory or oblivion."
>
> — Japanese Foreign Minister Hideki Tojo, Dec., 2, 1941

---

October of 1941 was a particularly troubling month for Washington diplomats. They and media pundits watched events in Europe, but ominous depredations also were taking place in the opposite direction from the United States. Four years earlier when in September, 1937, the Japanese indiscriminately bombed Nanking and committed other atrocities in Chinese cities, President Roosevelt had used the dedication of Chicago's Outer Drive Bridge as an opportunity to call for a "quarantine" of aggressor nations. In this address he named no nations, but there was no doubt he meant Japan, Italy, and Germany.[1]

The primary appeal of FDR's speech on that occasion lay in the suggestion that he could overcome aggressor nations by peaceful means. Many groups in America applauded the sentiment; newspapers and magazines liked taking economic and financial steps against Japan but warned that such actions should not permit the President to lead the nation into war. The Catholic Association for International Peace declared its support for a "concerted effort . . . to uphold the laws and principles of peace" without having to resort to war. The American Federation of Labor likewise endorsed the idea, proclaiming a national boycott of Japanese goods but declared its opposition to involvement in European or Asiatic wars.

Vacillations and weaknesses of American foreign policy toward Japan in 1940 and 1941 can only be explained by understanding that President Roosevelt and his advisers had concluded that dangers in Europe were greater and more immediate than those looming in Asia. In view of that position, Tokyo paid little attention to American protests, considering them nothing more than pleas for maintenance of the status quo and the employment of peaceful means.

Throughout 1941, while President Roosevelt and leaders in his Administration concentrated on Europe and worked slightly on hemisphere defense, they also had to try to prevent enlargement of incursions Japan was making into China and Southeast Asia. Anxious to take advantage of British weaknesses and French defeats, the Konoye Cabinet in Tokyo took further actions. Their aim was to cut off supply routes to China and strengthen their own economic position by preparing the way for incorporation of Indo-China into what Japanese leaders envisioned as a Greater East Asia Co-Prosperity Sphere. To achieve this end, the Japanese government asked Britain to close Chinese supply routes through Hong Kong and Burma, and also urged France to shut the Indo-China border.

In mid-year of 1940, President Roosevelt in a rare move had yielded to the urging of the more bellicose members of his Cabinet, Secretary of the Treasury Henry Morgenthau, Secretary of War Henry Stimson, Secretary of the Navy Frank Knox, and Secretary of the Interior Harold Ickes; he called them his "War Cabinet." With encouragement from these stalwarts, FDR had signed a Treasury Department proclamation limiting the export of all oil and scrap metal. The measure was aimed against Japan, but a limitation of some sort was necessary anyway in order for the U.S. to continue exporting those vital supplies to beleaguered Britain. The U.S. Department of State, therefore, interpreted the President's order to include only high-grade aviation fuel, and this interpretation allowed Japan to buy middle-grade octane gasoline which was entirely satisfactory for their planes.

In the fall of 1940, Japan had concluded a Tripartite Pact with Germany and Italy pledging to help each other if any of the three was attacked by a power not currently involved in either European or Sino-Japanese fighting. In effect, the treaty was to prevent the U.S. from joining Britain against Germany or in opposing Japan in creation of its East Asian sphere.

In Tokyo the Japanese Government was rent with its own internal dissensions. In the second half of July, 1940, the Konoye Cabinet had been restructured with appointments of Yosuke Matsuoka and General Hideki Tojo, both avowed expansionists, as Minister of Foreign Affairs and War Minister respectively. These two, along with other Nipponese militants, pressed French Indo-China into conceding transit rights for Japanese troops, permission to construct airfields, and to enact closer economic ties with expansionists in Tokyo.

Throughout 1940 and most of 1941, the U.S. State Department under leadership of Secretary of State Cordell Hull and with backing from the White House attempted negotiations with Japan aimed toward maintaining the status quo in Indo-China. Complicating the problems was the Vichy Government and its handling of French territories in North Africa.

In the spring of 1940, the conquest of Poland had been accomplished, and Nazi troops were sent into Norway and Denmark. Next came the German invasion of the Netherlands, Belgium, and Luxembourg — all taken easily. The last week of May, 1940, had seen the British Expeditionary Force — the men England had sent to France — caught between German forces and the English Channel. Entrapped British and French soldiers were saved through the bravery and determination of British civilians who commandeered every kind of boat imaginable and sailed to Dunkirk to evacuate 300,000 men who lived to fight another day. Nevertheless, *Wehrmacht* leaders agreed with Hitler: it was time for an all-out assault on France.

After the Germans had overrun the Low Countries and had entered France, the newly-installed British Prime Minister, Winston Churchill, was cementing his ties with President Roosevelt, and from London the former sent repeated descriptions of the plight of both England and France. FDR was sympathetic but too cautious to risk more outright help.

Resistance in France fell quickly in the face of the German invasion, and on June 21, 1940, Hitler received France's representatives in the same railroad car and in the same part of the Compiègne forest where Germany's envoys had signaled their capitulation in November 1918.

The French navy had sailed beyond Hitler's reach, but his terms demanded disarmament of most of the French military and surrender of the northern three fifths of the country to German control. Under capitulation terms, the French were to make available to the Germans all holdings in North Africa, including the port of Bizerte and the railroad from there to Gabes. France also agreed to sell trucks and guns to the Germans and to use the few ships remaining in French ports for the transport of German supplies across the Mediterranean. In West Africa, the important port of Dakar was put at the disposal of the Germans as a supply base for submarines, warships, and airplanes.

A puppet government was set up to govern this southern rump of France, and immediately factions began fighting among themselves as to who would be leaders of the shattered French forces. A spate of appeals from Churchill and French Premier Paul Reynaud came to the American President for immediate assistance, but Roosevelt, confronted by strong isolationist elements at home, was temporarily nonplused as to what he should do.

Major figures in the struggle for control of the satellite government set up to protect French interests in North Africa were Darlan, DeGaulle, Pétain, and Weygand. Jean François Darlan was a French admiral and opportunist who in collaborating with the Hitler regime hoped to become established in what he believed was inevitable, namely, a total German victory. Army General Charles DeGaulle was a Resistance leader who continued to oppose Nazis and all French collaborators. Henri Philippe Pétain was a French Army Marshal and was first chosen to head the rump government which became known as the Vichy Government, named after a city in central France. Maxim Weygand had been chief of staff to Marshal Foch in the First World War, and in the early stages of the Vichy Government was installed as its delegate general to French Africa and governor of Algeria.

The Vichy Government was authoritarian, and Pétain would later claim he had collaborated "honorably" with the Germans. His popularity, however, declined as he yielded to ever increasing harsh demands from Berlin without obtaining much in return. In 1942, Pétain was succeeded by Pierre Laval, a more outspoken advocate of collaboration with Germany, and the former Army Marshal became a mere figurehead.

All this was happening while in America the 1940 political campaign was underway. FDR's opponent, Wendell Willkie, refused to join with the isolationists firing their charges against Roosevelt, but he aimed and effectively employed attacks on FDR's economic measures and upon his "effrontery" in seeking a third term.

One of the mainstays in President Roosevelt's foreign policies was defense of the Western Hemisphere, and fundamental to this fact was control of the Panama Canal. The Tripartite Pact signed by Germany, Japan, and Italy in September, 1940, raised protection of the Panama Canal to paramount priority; the waterway had to be considered in every U.S. defense measure.

The Administration, the Congress, and the American people unanimously agreed that defense of the Canal, Latin American, and South American countries was essential. So the U.S., hoping to solidify more support, increased its imports from Latin America and South America by more than 30% during the first nine months of 1941.

The dangers of Nazi infiltration or splinter groups in the U.S. had fallen since war had begun in 1939, but two years later there still were concerns that Nazi groups might be infiltrating into South America. October 27, 1941, was designated Navy Day, and President Roosevelt used the occasion to assault again Nazi menaces. He asked Congress for further modification of the Neutrality Act which prohibited the arming of merchant ships engaged in foreign commerce, and he requested that vital Lend Lease goods be delivered in U.S. ships flying the nation's flag. Three weeks later the Congress approved both requests.

Addressing dangers of Nazi infiltrations, FDR in this Navy Day speech declared:

> I have in my possession a secret map made in Germany by Hitler's government . . . It is a map of South America and a part of Central America as Hitler proposes to reorganize it. . . . The geographical experts of Berlin, however, have ruthlessly obliterated all existing boundary lines; and have divided South America into five vassal States, bringing the whole continent under their domination And they have also arranged it that the territory of one of these new puppet States includes the Republic of Panama and our great life line — the Panama Canal.[2]

Such a dire warning was alarming, and it sparked an onrush of requests for more information; reporters wanted details. Could they see the map? Where had it come from? Who had made it? And a host of similar concerns. The White House and State Department rebuffed all questions, saying the map was a matter of diplomacy and national security; no further information would be given. From Berlin came an immediate announcement denying the plan and stating that Germany had never produced such a map.

It wasn't long before the charge began to die, and President Roosevelt's dramatic allegation was discounted; reputable observers concluded he must have been taken in by clumsy propaganda, a gullible trait unworthy of the nation's leader.[3]

Only a small percentage of Americans were concerned about matters in the Far East. Reflecting the mood of American citizenry, FDR and Secretary of State Cordell Hull had told American Ambassador Grew that the U.S. would not be forced out of China and would reinforce its forces at Manila and Pearl Harbor. Following this instruction, Grew, with FDR's explicit approval, bluntly had addressed an American-Japan Society luncheon in Tokyo stating that the U.S. highly resented Japanese actions in China and favored economic retaliation against further violations of American rights.

In September 1941 American Ambassador Joseph Grew in Tokyo wired Washington that further efforts to conciliate the Japanese Government with protests or expressions of disapproval were unlikely to be successful. Such warnings and Japanese maneuvering helped persuade FDR to take more action against the Pacific threat. Advisors told him that shipments of scrap and iron were endangering U.S. defenses and might leave its own forces without adequate supplies for six or nine months, so he asked Morgenthau to find ways of halting scrap shipments to Japan without denying them to Britain. The U.S. first tried a series of limited embargoes of oil and scrap iron, but these failed to halt Japanese advances. Finally on September 24, 1941, after Britain had shown likelihood of withstanding German air assaults and more Japanese forces had marched into Indo-China, the FDR Administration announced a full embargo on all scrap and iron.[4]

In early November, discussions were opened in Washington between Secretary of State Cordell Hull and two special Japanese envoys, Ambassador Kichisaburo Nomura and a special envoy, Saburo Kurusu. In the discussion, the Japanese envoys announced their government was demanding that the U.S. abandon China; lift the orders freezing Nipponese credits in the U.S.; resume full trade relations with the Japanese Empire; exert pressure to aid Japan in securing supplies from the Netherlands East Indies; and bring a halt to U.S. naval expansion in the Western Pacific.

Secretary Hull countered with a set of proposals that included the withdrawal of Japanese troops from China and Indo-China and the conclusion of a multi-lateral non-aggression pact. The U.S. proposals restated the following principles: 1) respect for the territorial integrity and sovereignty of all nations, 2) support of the principle of noninterference in the internal affairs of other countries, 3) support of the principle of equality, including equality of commercial opportunity, and 4) nondisturbance of the status quo in the Pacific except by peaceful means. In return, Hull promised to free all frozen Japanese assets and to resume treaty-based commercial relations.

The two envoys from Japan asked for two weeks in which their government could weigh the proposals. Their request was granted, and in the meantime, Japan rushed ahead with military and naval preparations in Asia and the Pacific.

That same month U.S. Naval Intelligence detected the signals indicating Japan was about to strike. Stationed in a basement room at Pearl Harbor, Joseph Rochefort, Chief of the Navy's Combat Intelligence Unit, studied radio transmissions from Japanese troops occupying the island of Chichi Jima, two hundred and fifty miles north of the larger Iwo Jima. When translated, the messages revealed that Japan was planning a "two-prong" attack, one going east from Japan, the other south. Rochefort compiled information he and his staff had gathered and forwarded it to the Chief of Naval Operations. On November 27, 1941, the U.S. Chief of Naval Operations wired an urgent dispatch to all Pacific stations:

THIS DISPATCH IS TO BE CONSIDERED A WAR WARNING.

NEGOTIATIONS WITH JAPAN LOOKING TOWARD STABILI-ZATION OF CONDITIONS IN THE PACIFIC HAVE CEASED AND AN AGGRESSIVE MOVE BY JAPAN IS EXPECTED WITHIN THE NEXT FEW DAYS.[5]

Reports later would show that Japan had launched another assault an hour and twenty minutes before the strike at Pearl Harbor. In this opening salvo, Japanese General Yamashita landed 20,000 troops on the east Malaya, where Britain's vastly outnumbered 88,000 men were forced into quick surrender.

At the conference which had sired the Atlanta Charter, Churchill had pressed Roosevelt to join in issuing parallel warnings to Japan from America, Britain, and Holland. The warning, according to the Prime Minister, would announce that any further encroachments in the Southwest Pacific would compel countermeasures that might lead to war. At that time Roosevelt would not make such a commitment. The reasons behind his reluctance are unclear, but most probably they were because his concentration was almost entirely upon Europe, and innate arrogance led to his confidence that he could personally "work something out" with the Japanese. At any rate, the most FDR would do at Placentia Bay in regard to Japan was to promise to maintain economic pressures against that nation in "full force."

FDR returned to Washington, and in conversation with Japanese Ambassador Nomura declared that if Japan would suspend its expansionist activities, the U.S. was ready to join in informal exploratory discussions about economic matters. FDR also suggested he would be receptive to a meeting with Prince Konoye of Japan in Juneau, Alaska, sometime around the middle of October.

Secretary Cordell Hull and other advisors cautioned the President that he and Nomura should resolve fundamental differences before such a meeting should take place. The advisors, some of whom by this time perhaps were aware of FDR's habits of grandstanding and overlooking details, feared that such a meeting would produce only vague positions which could be bent in any direction.

In early September an Imperial Conference of military leaders in Tokyo firmly set Japan on the road to war. Leaders in Tokyo agreed that the U.S. and Britain were not to interfere with Japan's efforts in China. Neither the U.S. nor Britain was to do anything which might threaten Japan's interests in the Far East, and the two Western nations were to cooperate with Japan's efforts to secure adequate supplies of raw materials to assure her economic well-being.

In mid-October, 1941 Prince Fumimaro Konoye resigned as Head of the Japanese Cabinet, and his place was taken by General Hideki Tojo, War Minister. Japanese incursions into China increased, and in that scattered nation Generalissimo Chiang Kai-shek kept international wires buzzing with messages to the U.S. asking for additional help, contending that the closing of the Burma Road in July, widespread inflation, and Communist infiltrations were sapping China's resolve and ability to fight.

Conditions in Southeast Asia worsened throughout 1941. During the period, FDR did not want to take any action which would weaken or endanger the help his Administration was sending to Europe. Hoping to curb Japan, he relied instead on "moral steps," — steps which history would show were inconsequential.

The British pressed Roosevelt to go beyond these "moral steps," but FDR continued to aim for peace with Japan through diplomatic talks, limited displays of naval strength, and additional aid to the forces of Chang Kai-shek.

By this time, Ambassador Joseph Grew was abandoning his hope that the status quo in Asia could be preserved by economic measures only; he and his military attachés believed the point had been reached when stronger measures were necessary. One message cautioned that a serious infraction could occur "by some sudden stroke by the [Japanese] Navy or Army without prior authorization or knowledge of the Government." In numerous telegrams to Secretary Hull with requests that the President be informed, he repeated earlier warnings about moves of the new regime in Tokyo, and he cautioned that even more drastic actions were about to be taken. In the first week of November, 1941, Ambassador Grew alerted Washington that Japan might take action and "an armed conflict with the U.S. might come with dangerous and dramatic suddenesss."[6]

Grew's official reports were increasingly somber; his diary entries even more so. In those while reviewing events between August and December, 1941, he wrote:

> Our own telegrams brought no response whatsoever; they were never even referred to, and reporting to the Department was like throwing pebbles into a lake at night; we were not permitted to see even the ripples. For all we knew our telegrams had not in any degree registered. Obviously I could only assume our recommendations were not welcome, yet we continued to express our carefully considered judgment as to the developing situation, a judgment which subsequent events prove to have been all too accurate.[7]

# Chapter 24. Infamy

> "Yesterday, December 7, 1941 — a date which will live in infamy — the United States of America was suddenly and deliberately attacked by naval and air forces of the Empire of Japan." [115]
>
> — President Franklin Roosevelt, December 8, 1941.

In the middle of the nineteenth century, Commodore Matthew Perry opened long-slumbering Japan to world commerce. Nipponese leaders, realizing that European powers had occupied India, China, Africa, Australia, the Indies, and other areas surrounding Japan, began moving their country from feudalism to industrialism. Along with the move toward industrialism, Japan promoted its military tradition and sent its future army officers to Germany for training and its future naval leaders to England.

With help from U.S. President Teddy Roosevelt, uncle of FDR, Japan was strong enough to defeat Russia in a short war ending in 1904. The U.S. Navy then started displaying its strength in Manila Bay, Guam, Hong Kong, and the Yangtze, thus alarming the Japanese already wary of the Dutch in the Indies, the British in China, and the French in Indo-China. When the U.S. seized the Philippines in 1898, Japanese leaders began casting America in the role of adversary.

Japanese warlords sent troops into Manchuria in 1931. Americans and Europeans who noted the event deplored it but took no action except to declare Japan "an outlaw nation." Six years later Nipponese troops crossed the Marco Polo Bridge ten miles west of Peiping and marched into China, starting a war between the two countries which would last eight years. In a pattern all-too typical, Prime Minister Prince Konoye expressed regret but did not prevent his army from marching ever farther into the invaded China. Again, America and Western Powers, led by Roosevelt, stood aside, endeavoring to administer foreign policies constructed on morality and neutrality alone.

The Chinese government asked the U.S. to mediate, but FDR's administration turned down the plea. If the U.S. officially recognized that a war between China and Japan existed, the Neutrality Act would apply, and the U.S. would not have been able to send arms or aid to China. Such aid would have been construed as helping one of the belligerents, and in consequence Japan would be stronger. Japan did not need arms from the U.S. What it needed was oil, scrap iron, and other raw materials, which America kept supplying in abundance.

At the end of January, 1941, Joint Military Staff Conferences between the U.S. and Great Britain got underway in Washington. Discussion in these meetings centered on three goals: 1) to devise ways of keeping sea lanes open to Britain, 2) to allocate and station combined forces that would show a defense to Germany and Japan, and 3) to provide for coordinated military operations should the U.S. get into a war in either the Atlantic, the Pacific, or both.

American spokesmen in the conferences were General George Marshall, Chief of Staff for the Army, and Admiral Harold Stark, Chief of Naval Operations. Just days after the conferences ended, Admiral Stark sent a message to all his fleet commanders warning: "The question of our entry into the war now seems to be *when* and not *whether*" [italics mine].[1] Stark's alarm was not shared with President Roosevelt or the State Department.

At the beginning of July, 1941, the Japanese Emperor met with the chief figures of his civil and military government, and it was this Imperial Conference which adopted and set in motion plans which six months later resulted in war between Japan and the United States. The main argument in this historic conference was advanced by Hideki Tojo, War Minister and General. The conferees agreed to instruct the nation to get ready for war, and the following steps were enacted immediately: 1) Economic resources of the nation were to be organized for war. 2) The Army began operational moves into Malaya, Java, areas within the Netherlands East India, Borneo, and the Philippines. 3) The Navy was to develop corresponding plans, among them to practice the Pearl Harbor attack, conceived in the preceding January. Airplanes were to practice coming in low over the mountains, dive bombing, and the use of newer torpedoes designed to operate in shallow waters.

Negotiations between the U.S. and Japan continued throughout the summer of 1941 and grew more frantic each month. Prince Konoye noted in his diary that "if by the early part of October, there was no reasonable hope of having its terms accepted, Japan should decide for war."[2]

In the middle of October, the Konoye Cabinet fell and was replaced by one headed by the more combative General Tojo. Under his leadership, Nipponese diplomats insisted that the next move was up to the Americans, but Washington administrators led by FDR would not budge from restrictions on Japanese assets in the U.S.; nor would the U.S. relinquish its ban of permitting oil to be sold to Japan. Washingtonians were fully conscious of Japan's tripartite alliance with Germany and Italy. Hence, in the early fall of that fateful year negotiations between the U.S. and Japan came to a complete deadlock.

In America, a few military advisors were beginning to believe that hostilities between Japan and the U.S. were certain to break out; indeed, U.S. Pacific bases had been put on alert several times in the fall of 1941, but conventional thinking accepted FDR's conviction that any really dangerous movements by Japan would first be upon the Philippines, if any indeed any such military actions were launched at all. Such complacency was confusing to the two major army and navy commanders at Pearl Harbor, and as a result, on the fateful morning of December 7, 1941, army personnel were not on the alert. and navy crews were not aboard their assigned vessels.

Japanese planning for the Pearl Harbor attack was started very early in 1941 under the auspices of Admiral Isoroku Yamamoto, Commander of the nation's Combined Fleet, and in February of that year Yamamoto had begun picking leaders for the attack. Within a month Captain Minoru Genda was chosen to develop tactics for the actual strike. Genda, a crack young airman, deemed the strike risky but not impossible. Over the next several months, more intelligence was collected, maps were studied, mockups prepared, pilots trained, and equipment gathered. It was November 5, 1941, before the plan in its final form was approved by Emperor Hirohito.

Vice Admiral Chuichi Nagumo, Commander of the First Air Fleet aboard the flagship *Akagi*, was selected to lead the attack. Young Mitsuo Fuchida was picked to be commander of all air groups of the First Air

Fleet. One by one, other key persons were chosen. Meanwhile, pilots and navy crewmen began intensive training for the secretive venture.

A problem that Japanese strategists had to solve was how to make torpedoes effective in the shallow waters of Pearl Harbor. A torpedo bomber needed a long, level flight, and when released, its conventional missile would plunge nearly 100 ft. into the water before leveling off to make passage toward the hull of a targeted ship. In Pearl Harbor the average depth was only 42 ft. Borrowing an idea from the British carrier-based attack on the Italian naval base at Taranto, Japanese manufacturers were able to produce torpedoes that would dive to a depth of only 35 ft. in the water, and military strategists managed to fashion auxiliary wooden tail fins to keep the torpedo horizontal during its fall. Also added was a breakaway nose cone made of very soft wood which would cushion the impact when the dropped torpedo first hit the water.[3] With the depth problem solved, and with these torpedo modifications having been developed, attack plans proceeded rapidly.

Allegations have been made by historians such Charles Beard and Charles T. Tansill as well as former armed forces personnel that some members of the Roosevelt administration, including FDR himself, had advance knowledge of the attack and purposely ignored it in order to gain public and Congressional support for America to enter the war on the side of the Allies. American leaders were charged with deliberately exposing Pearl Harbor in order to force the U.S. into the war. (Such assertions were almost certain to arise after some of the mistakes and lapses of FDR and his administration were exposed, but most students of the period believe such charges go beyond any factual evidence yet discovered.)

Admittedly, the attack took place before any formal declaration of war was made by Japan. Tokyo transmitted a 5,000-word notification to the Japanese Embassy in Washington, but transcribing the message took too long for the Japanese Ambassador to deliver it.

Conventional wisdom has held that Japan attacked without any official warning of a break in relations solely because of bumbling that delayed delivery of this translated document to the American Secretary of State and that Washington diplomats were completely unaware of the impending assault. In fact, however, U.S. code breakers already had translated and deciphered most of the message hours before the 1:00 P.M. deadline and before the Japanese ambassadors met with Secretary Hull. Takeo Iguchi, a law professor at the International Christian University in Tokyo, discovered documents that pointed to vigorous debate inside the government over whether to notify Washington that it was Japan's intention to break off negotiations. Iguchi presented a diary in which the entry on December 7 stated, "Our deceptive diplomacy is steadily proceeding toward success." Iguchi further asserted, "The diary clearly shows that the army and navy did not want to give any proper declaration of war or indeed prior notice even of the termination of negotiations . . . and they clearly prevailed.[4]

On the morning of December 7, Secretary of the Navy Frank Knox in Washington had met with Secretary of State Cordell Hull and Secretary of War Henry Stimson and had returned to his own office. At 1:00 P.M., Washington time, a naval commander appeared at Knox's door with the message: "We are being attacked in Hawaii. This is no drill."

Knox could not believe it and blurted, "It can't be true. They must mean the Philippines." He asked for immediate confirmation, and Admiral Harold Stark replied, "No, sir. It's true! It's Pearl Harbor."[5]

On November 20, 1941, a Japanese task force of 31 ships had been assembled: six aircraft carriers, two battleships, two heavy cruisers, one light cruiser, nine destroyers, three submarines, and eight tankers. The aircraft consisted of 432 planes to be used as follows: 39 for combat air patrol, 40 for reserve, and 353 for the raid itself. The plan was for the aircraft to attack in two separate waves.

Five days later on November 25, Admiral Yamamoto ordered the force to depart for Hawaii. Its course would be SSE to a point 650 north of the island of Oahu. There all planes would be gassed up and readied; naval ships would be refueled, and accompanying tankers could withdraw for safety while the attackers would swing to the right and head directly south toward Pearl Harbor.

Air crews were ordered to select battleships and aircraft as primary targets and cruisers or destroyers if the primaries were not available. Dive bombers were to attack ground targets (hangars and buildings), and fighters were to strafe and destroy as many parked aircraft as possible to ensure they did not get into the air to strike back.

When the attackers were within 500 miles of their target, a message from Honolulu and relayed from Tokyo to Nagumo aboard the *Akagi* disclosed that moored in Pearl Harbor were 9 Battleships, 3 Class-B Cruisers, 3 Seaplane Tenders, and 17 Destroyers. Just entering the Harbor were an additional 4-Class-B Cruisers, and 3 Destroyers. No aircraft carriers were in port, but everything there appeared quiet and undisturbed. There were no signs of alerts or undue wariness; Tokyo planners were quite satisfied.

After the war, some historians speculated that such intelligence must have come from Japanese spies planted in Hawaii, but the Islands' 160,000 people of Japanese blood pulled no sabotage, probably no important espionage. No tangible evidence was ever discovered to support claims of undercover spying. The Japanese Consul General Nagao Kita had been given proper diplomatic credential by the U.S. and was living in Honolulu along with an authorized staff of more than 200 persons. He could look out his office windows or drive down one of several roads to the nearby harbor and get a perfect view of the big ones in Battleship Row as well all destroyers, tenders, minesweepers, and lesser vessels moored to the docks of Pearl Harbor itself. Why bother with undercover spies?

The Japanese planned to hit Pearl Harbor with planes staggered in two waves. The first wave of Japanese planes was made up of 40 torpedo planes, 51 dive bombers, 49 level bombers, and 43 fighters flying as escort. A second wave was to be launched an hour and fifteen minutes after the first and would be comprised of 80 dive bombers, 54 high level bombers, and 36 more fighters. That left 39 planes to guard the task force just in case the Americans were able to mount an immediate counter attack.

Admiral Husband Kimmel, Commander of the Pacific Fleet, was at home when a duty officer phoned him the shocking news: *"There's a message from the signal tower saying the Japanese are attacking Pearl Harbor. This is no drill!"* The admiral slammed down the receiver and dashed outside, buttoning his white uniform jacket as he ran.

General Walter C. Short had been appointed to command the Hawaiian Department of the U.S. Army in February, 1941, and upon his first appearance at Pearl Harbor Admiral Kimmel had ordered a navy review as an *aloha* gesture for the new commander. General Short and Kimmel thereafter became friends, often playing golf, bridge, or sharing dinners and drinks with their wives at their respective Officer Bars.

Short was at home on the morning of December 7, and when he heard the first bombs he remarked to his wife that "the Navy must be having some battle practice." A few minutes after 8 o'clock, an aide ran in to tell him, "Sir! This is the real thing."[6]

At 7:48 A.M. Hawaiian time, Commander Fuchida and his accompanying planes were fifty miles from the northwest shore of Oahu. Convinced that his formations were still undetected, Fuchida fired his signal pistol. The attack finally could begin — *Tora, tora, tora* — *Tiger, tiger, tiger.*

Dive bombers climbed to 12,000 ft.; horizontal bombers spiraled down to 3500 ft., and torpedo planes dropped until they barely skimmed the water. All pilots were anxious for the honor of leading the assault, and at a point roughly opposite Haleiwa on the northwest shore of Oahu, the planes started to make their runs onto the targets.

Through a mix-up of signals, dive bombers instead of torpedo planes went in first. The mistake was of no consequence because the Pacific Fleet had been caught napping. Back on the deck of the *Akagi*, Admiral Nagumo upon hearing Fuchida's message of "*To, to, to*" — the first syllable of *totsugekiseyo* (charge), smiled and silently shook hands with another admiral standing by his side. Yamamoto's madcap venture implemented by Genda's strategy was proving to be a success.

Five hundred miles to the south of the *Akagi*, the attack got underway, and Commander Fuchida sat among thin clouds watching horizontal and dive bombers go in. They were followed by torpedo bombers who split into two groups: one heading for the west side of Pearl Harbor, the other flying southeastward toward Hickam Field before swinging toward Battleship Row. Each group attacked in formations of twos and threes, and every pilot had been given orders to make certain he had closed in on his target, even at the risk of his life.

The horizontal bombers approached Battleship Row from the south, and the mammoth vessels looked like ducks sitting in a line. As they neared the targets, Commander Fuchida traded positions with the lead plane in his squadron. Fuchida's plane had a specially trained bombardier, and when he released his bombs other planes would follow suit; all the squadrons were to operate the same way.

Fuchida's personal target was the U.S.S. *Nevada*, at the head in the row of five battle wagons pointing northeast, but on his initial pass a few thin clouds covered that ship. He would have to try again, and on his second pass too much smoke swirled over the *Nevada*. He switched targets and chose the U.S.S. *Maryland*, fourth in line. In post attack briefings Fuchida would report that he thought he had two hits on her.[7]

For the United States, it was the most one-sided battle in its history. The first bombs fell at 7:55 A.M., and the attack lasted two hours, ending shortly before 10:00 A.M. To service men and women as well as Hawaiian citizens the two-hour assault must have seemed continuous, but in truth the fighting was sporadic. There was a slight lull around 8:40 A.M. — likely the period between the two attack waves. The most stunning and devastating instance of it all was the blowing up of the U.S.S. *Arizona*

— a tragedy which occurred within 15 minutes after the first bombs were dropped.

The cost in American ships was high — more than eighteen vessels sunk or seriously damaged. Sunk or lost outright were the two battle-ships *Arizona* and *Oklahoma*, the target ship *U.S.S. Utah*, and the destroy-ers *Cassin* and *Downes*. Sunk or later beached and salvaged were the bat-tleships *West Virginia*, *California*, and *Nevada*, and the mine-layer *Oglala*. Battleships that suffered major damage were the *Tennessee*, *Maryland*, and *Pennsylvania* along with the cruisers *Helena*, *Honolulu*, and *Raleigh*. Other vessels shattered were the destroyer *Shaw*, the seaplane tender *Curtiss*, and the repair ship *Vestal*.

Beyond the stricken seagoing vessels were air fields and planes in their hangars or on their ramps. More than 188 planes were destroyed — 96 Army and 92 Navy; an additional 128 Army and 31 Navy aircraft were damaged. Hardest hit were fields at Kaneohe and Ewa; of the 82 planes caught on the ground at these two fields only one was able to fly after the raid.[8]

Military targets — ships, docks, supplies, air field, and planes — suf-fered most of the destruction, but the city of Honolulu did not escape completely. In that swelling metropolis there was an estimated $500,000 worth of damage.

For the Japanese, it appeared to be an unmitigated triumph. The Japa-nese strike force lost only 29 planes — 9 fighters, 15 dive bombers, and 5 torpedo planes. In addition, there was the loss of one submarine with its entire crew as well as nine men aboard midget subs which failed to achieve any significant impact. Planning by the Empire of the Rising Sun had paid off; Americans through mistaken judgments, lapses, and care-lessness had made the sneak assault possible.

## Chapter 25. FDR: A Reckoning

> Character [ethos] is the most potent of all means of persuasion.
>
> —Aristotle, *Rhetoric*, Book 1.

At the beginning of the fourth decade of the twentieth century, peace everywhere was threatened. The whole world was in flux; although the Spanish Civil War had ended, World War II had broken out in Europe; *Luftwaffe* planes were bombing England; Japanese forces had invaded China and Indo-China. The world had moved to a global economy, and the balance of power was shifting. The United States, new to its role as a truly great industrial power, was inescapably involved in the affairs of other nations through heritage, diplomatic ties, vast flows of resources, and extensive commerce links. Franklin Roosevelt realized this fact earlier than most politicians, and he used persona and persuasion, buttressed by guile, and outright deceptions in several instances, to bring American voters along.

Was he a great President? Does he belong in an American pantheon along with Washington and Lincoln? What makes for greatness, anyway?

According to the writings of William Shakespeare, some men are born great, others achieve greatness, and some have greatness thrust upon them. Franklin Roosevelt's life fits into each of the three categories. The bard of Avon might have added (but didn't) that some persons outlive greatness; yet that is what happened to Franklin Roosevelt.

Judgments on what makes greatness come to us from many sources, and in taking such measurements savants look into the character of the person being examined. Character is not an easy word to define; even an average-sized modern dictionary may offer as many as fourteen differing definitions, many of which are something akin to "a description of a person's attributes, traits, or abilities." Ancient Greek writers extolled the importance of *ethos*, a complex noun used almost as a synonym for our modern character. Aristotle, sage of long-ago Athens, asserted that ethos was the sum of all attributes which makes a person worthy of being believed.[1]

With the guideline of Aristotle's ethos in mind, let us take a quick review of Franklin Roosevelt.

Born to the purple with ancestors who had gained material wealth and enviable reputations, Franklin grew up as a child of privilege with a background impossible for persons in families with average incomes to appreciate. In the 1930s, when his country was on the verge of anarchy — more threatened than at any time since the Civil War — with matchless persuasion he led the citizenry into adoption of measures which brought the nation through the perilous times.

Franklin Roosevelt had overcome the debilitating effects of polio and had proved himself a formidable politician in the 1920s, winning the Governorship of the Empire State in 1928. He had saved his country during the stark years of its greatest Depression when every state teetered on the brink of economic disaster. No one could be sure whether the improvement had come from his leadership or from rearmament programs beginning to sweep the world, including the U.S. Indeed, anyone with a plan then might have gained a following, but only a person with eloquence and undaunted faith in himself could win public enthusiasm. Willing to use government funds for citizen relief, FDR amassed a troop of absolutely loyal lieutenants in and out of Congress; he listened to his Brain Trust and grasped ideas from others even when he did not fully understand mechanics or implications in those ideas. Nor was he afraid to use executive powers to set up agencies to help those who could not help themselves. As a person who had never known economic hardships, Roosevelt might not have realized all he risked when he stepped out of his class and endorsed pump priming — the use of government funds to stimulate private business — yet he did so. Except for mistaken beliefs in his own invincibility during the Supreme Court fiasco, his first eight years in the White House were unmitigated triumphs — worthy of the adjective great — none but inveterate haters of FDR, of which there were quite a few, can ever deny that.

With the coming of World War II, America's productive capacity thrust the United States into the forefront of the world's great powers, and by virtue of that power alone, the nation's Chief Executive — no matter who that person might be — became an unchallenged authority; thus greatness was thrust upon Roosevelt.

Biographers tend to laud only their central character, and there is no denying that for more than twelve years Franklin Roosevelt dominated American politics and diplomacy. Successes as well as shortcomings must be attributed to him and his administrations. Programs of the New Deal and commitments in international relationships either were initiated or approved by him alone. Nevertheless, in attacking domestic problems, he constantly was nagged into action by his persistent wife, Eleanor.

What had made FDR choose Eleanor? No matter whether it was young romantic love or political calculation, it was the wisest decision he ever made. There would be estrangements in their marriage, particularly after Eleanor's discovery of Franklin's first involvements with Lucy Mercer, but the Roosevelt couple reconciled differences enough to set up an unusual arrangement — not genuinely married but a compatible twosome living apart.

From Eleanor came constant insistence for civil rights. She was unrelenting in prodding her husband for greater support of the underprivileged, for improving the plights of women, factory workers, the aged and infirm, and for minorities in every class. Much of the acclaim given Franklin for championing the nation's liberal causes more rightly ought to go to Eleanor and her dogged determination to help those unable to help themselves.

Other persons who influenced FDR and his programs included Frances Perkins, one of Franklin Roosevelt's appointees when he was Governor of New York and later the Secretary of Labor in his Cabinet. More than any other one person, Perkins was responsible for developing and helping establish the Social Security System in 1935, and she was one of only two appointees who stayed with FDR throughout his terms as President.

Another loyal lieutenant to FDR throughout his presidencies was curmudgeonly Harold Ickes, Secretary of the Interior. Harold Ickes was a faithful aide, an unabashed Democrat, a good phrase-maker, and a budget-minded administrator as head of the gigantic Public Works Administration (PWA), established in 1933 during Roosevelt's first Hundred Days.

Henry Wallace of Iowa proved to be far-sighted and effective in his role as Secretary of Agriculture, and it was only after being passed over for the Vice-Presidential slot in 1940 that his standing with Roosevelt began to sag.

There were others who helped bring FDR's ideas into fruition. David Lilienthal made the TVA a model of success. Henry Morgenthau, Secretary of the Treasury, liked to think he was closest to Roosevelt and indeed did share many lunches with his former neighbor from Hyde Park. Except for straying well beyond his Cabinet responsibilities and proposing a short-sighted plan for utter destruction of Germany as a sovereign government and turning it into an agricultural province, Morgenthau was invaluable to Franklin Roosevelt.

There were others: personal emissary Harry Hopkins, Cordell Hull, Felix Frankfurter, Samuel Rosenman, Raymond Moley, and James Byrnes to name a few. The list could go on, but none equaled the impact of Eleanor, and we should remember, too, that FDR made the final judgments himself, irrespective of what others told him.

Those who earn the award of greatness may have to go against prevalent public opinion and — as Webster phrased it — "push his own skiff out from the shore." In doing so, a leader may risk and sometime lose his elected seat; (witness the careers of John Quincy Adams, Henry Clay, or Abraham Lincoln when in debates with Stephen Douglas he agreed that "the right of property" was expressly stated in the Constitution but boldly asserted that "property in a slave" was not contained therein. Ownership of a human being was different from ownership of acres of land, buildings, cattle, and livestock. His was a shocking assertion to many at the time.

Presidents with more executive authority than candidates or other elected officials run greater risks when taking actions contrary to what the public then expects or may even be demanding. That's what George Washington did in 1794 when his advisors and the press of his day were rabidly denouncing the Treaty signed in London by American Ambassador John Jay.

The Treaty was the most contentious and significant matter to come before the fledgling government and was submitted to the U.S. Senate in June. Then followed two months of horrendous debate both in and out of Congressional chambers. President Washington, besieged by persons and press urging him to veto the Treaty, signed it in August making it the nation's law.

Denounced for his acquiescence, Washington defended his action in a formal letter he sent to Edmund Randolph:

> I have weighed with attention every argument which has at any time been brought into view. But the constitution is the guide which I will never abandon... While I feel the most lively gratitude for the many instances of approbation from my country, I can no otherwise deserve it than by obeying the dictates of my conscience.[2]

Washington was the dominant figure to come out of the American Revolution and the only person who could have held the new country together during its tumultuous and fractious first decades. Widely revered, the attacks he suffered for endorsing the hated Jay's Treaty threatened even his known imperviousness. To Thomas Jefferson he wrote:

> I am accused of being the enemy of America, and subject to the influence of a foreign country . . . .and every act of my administration is tortured, in such exaggerated and indecent terms as could scarcely be applied to Nero, to a notorious defaulter, or even to a common pickpocket.[3]

Abraham Lincoln, too, both as a senatorial candidate and later as President came under intense public pressures to bow to demands from within and outside his own party. In his first year in the Presidency when war for the North was going badly, both Houses of Congress had passed resolutions declaring the war was not for any purpose of conquest or subjugation, or of "overthrowing or interfering with the rights or established institutions" of the Southern States; it was solely "to preserve the Union with all the dignity, equality, and rights of the several States unimpaired."

As a young man, Lincoln had been appalled when he witnessed a slave auction in Mississippi. As President, he issued the Emancipation Proclamation in September, 1862, to take effect in the following January. Although the measure gratified a few radical Republicans, it was lambasted by moderates and conservatives. Lincoln's announcement went against prevailing opinion; it undoubtedly cost him the support of many moderates and conservatives, and contributed to Republican defeats in the congressional election of 1862. Judgments contrary to prevailing opinions are the stuff from which greatness is made.

Throughout his first eight years in the Presidency, Franklin Roosevelt was not intimidated by public sentiment. He went against the prevailing tide which preached that the business of America was business and leaders in that sector knew best. He courageously used public addresses, press conferences, and fireside chats to bring voters around to his points

of view. Many biographers pay tribute to his skill in public persuasion..
One writer, David Halberstam, captured the essence of FDR as the first
Media President:

> He [FDR] was the first great American radio voice. For most Americans of
> this generation, their first memory of politics would be sitting by a radio
> and hearing that voice, strong, confident, totally at ease. . . . Most Ameri-
> cans in the previous 160 years had never even seen a President; now almost
> all of them were hearing him, in their own homes. It was literally and figu-
> ratively electrifying.[4]

Only after he was assured of public support did FDR announce foreign policy measures. Throughout his first two terms he wanted to assure himself of solid support before enacting a measure. His fireside chat
explaining Lend Lease, in which he used a homely analogy of granting
a garden hose to help a neighbor put out a fire, was a splendid example
of his sophistry in marshaling public opinion. Another example can be
seen in his transfer of destroyers to Britain; before taking that executive
action he called in Republican leaders from the Congress to make certain
they would not mount major opposition to his move.

He boasted numerous times, "I'm a good horse trader." Actually, he
was outguessed often by Churchill, Stalin, and Chiang's minions, including Madame Chiang. If FDR had been a horse trader, he would have given
away the farm and swapped a prize stallion for a Missouri mule!

Near the end of the nineteenth century, a Catholic historian in England, John Emerich Edward Dahlberg Acton, usually referred to simply
as Lord Acton, wrote a dictum widely quoted: "Power tends to corrupt;
absolute power corrupts absolutely."[5] Acton's observation applies to
Franklin Roosevelt, for by the time he started his third term FDR was a
changed leader.

In the worst of the Depression years, FDR knew voters were desperate, ready to accept almost any and every promise that gave a sliver of
hope in bringing them out of the depths of the Depression. In those years
he explained, educated, and encouraged through public speeches and
fireside chats to bring voters to his way of thinking.

Few have described FDR's handling of public opinion better than political scientist Edwin Hargrove, who noted:

> In his leadership of public opinion, FDR oscillated from the heroic to the
> cautious. With his sensitivity to public moods, he was forthright as a
> leader when crisis was high and public sentiment was ripe for heroic lead-
> ership. This was the case when he first entered public office and embarked
> on the dramatic legislative leadership of the first hundred days. . . . At

other times, he was more cautious and gradually prepared the public for a new departure. For example, he held off on social security legislation in order to . . . educate people that it was not alien to the American tradition of self-reliance. He did this by blending press conferences, a message to Congress, two fireside chats, and a few speeches in which he progressively unfolded the Americanness of the plan. . . He did this kind of thing with artistry, and the artistry was an extension of his own empathy and ability to act to win over others.[6]

After most New Deal measures were in place, confidence in government had returned. As one success piled on top of another, FDR knew he had won public approval; he had overcome all rivals; his self-confidence mounted, and his attitudes changed.

He had reasons for pride. Through press conferences he had manipulated subservient reporters, had helped engineer a remarkable economic recovery for the nation, had amassed solid backing in the Congress, and had triumphed in three presidential elections. These laurels convinced him he could act by fiat; whatever he did would be accepted, and any persuasion, if necessary, could be relegated to subordinates.

Supremely confident in his own skills, FDR seldom bothered to read or consider the fine print in pacts or programs — those details were matters for lesser persons. If he endorsed an idea, it had to be successful. He boasted of his skill as a negotiator, but in truth he overlooked provisions and inherent clauses in agreements, leaving implementation to others and shunting to them questions unresolved.

FDR was not above deception. He was faithless in his own marriage (although he was not the only President to fall into that pit). Many voters seem willing to write off indiscretions and are ready to forgive marital transgressions of elected officials. Grover Cleveland, the nation's 22nd President, before his elevation to the office, had a liaison with a young widow. The woman admitted she had had relations with other men, and Cleveland had no real evidence that he was the father of her child. Nevertheless, he accepted responsibility for it and contributed to the child's support even though he never saw or contacted the mother again. Political enemies made the most of Cleveland's liaison, and during the campaign of 1884 they paraded the streets singing:

"Ma, Ma, where's my Pa?"

"Gone to the White House, Ha, Ha, Ha."

Fourscore years later, readers, television viewers, and *paparazzi* everywhere were titillated and ready to forgive handsome President Jack Kennedy's affairs with society queens and Hollywood stars.

Franklin Roosevelt's romantic peccadilloes were not so flagrant as others and perhaps had no effect upon his ability to lead the nation. His leadership from 1933 until 1940 is unquestionable. From that latter date, however, the picture grows murkier. His physical resistance, which once seemed indefatigable, showed signs of weakening, and close associates noticed the changes along with a slower decline of his powers of concentration and mental acuity. Along with these deteriorations came further evidence of his unshakable self confidence and willingness to act by executive orders.

Upon enactment of the one-year draft in 1940 when war jitters were spreading across America, Roosevelt had said, reiterating the vow in 1941, "Your boys are not going to be sent into any foreign war." To associates he qualified the repeated promise by saying, "Of course, if we were attacked, it would not be a foreign war." From such statements, revisionist historians allege that FDR was not being forthright in his intentions.

Chief among such critics was Robert B. Stinnett, author of *Day of Deceit*. Stinnett's book spurred others to make allegations that FDR adopted measures deliberately meant to provoke Japan into an act of war. Citing information first withheld but later gleaned under the Freedom of Information Act, Stinnett, John Toland, and others have written that FDR knew war with Japan was inevitable, but he was determined to make that country commit the first overt act so that isolationist Americans would be galvanized into action.[7]

There is no question that well in advance of Pearl Harbor, FDR, military and State Department leaders were in agreement that a victorious Germany would threaten the security of the United States. Yet according to nearly every poll, the majority of Americans wanted nothing to do with Europe's war. There also is general agreement that FDR and Administration officials believed that before America would get into actual war, Germany or Japan would have to commit an act dangerous enough to override isolationist sentiment.

In the context of such reasoning, some historians and writers have asserted that FDR knew an attack on Pearl Harbor attack was coming. Others, perhaps more charitable, reply that FDR must have believed in measures he pushed through, doing so because he was convinced that if only he could sit across the table from other government leaders, he could win any and all to his points of view. He had captured public allegiance, and his triumphs in America when added to his innate confidence convinced him he could manage men from other countries equally well if he could get them to listen to him.

U.S. Intelligence staff had broken the Japanese diplomatic code in the summer, and there is ample evidence showing that Washington officials including FDR learned in late November 1941 that a Japanese naval force was at sea and en route eastward. The broken codes, warnings from Ambassador Grew, and friendly allies had mounted to a level that all privy to them could not fail to realize that Japan was preparing for war.

Yet with these facts, it cannot be proved that FDR had definite knowledge that Pearl Harbor was going to be attacked on December 7. He and other planners believed when the attack came it would be farther west — lands in Southeast Asia, on island territories, or the Philippines.

With war in the offing, if FDR did not actually lie to American voters, he certainly was careless with the truth. His statements about having a map showing Nazi plans to take over portions of South America, his exaggeration and misstatements of disasters in the Atlantic shipping crises, and his unequivocal promises not to send American soldiers overseas are examples of manipulations or distortions.

Even more dramatic are lapses in administrative duties to permit failures to transmit alerts down through channels to respond adequately to numerous warnings about aggressive moves taken by Japan — that country's incursions into China, the rape of Nanking, naval build-ups, military actions into Indo-China, Nipponese double talk — and U.S. intelligence findings which would have led a more responsible administration to install adequate defensive measures and make certain all army and naval forces were on guard.

Supremely confident in his own skills, FDR seldom bothered to read or consider the fine print in pacts or programs — those details were matters for lesser persons. If he endorsed an idea, it had to be successful. He boasted of his skill as a negotiator, but in truth he overlooked provisions and inherent clauses in agreements, leaving implementation to others and shunting to them questions unresolved.

Of course, in weighing wartime mistakes or lapses one cannot ignore Roosevelt's declining health — a decline hastened by a lifetime of heavy smoking. His blood pressure had been worrisome for more than ten years, and by the time war broke out he was wasting away from heart disease and hardening of the arteries. His closest adherents and doctors at Bethesda Hospital knew the truth about his precarious health soon after 1940, but that knowledge was carefully withheld.

In the campaign of 1944 he had lost his zip, and several on his staff said he looked "positively awful." After his victory that November, he seemed to develop a lassitude about American politics, paying little attention to intra-party rivalries, and he could not be led into conversation about a possible successor. Indeed, he must not have viewed anyone as his successor, not even his new Vice President.

Although by wire he complimented Harry Truman for helping in the campaign, it had been a routine message of small significance. He did not take Truman into his circle of advisors or share with him on-going problems or any matters of foreign policy. FDR's failure in 1944 to acquaint his Vice President with any of the major unresolved problems, foreign and domestic, is a serious lapse of judgment.

In January of 1945, FDR told some confidants of personal items from his collection he wanted each to have in case of his death. The beneficiaries would smile, take it jokingly, and change the subject although several wrote or said later that during this time the Boss was a very sick man.

On January 9, 1945, FDR asked Edward Stettinius, titular Secretary of State, to come in for a confidential talk, and after the two shared lunches served on trays, FDR asked Stettinius for complete secrecy. Then he told the Secretary that the U.S. was on the verge of perfecting an atomic bomb — a bomb which if it worked would be so powerful as to destroy New York City in one fell swoop. FDR advised Stettinius to consult the War Department in the matter, but he never so much as mentioned the important project to his Vice President and legal successor.

At the Yalta Conference the next month, Lord Moran, Churchill's personal physician, watching Roosevelt, observed, "To a doctor's eye, the President appears a very sick man. He has all the symptoms of hardening of the arteries to the brain in an advanced stage. . . I give him only a few months to live."[8]

A week after FDR returned from the Yalta Conference, he invited Vice President Truman to an informal luncheon for the two at the White House. Nothing of consequence was discussed, and Truman would write of the meeting:

> I met with the President a week later and was shocked by his appearance. His eyes were sunken. His magnificent smile was missing from his care-worn face. He seemed a spent man. I had a hollow feeling within me, for I saw that the journey to Yalta must have been a terrible ordeal.[9]

It was not unusual for Lucy to be invited to Warm Springs when Franklin was there. Eleanor did not like the southern attitude around Warm Springs, and preferred to stay either in Washington, Hyde Park, or follow her increasingly heavy personal business. Such was the case at Thanksgiving, 1944, after the Democratic Convention in July had nominated FDR for an unprecedented fourth term (along with endorsing his selection of Harry Truman as a running mate). Eleanor was at Hyde Park awaiting Franklin's arrival from Georgia; they were scheduled to depart for San Diego a few days afterwards.

On the Sunday following Thanksgiving that year, FDR at Warm Springs told associates that he proposed to drive Mrs. Rutherfurd, who was one of several guests in the house reserved for visitors, part way back to her own home near Aiken. The driving distance would be about twenty-five miles. He and Lucy were alone in his personal car with a Secret Service car driven in front of them and another behind. The December morning was pleasurable with its crisp, sparkling air. They drove slowly, taking almost an hour for the twenty-five miles. FDR was in a jaunty, talkative mood, and the two of them must have reminisced about former times. Yet it probably had its sadness for Lucy because there were signs she could not have failed to notice. The strains of office had exacted a heavy toll from her former handsome, virile lover, and now he appeared so ill, haggard, and fragile.

In the first week of April, 1945, President Roosevelt was at Warm Springs with most of his personal staff there to assist him with correspondence and the day-to-day problems of his office. He had come back from the Yalta Conference ill and utterly exhausted. The restful days at Warm Springs were just what he needed. He had telephoned Eleanor at Hyde Park on Saturday, April 7th. By Monday, he was somewhat rejuvenated, and he told aides he wanted to go for a drive. Late in the afternoon, he was wheeled into his specially equipped Ford, and he drove out the gates at Warm Springs with one Secret Service car ahead of him and another behind. The three car procession turned right on old Route 41, going through the little towns of Manchester and Woodland before that highway made its junction with Route 208. There a Cadillac was parked, and when FDR stopped his car, a tall lady got out, came over, and entered his Ford where he and she exchanged a brief kiss. Lucy beckoned for her own companion, Elizabeth Shoumatoff, a portrait painter she had commissioned to paint FDR, to join them, and the three cars then turned and headed back to Warm Springs.

Nearly every biography of President Franklin Roosevelt will confirm details of his final days at Warm Springs, and as Eleanor would soon learn, the two women along with several staff members were at the Georgia retreat with President Roosevelt at the time of his death, the dire day of April 12, 1945.[10]

Article II, Section I, of the U.S. Constitution reads: "The executive power shall be vested in a President of the United States of America. He shall hold his office during the term of four years . . ." Presidents were allowed to be re-elected for a second term of four years, and until 1940 none had served more than eight years. Thus Presidents were judged for either four or at most eight years. Franklin Roosevelt was President for twelve and one-quarter years.

If presidential administrations are judged separately, FDR earned an undeniable "great" for his first two terms. Vigorous leadership and New Deal programs pulled the country away from the brink of absolute disaster. FDR's subsequent terms, however — from 1941 until his death in April, 1945 — raise questions about the label greatness.

To millions, Franklin Roosevelt's reputation for greatness will never be lessened; others may examine the last three and three-quarter years of his life and conclude that waning acumen, supreme personal arrogance, and unbridled authority combined to make "great" an inappropriate adjective for his entire career.

President Roosevelt was a great leader for eight years — no questions about that. During those terms he brought new ideas and programs into American government. He chose eloquent phrases, stirred hopes and dreams of people everywhere, and rescued an endangered nation. Then he overused his illustrious position, was lax in carrying out designated responsibilities, and through carelessness made grandiose commitments that successors had to face and rectify.

Even one term in the Presidency, exacts a heavy toll, and twelve years in the office for Franklin Roosevelt were devastating. In a final judgment, his decline in physical and mental health during 1941-1945 permitted lapses, decisions, or mistakes which not only weakened our military defense but undermined the very peace he thought he had set up for the war's aftermath.

As a youth and budding politician, he had given great promise, and for two terms in the nation's highest executive office he more than fulfilled them. Unreconstructed supporters will remember only his periods of full bloom — times when he was daring and effective — in the very prime of his life. More careful observers will see the bloom begin to fade in 1940 and progressively wilt until his death in 1945.

# Franklin Delano Roosevelt Chronology

Born January 30, 1882
Parents, James and Sara Roosevelt
Place of Birth, Hyde Park, New York
Tutored at Home until 1896
Enrolled at Groton, private school in Massachusetts, 1896
Harvard College, 1899–1903, graduating with a BA
Law College, Columbia University 1904–1907
Married Eleanor Roosevelt, March 17, 1905
Private law practice 1907–1910
Elected to New York Senate 1911–1913
Assistant Secretary of the Navy 1913–1920
Vice Presidential Nominee, Democratic Ticket, 1920
Stricken with Polio, 1921
Delivered "Happy Warrior" Speech supporting Alfred Smith for Presidency, 1924
Purchase of "little White House" at Warm Springs, Georgia, March, 1926
Elected Governor of New York State, 1928
Historic Flight to Address Democratic Convention in Chicago, July, 1932
Elected to the U.S. Presidency, November, 1932; inaugurated March 4, 1933
Re-elected to U.S. Presidency 1936; inaugurated January 20, 1936
Re-elected to U.S. Presidency 1940; inaugurated, January 20, 1941
Re-elected to U.S. Presidency 1944; inaugurated, January 20, 1945
Died, Warm Springs, Georgia, April 12, 1945
Significant Legislation And Events During FDR's Presidencies

"Bank Holiday" Declared for March 5, 1933

First "Fireside Chat" Delivered on March 12, 1933

"Hundred Days" Congressional Session, March 9 until June 16, 1933

Civilian Conservation Corps created, March 31, 1933

Agricultural Adjustment Act, May 12, 1933

Federal Emergency Relief Act, May 12, 1933

Tennessee Valley Authority Established, May 18, 1933

Took U.S. off gold standard, "Gold Repeal," June 5, 1933

Home Owners Loan Corporation Enacted, June 13, 1933

Federal Deposit Insurance Corporation Created, June 16, 1933

Farm Credit Administration Authorized, June 16, 1933

National Recovery Administration (NRA) and Public Works Administration (WPA) created, June 16, 1933

Recognition of U.S.S.R., November 16, 1933

Repeal of Prohibition, December 5, 1933

Securities and Exchange Commission Authorized, June 6, 1934

Federal Communications Commission Created, June 19, 1934

Federal Housing Administration Authorized, June 28, 1934

Works Progress Administration Established (WPA), April 8 1935

Vetoed World War I Veterans' Bonus Bill, 1935

Rural Electrification Administration Passed by Congress, 1935

Wagner Labor Relations Act Passed, July 5, 1935

Neutrality Act Passed, August 10, 1935

Social Security Act Passed, August 14, 1935

Signed Public Utilities Act, 1935

Supreme Court "court packing" controversy began, February 7, 1937

Revision of Neutrality Act, "Cash and Carry" provisions, 1937

Fair Labor Standards Act Passed, June 25, 1938

Recommended $535 million defense program, 1939

Repeal of Arms Embargo Passed by Congress, 1939

Approved Alien Registration Act, 1940

Fifty destroyers sent to Britain Announced, September 3, 1940

One-year Selective Training and Service Act Approved, September 16, 1940

"Four Freedoms" Enunciated, January 6, 1941

Lend Lease Act Passed, March 11, 1941

U.S. troops sent to Iceland by Executive Order, July 7, 1941

Ordered Embargo on shipment of scrap iron, gasoline, and froze Japanese assets, 1941

Extension of Selective Service Act, 1941

Roosevelt and Churchill confer at Newfoundland Bay, August 9, 1941; subsequent joint announcement of Atlantic Charter, August 14, 1941

Japan attacks Pearl Harbor, December 7, 1941

Executive Order Issued for Evacuation and Internment of citizens with Japanese ancestry, February, 1942

Executive Order sending American Expeditionary Forces to Northern Ireland, January 26, 1942

MacArthur named commander of Allied forces in Australia and southwest Pacific

Women's Auxiliary Army Corps authorized, May14, 1942

Allied Invasion of North Africa, October-December 1942

Self-sustained nuclear chain reaction demonstrated at Chicago, December 2, 1942

Roosevelt and Churchill confer at Casablanca, January 14-24, 1943

Roosevelt and Churchill confer at Quebec, 1943

"Pay-as-you-go" Income Tax Signed, 1943

Roosevelt, Churchill, Chiang-Kai-shek confer at Cairo, 1943

Roosevelt, Churchill, and Stalin confer at Teheran, November 28-December 1, 1943

D-Day Invasion of France, June 6, 1944

G. I. Bill of Rights for Returning Servicemen Approved, June 22, 1944

Dumbarton Oaks Conference on postwar international organization, Aug.-Oct., 1944

Roosevelt, Churchill, and Stalin confer at Yalta, February 4-11, 1945

Address to Congress on the Yalta Conference, March 1, 1945

# BIBLIOGRAPHY

## BOOKS

Allen, Frederick Lewis. *The Big Change: America Transforms Itself 1900-1950*. New York: Harper and Rowe, 1952.

Beschloss, Michael R. *Kennedy and Roosevelt*. New York: W. W. Norton & Co., 1980.

Blum, John Morton. *From the Morgenthau Diaries*. Boston: Houghton Mifflin Co., 1955.

Brands, H. W. *The Privileged Life and Radical Presidency of Franklin Delano Roosevelt*. New York: Anchor Books (Division of Random House), 2009.

James MacGregor Burns. *The Lion and the Fox*. New York: Harcourt and Brace, 1956.

_____ *The Soldier of Freedom*. New York: Harcourt Brace Jovanovich, 1970.

Churchill, Allen. *The Roosevelts: American Aristocrats*. New York: Harper & Rowe, 1965.

Cole, Wayne S. *Charles A. Lindbergh and the Battle Against Intervention in World War II*. New York: Harcourt, Brace, and Jovanovich, 1974.

_____. *Roosevelt and the Isolationists 1932-45*. Lincoln, Nebraska: University of Nebraska Press, 1983.

Feis, Herbert. *The Road to Pearl Harbor*. Princeton, NJ, Princeton University Press, 1950.

Davis, Kenneth S. *FDR: The Beckoning of Destiny 1882-1928*. New York: Random House, Inc., 1971.

Gallagher, Hugh Gregory. *FDR'S Splendid Deception*. New York: Dodd, Mead, & Co., 1985.

Grew, Joseph C. *Ten Years in Japan*. New York: Simon and Schuster, 1944.

Hull, Cordell. *The Memoirs of Cordell Hull*. 2 vols. New York: Macmillan, 1948.

Kimball, Warren F. *The Most Unsordid Act: Lend-Lease 1939-1941.* Baltimore: The John Hopkins Press, 1969.

Langer, William L. and S. Everett Gleason. *The Undeclared War 1940-1941.* New York: Harper & Brothers, 1953.

Lash, Joseph P. *Eleanor and Franklin.* New York: W. W. Norton and Co., Inc., 1971.

Leach, William R. *Land of Desire, Merchants, Power, and the Rise of a New American Culture.* New York: Knopf Doubleday Publishing Group (Vintage Series), 1994.

Manchester, William. The *Glory and the Dream: A Narrative History of America 1932–1972.* New York: Little Brown & Company, 1974. Republished by Bantam Books, 1990.

Manchester, William. *American Caesar: Douglas MacArthur 1880–1964.* New York: Dell Publishing Co., 1978.

Meacham, Jon. *Andrew Jackson: American Lion.* New York: Random House, 2008.

_____ Franklin and Winston: *An Intimate Portrait of an Epic Friendship.* New York: Random House, 2003.

McKenna, Marian C. *Franklin Roosevelt and the Great Constitutional War: The Court-Packing Crisis of 1937.* New York: Fordham University Press, 2002.

Miller, Donald L. *Masters of the Air.* New York: Simon & Schuster, 1996.

Miller, Nathan. FDR: *An Intimate History.* New York: Doubleday and Co., Inc., 1983.

Morgenthau, Henry. *From the Morgenthau Diaries 1938–1941.* John Morton Blum, ed. "The Role of Henry Morgenthau," Boston: Houghton Mifflin Co, 1965.

Morgan, Ted. *FDR: A Biography.* New York: Simon & Schuster, 1985.

Morison, Samuel Eliot. *The Oxford History of the American People.* New York: Oxford University Press, 1965.

_____. *The Battle of the Atlantic, September 1939–1943.* Annapolis, Maryland: Naval Institute Press, 1947.

Mowry, George E. *The Urban Nation 1920–1960.* New York: Hill and Wang, 1965.

*No End Save Victory,* ed. Robert Cowley. New York: G. P. Putnam's Sons, 2001.

*Public Papers and Addresses of Franklin D. Roosevelt.* Samuel I. Rosenman (ed.). 13 vols. New York: Random House and Harper & Brothers, 1938-50.

Rhodes, Richard. *The Making of the Atomic Bomb.* New York: Simon & Schuster, 1986. Roosevelt, Sara Delano. *Diary of Sara Delano Roosevelt.* Franklin Roosevelt Library, Hyde Park, N.Y.

Rosenman, Samuel I. (ed.) *The Public Papers and Public Addresses of Franklin D. Roosevelt, 1932–1945.* 13 vols. New York: Random House, 1938-1950.

Schlesinger, Arthur Jr. *The Politics of Upheaval: The Age of Roosevelt.* Boston: Houghton Mifflin Company, 1960.

Sherwood, Robert. *Roosevelt and Hopkins,* 2 vols. New York: Bantam Books, 1948.

Smith, Amanda. *Heritage to Fortune: The Letters of Joseph P. Kennedy.* New York: Viking, 2001.

Toland, John. *Adolf Hitler.* New York: Ballantine Books, 1976.

Underhill, Robert. *The Bully Pulpit: From Franklin Roosevelt to Ronald Reagan.* New York: Vantage Press, 1988.

Walimont, Walter. *Inside Hitler's Headquarters.* Washington: Praeger Publishing, 1964.

## NEWSPAPERS, JOURNALS, MAGAZINES, AND DIARIES

*Ames Tribune*

*Chicago Tribune*

*Des Moines Register*

*Life Magazine*

*New York Times*

*Public Opinion Quarterly*

*Time Magazine*

*U.S. News & World Report*

*Vital Speeches*

*Washington Post*

# Notes

## Chapter 1 — Europe After World War I

[1]*Encyclopedia of World History*, William L. Langer, ed. Boston: Houghton Mifflin Co., 1940, p. 761.

[2] John Toland. *Adolf Hitler*. New York: Ballantine Books, 1976, p. 178.

[3]Toland, *op. cit.*, p. 33.

[4]*Time*, February 6, 1933. Also, quoted by H. W. Brands, *The Privileged Life and Radical Presidency of Franklin D. Roosevelt*. New York: Anchor Books, p. 357.

## Chapter 2 — America's Great Depression

[1]George E. Mowry, *The Urban Nation 1920-1960*. New York: Hill and Wang, 1965, p. 64.

[2]William R. Leach. *Land of Desire, Merchants, Powers, and the Rise of a New American Culture*. New York: Knopf Doubleday Publishing Group (Vintage Series) 1994, p. 375.

[3]*World Almanac and Book of Facts for 1940*. E. Eastman Irvine, ed. New York: New York World-Telegram, 1940. P. 640.

[4]William Manchester, *The Glory and the Dream 1932-1972*. New York: Bantam Books, 1975, p.p. 36-37.

[5] *Des Moines Sunday Register*, October 27, 1996, S. 2A. p.7.

## Chapter 3 — Franklin Roosevelt: the Early Years

[1]These two sentences can be seen in a handwritten diary of James Roosevelt [Franklin's father] displayed in the Franklin Delano Roosevelt Library at Hyde Park, N.Y.

[2] Sara Roosevelt. *My Boy Franklin*. New York: Ray Long and Richard Smith, 1933, p. 12.

[3] Eleanor Roosevelt, *This is My Story*. New York: Harper & Row. 1937, pp. 1921.

### Chapter 4 — FDR: Emerging Politician

[1] This remark by "Big Tim" Sullivan is quoted by several FDR biographers. For examples, see H. W. Brands, *The Privileged Life and Radical Presidency of Franklin Delano Roosevelt*. New York: Anchor Books, 2009, p. 56 or Geoffrey C. Ward, *A First Class Temperament: The Emergence of Franklin Roosevelt*. New York: Book-of-the-Month Club, 1989, p. 131.

[2] Caroline Bird. *The Invisible Scar*. New York: McKay Publishing, 1966, p. 36.

### Chapter 5 — Seizing the Crown

[1] *New York Times*, March 5, 1933. Hereinafter referred to as NYT.

[2] Robert Sherwood. *Roosevelt and Hopkins: An Intimate Portrait*. New York: Harper & Brothers, 1948. P. 70.

### Chapter 6 — Advisors and Aides

[1] Niccolo Machiavelli, *The Prince and the Discourses*. New York: Modern Library, 1940, pp. 85-86.

[2] Sherwood, *op. cit.*, p. 31.

[3] John Morton Blum, *Roosevelt & Morgenthau: Revision from the Morgenthau Diaries*. Boston: Houghton Mifflin Company, 1970, p. 22.

[4] Blum, *op. cit.*, p. 127.

[5] Adolf A. Berle, Papers and Diary, October 29, 1940.. Franklin D. Roosevelt Library, Hyde Park, N.Y. Also, see Rosenman, *Working with Roosevelt*, pp. 222-55.

### Chapter 7 — First Media President

[1] Leo Rosten. *The Washington Correspondents*. New York: Harcourt, Brace, and Co., 1937, pp. 47-60.

[2] Jon Meacham. Franklin and Winston: An Intimate Portrait of an Epic Friendship. New York: Random House, 2004. p. 27.

### Chapter 8 — Supreme Court Imbroglio

[1] *Encyclopedia of American History*. Richard B. Morris, ed. New York: Harper & Brothers, 1953, p. 345.

[2] Nathan Miller. *FDR: An Intimate History*. New York: Doubleday & Company, Inc., 1983, pp. 370-73, *passim*.

[3] The speech was delivered by W. J. Cameron, speaking over CBS on the Ford Hour, 1936.

[4]H. L. Mencken. "Three Years of Dr. Roosevelt," *American Mercury*, March 1936.

[5]Arthur M. Schlesinger, Jr. *The Politics of Upheaval*. Boston: Houghton Mifflin Co., 1960, p.580.

[6]Joseph Nathan Kane. *Facts About the Presidents*. Permabook Edition, Pocket Books, Inc., New York: 1959, p. 343.

[7]Rosenman, *op. cit.*, pp. 158-59.

## Chapter 9 — Europe's War

[1]Toland, *op. cit.*, pp. 816-17.

[2]This statement by Churchill is quoted in numerous sources. My reference is found in "Bloody Marvelous," an essay by Anthony Bailey in *No End Save Victory*, ed. Robert Cowley. New York: G. P. Putnam's Sons, 2001. p. 40.

[3]William R. Leach. Land of Desire, Merchants, Powers, and the Rise of a New American Culture. New York: Knopf Doubleday Publishing Group (Vintage Series), 1994. p. 375.

[4]Wayne Cole, *Roosevelt and the Isolationists 1932-1945*. Lincoln, Nebraska: University of Nebraska Press, 1983, p. 380.

## Chapter 10 — Third Term

[1]Geoffrey C. Ward. *Before the Trumpet: Young Franklin Roosevelt 1882-1905*. New York: Book-of-the-Month Club, 2005.p. 5.

[2]Hazel Rowley, *Franklin and Eleanor*. New York: Farrar, Straus, and Giroux, 2010. p. 237.

[3]Cole, *op. cit.*, pp. 386-87.

[4]Rosenman, *op. cit.*, p. 201.

[5]Francis Sayre Papers, Hull, Cordell. *Memoirs of Cordell Hull*, vol. I, pp. 858-60.

[6]Rosenman, *op. cit.*, pp. 211-12.

[7]*The Public Papers and Addresses of Franklin D. Roosevelt*. Vol. 9. Samuel I. Rosenman, ed. New York: Random House, 1938. p 407. Hereinafter referred to as FDR Papers.

[8]Frances Perkins, *The Roosevelt I Knew*. New York: Viking Press, 1946 .p. 117.

[9]Jean Edward Smith, *FDR*. New York: Random House Paperback Books, 2007. pp. 473-74.

[10]Sherwood, *op. cit.*, p. 228.

## Chapter 11 — Lend Lease

[1]Sherwood, *op. cit.*, p. 224.

[2]NYT, January 1, 1941, p. 1.

[3]*Ibid.*

[4]*FDR Papers*, Vol.9, pp, 607-08.

[5]NYT, January 7, 1941, Sect 1, p.4.

[6]*Churchill, Winston S., and Franklin D. Roosevelt: The Complete Correspondence.* Warren F. Kimball, ed. 3 vols. Vol. I. New Jersey: Princeton University Press, 1984. p. 131.

[7]Ibid.

[8]*Public Opinion Quarterly*, March 9, 1941, Vol. 5, N. 1. Princeton, New Jersey: School of Pubic Affairs Princeton University, p. 158.

## Chapter 12 — Intervention or Isolation

[1]Michael R. Beschloss. *Kennedy and Roosevelt: The Uneasy Alliance.* New York: W. W. Norton & Company,1980., p. 153.

[2]*Ibid.*, pp. 154-60.

[3]Beschloss, *op. cit.*, p. 174.

[4]Cole, *op. cit.*, pp. 466-67.

[5]Leo Rosten. *The Washington Correspondents.* New York: Harcourt, Brace, and Co., 1937. Pp. 47-50.

[6]FDR Papers, 1940, pp. 711-12.

[7]Warren F. Kimball, *The Most Unsordid Act: Lend-Lease 1939-1941.* Baltimore: The John Hopkins Press, 1969, pp. 77-104.

[8] Cole, *op. cit.*, pp. 380-81.

[9] Chicago Tribune, September 5, 1940, p. 3.

[10]*Des Moines Register and Tribune*, September 12, 1941.

[11]Cole, *op. cit.*, p. 466.

[12]*Public Opinion Quarterly*, March 1941, Vol. 5, No. 1. Princeton, New Jersey: School of Public Affairs Princeton University, p. 158.

[13]*Public Opinion Quarterly*, September 1941, Vol. 5, No. 2, p. 160.

[14]*Public Opinion Quarterly*, September, 1940, pp. 440-45.

## Chapter 13 — Barbarossa

[1]Richard B. Morris, ed. *Encyclopedia of American History.* New York: Harper & Brothers, 1953. pp. 365-66.

[2]As quoted by John Toland, *Adolf Hitler.* New York: Ballantine Books, 1976. p 921.

[3]Morris, *op. cit.*, pp. 366-67.

[4]See, for example, John Erickson and David Dilks, eds., *Barbarossa: The Axis and the Allies.* Edinburgh, Scotland: Edinburgh University Press, 1944 (hardcover) or 1998 (softcover).

[5]Quoted by William L. Langer and S. Everett Gleason, *The Undeclared War 1940-1941.* New York: Harper & Bros., 1953, pp. 145-46 and as taken from Fuehrer Conferences, 1941 (Conference of January 8 and 9, 1941.).

[6]As quoted in NYT, June 24, 1941.

[7]Text in the official Soviet publication: *Soviet Foreign Policy During the Patriotic War* (New York), vol. I, 21 ff. As quoted in William L. Langer and S. Everett Gleason, *op. cit.*, pp. 535-36.

[8]WalterWalimont, *Inside Hitler's Headquarters.* Washington: Praeger Press, 1964, p. 180.

[9]Morris, *op. cit.*, pp. 366-67.

*Chapter 14 — Troubled Waters*

[1]Richard B. Morris, *op. cit.*, pp. 365-66.
[2]Churchill's request at this time for "tools" rather than "armies" is quoted by several historians. For examples, see Kenneth S. Davis, *FDR: the War President 1940-1943*, New York: Random House, 2000, pp. 101-02. Also H. W. Brands, *op. cit.*, p. 582; Robert E. Sherwood, *op. cit.*, pp. 261-62; Winston Churchill, *The Grand Alliance*. Boston: Houghton Mifflin, 1950, p. 128.
[3]NYT, March 11, 1941.
[4]*FDR Papers*, vol. 10, pp. 255-64; Sherwood, *op. cit.*, pp. 290-91.
[5]NYT, July 8, 1941.
[6]PPA, 1941, pp. 227-30
[7]Rosenman, *op. cit.*, p. 288.
[8]Arthur Krock in an address to the alumni of Columbia College on November 5, 1941. Quoted by Charles A. Beard. *President Roosevelt and the Coming of the War 1941*. New Haven, Connecticut: Yale University Press, 1968, pp. 149-50.
[9]*Nothing to Fear: Selected Addresses of Franklin Delano Roosevelt 1932-1945*. B. D. Zevin, ed. Boston: Houghton Mifflin Co., 1946, p. 293. Hereinafter referred to as NTF Addresses.
[10] *Ibid.*
[11] As quoted in NYT, Nov. 1, 1941.

*Chapter 15 — Americana 1941*

[1]*World Almanac and Book of Facts 2007*. New York: World Almanac Books, 2007, p. 123.

*Chapter 16 — The Labor Front*

[1]Doris Kearns Goodwin, *No Ordinary Time*. New York: Simon & Schuster, 1994, p. 225.
[2]*Ibid.*, pp. 248-53.
[3]*Ibid.*, pp. 228-30.
[4]Kenneth S. Davis, *op. cit.*, p. 326.
[5]*FDR Papers*. Vol. 9., pp. 494-95.

*Chapter 17 — From Marriage to Alliance*

[1]Numerous biographies attest to the unusual marital arrangement adopted by Franklin and Eleanor following her discovery in 1918 of his affair with Lucy Mercer. For examples, see Joseph Lash, *Eleanor and Franklin*, pp. 302-03; Goodwin, *op. cit.*, pp. 18-19; Jean Edward Smith, *FDR*, pp. 159-63; Kenneth S. Davis, *FDR: the Beckoning of Destiny*, pp. 483-95, et al.

[2]Letter from Sara D. Roosevelt to Eleanor Roosevelt, March 14, 1915; found in Sara D. Roosevelt Journals, Halsted Collection, Franklin D. Roosevelt Library, Hyde Park, N.Y.

[3]Joseph P. Lash, *op. cit.*, p. 303.

[4]Quoted from an interview with Alice Longworth, Lash, *op. cit.*, p. 309.

[5]For example, note the death of Quentin Roosevelt, youngest of Theodore's four sons. Cf. Geoffrey C. Ward. *A First Class Temperament: The Emergence of Franklin Roosevelt.* New York: Book of the Month Club, 1989, pp. 387-89.

[6]Lash, *op. cit.*, pp. 309-11. Also, see Joseph Alsop, *FDR: A Centenary Remembrance.* New York: Viking Press, 1st edition. 1982., pp. 67-74.

[7]Michael Teague, *Mrs. L. Conversations With Alice Roosevelt Longworth.* Garden City, New York: Doubleday, 1st edition, 1981, p.158.

[8] Bishop, Jim. *FDR'S Last Year: April 1944-April 1945.* New York: Pocket Books, Simon & Schuster, 1975, p. 753.

## Chapter 18 — Empire of the Rising Sun

[1]Iris Chang, *The Rape of Nanking.* New York: Penguin Books, 1998, p. 4.

[2]William Manchester, *The Glory and the Dream.* New York: Bantam Books, 1975, p. 254. Also, see *Time*, January 12, 1945 and *Time*, January 31, 1945.

[3]Foreign Relations of the United States, Nov. 3, 1941, vol. 2, pp. 701-04.

[4]*Washington Post*, February 6, 1941.

[5]*Time*, February 10, 1941.

[6]As quoted by William E. Leuchtenburg, *Franklin D. Roosevelt and the New Deal*, New York: Harper and Row, p. 308.

## Chapter 19 — Atlantic Charter

[1]Several biographies of both men refer to these earlier meetings. For examples, see Amanda Smith, ed. *Heritage to Fortune: The Letters of Joseph P. Kennedy.* New York: Viking, 2001, p. 411; Jon Meacham, *Franklin and Winston: An Intimate Portrait of an Epic Friendship.* New York: Random House, 2003, pp. 3-5.

[2]Columbia Oral History Project, Butler Library, Columbia University, quoted by Ted Morgan in *FDR: A Biography.* New York: Simon & Schuster, 1985, p. 598.

[3]Winston Churchill, *The Second World War*, vol. III., *The Grand Alliance.* Boston: Houghton Mifflin Co., 1950. pp. 390-93.

[4]John Morton Blum, *From the Morgenthau Diaries: Years of Urgency.* Vol. II. Boston: Houghton Mifflin Co., 1965, p375.

[5]Sherwood, *op. cit.*, p. 236.

[6]Halifax to Churchill, Oct. 11, 1941. Found in Premier Files, Prime Minister Winston S. Churchill Manuscripts, Public Records Office, London, England, and cited by Robert Dallek in *Franklin Roosevelt and American Foreign Policy 1932-1945.* New York: Oxford University Press, 1995, p. 289.

[7]*Ibid.*, pp. 285-86..

## Chapter 20 — Enter the Scientists

[1]Max Planck, *Scientific Autobiography*. New York: Philosophical Library, 1949, p. 13.

[2]Niels Bohr, "Neutron Capture and Nuclear Constitution," *Nature*. vol. 137. Baltimore, Md., 1936. p. 344.

[3]*NYT*, April 30, 1939, p. 35.

[4]The final draft of this letter is dated August 2, 1939, and is located in the "America Since Hoover" Collection at the Franklin D. Roosevelt Library, Hyde Park, New York.

[5]Accounts of this historic meeting when Sachs transmitted Einstein's letter to FDR can be found in numerous histories or biographies. My account is taken largely from Richard Rhodes, *The Making of the Atomic Bomb*. New York: Simon & Schuster, 1986. pp. 291-315, *passim*.

## Chapter 21 — Undeclared War 1941

[1]Morris, *op. cit.*, pp. 482-83.

[2]*Public Opinion Quarterly*, Vol. V. 1941, pp. 481-85.

[3]Quoted by Robert Dallek, *Franklin Roosevelt and American Foreign Policy, 1932–1945*. New York: Oxford University Press, 1995, p. 276.

[4]*FDR Papers*, 1941, pp. 272-76.

[5]An Analysis of Newspaper Opinion, *Public Opinion Quarterly*, V, 1941, pp. 448-55.

[6]*NYT*, August 9, 1941 and August 13, 1941.

## Chapter 22 — Russia: the Enigma

[1]Frederick Lewis Allen, *Only Yesterday*. New York: Harper and Row, 1931, pp. 46-49.

[2]As quoted by Robert Dallek, Franklin D. Roosevelt and American Foreign Policy 1932-1945. Pp211-12. Also, see A World at Arms: A Global History of World War II. Cambridge, England: Cambridge University Press, 2005.

[3]*NYT*, June 22, 1941.

[4]*NYT*, June 24, 1941. Also quoted in numerous other sources. For examples, see David McCullough, *Truman*. New York: Simon & Schuster, 1992, p. 262. Robert J. Donovan, *Conflict and Crisis: Presidency of Harry S Truman 1945-1948*. New York: W. W. Norton & Company, 1977, p. 36.

[5]Sherwood, *op. cit.*, pp. 333-40.

## Chapter 23 — Japan: Expansion and Perfidy

[1]Nothing to Fear: Selected Addresses of Franklin Delano Roosevelt 1932-1945. B. D. Zevin (ed.). Boston: Houghton Mifflin Co., 1946, pp. 110-15.

[2]*Ibid.*, p. 297.

[3]Langer and Gleason, *op. cit.*, p. 595.

[4]*Morgenthau Diaries*, Vol. 308, September 24, 1940. Boston: Houghton Mifflin Company, 1965, pp. 42 ff. 220 ff Also, see Jean Edward Smith, *FDR*. New York: Random House Trade Paperback Edition, 2008, pp. 506-10.

[5]As quoted by James Bradley in *Flyboys*. New York: Little, Brown, and Co., p. 77.

[6]*Foreign Relations*. U.S. Department of State. Japan. II, pp. 701-04.

[7]Herbert Feis, *The Road to Pearl Harbor*. New York: Atheneum Edition, 1966, p. 298 and especially ff. 4 on same page.

## Chapter 24 — Infamy

[1]Hearings in the U.S. Congress, Joint Committee on the Investigation of the Pearl Harbor Attack, Part 17, p. 2463.

[2]As quoted by Herbert Feis, The Road to War. Princeton University Press: Princeton, New Jersey, 1950, p. 278.

[3]Robert Gannon. Hellions of the Deep: Development of American Torpedoes During World War II. University Park, PA: Penn. State Press, 1996, p. 49.

[4]Howard W. French, "Pearl Harbor Truly a Sneak Attack," *New York Times*, December 9, 1999.

[5]As quoted by Gordon W. Prange, *At Dawn We Slept: the Untold Story of Pearl Harbor*. New York: Penguin Books, 1981. P. 527.

[6]Ibid., p. 525.

[7]Walter Lord, *Day of Infamy*. New York: Henry Holt & Co., 1957, p. 114.

[8]Ibid., p. 212.

## Chapter 25 — FDR: A Reckoning

[1]Lane Cooper, *The Rhetoric of Aristotle*. New York: D. Appleton-Century Co., 1932., p. 8 and *passim*.

[2]Smith, Richard Norton. *Patriarch*. Boston: Houghton Mifflin Co., 1993, p. 237.

[3]Quoted by John F. Kennedy, *Profiles in Courage*. New York: Harper & Brothers, 1955. p. 232.

[4] David Halberstam. *The Powers That Be*. New York: Knopf, 1979, p. 15.

[5] Lord Acton, originally in a letter to Bishop Mandell Creighton, April 5, 1887. *Historical Essays and Studies*, ed. J. N. Figgis and R. V. Laurence. London: Macmillan & Co., 1907.

[6]Edwin C. Hargrove. *The Power of the Modern Presidency*. Philadelphia: Temple University Press, 1974. P. 53.

[7]Robert B. Stinnett, *Day of Deceit*. New York: Touchstone, Rockefeller Center, 2000. See also John Toland. *Infamy: Pearl Harbor and Its Aftermath*. Garden City, New York: Doubleday, 1982.

[8]Bishop, *op. cit.*, p. 394.

[9]Harry S Truman Memoirs. *Year of Decisions*. Vol. 1. New York: Doubleday & Co., Inc., 1955, p.2.

[10]Bishop, *op. cit.*, pp. 748-802 passim.

*Also by Robert Underhill*

The Truman Persuasions
Blechhammer on the Oder
I'll See You Again
The Bully Pulpit
FDR and Harry
Eden So Near (Novel)
Alone Among Friends
A Doctor and His Wife
Jack Shelley and the News
Meanwhile At Home
Life With Alexander
First the Black Horse

# INDEX